Field Guide to Rivers & Streams

Discovering Running Waters and Aquatic Life

RYAN UTZ, PhD

FALCON

ESSEX, CONNECTICUT

To the Sturges family, who nurtured my love of rivers by sharing Allegheny River watershed outdoor adventures in our youth, and to Ed Freeman, whose emotional support over the decades and guidance with the visual arts lie behind each page of this work.

An imprint of Globe Pequot, the trade division of
The Rowman & Littlefield Publishing Group, Inc.
4501 Forbes Blvd., Ste. 200
Lanham, MD 20706
www.rowman.com

Distributed by NATIONAL BOOK NETWORK

British Library Cataloguing-in-Publication Information available

Library of Congress Cataloging in Publication Data available
ISBN 978-1-4930-6038-2 (paper : alk. paper)
ISBN 978-1-4930-6039-9 (electronic)

♾™ The paper used in this publication meets the minimum requirements of American National Standard for Information Sciences—Permanence of Paper for Printed Library Materials, ANSI/NISO Z39.48-1992.

CONTENTS

ACKNOWLEDGMENTS

I am most indebted to the excellent naturalist artists willing to share their photographic work in the following pages. Zach Alley, Andrea Kautz, Konrad Schmidt, Scott Smith, Ryan Douglas, Julia Wood, Brian Zimmerman, and others worked hard to create the invaluable images that help identify our precious native North American species. Online resources that some of these artists maintain, especially www.macro invertebrates.org and https://ncfishes.com, provide excellent identification and natural history information, including for many rare species not covered here. I also thank Tim Pearce for the invitation to photograph bivalve mollusks from the outstanding malacology collection at the Carnegie Museum of Natural History. The brilliant Julia Barnes provided encouraging moral support and helpful feedback on writing.

INTRODUCTION

The reverence for flowing bodies of water across cultures draws from many emotions. With a river in view, we feel the excitement of exploration, deference for the power of nature wrought by floods, eagerness to observe the many strange animals inhabiting the depths, or perhaps a primordial comfort that watching moving water can convey. Most civilizations possess ancient origins along a specific river: the Tigris and Euphrates watered the wheat fields of Mesopotamia; the Yangtze delivered vital rich soils to ancient China; and Cahokia, the largest known pre-Columbian indigenous city north of Mexico, rose along the banks of the Mississippi. Each of these legendary waterways delivered not only wealth through trade and the spread of ideas but also catastrophic floods capable of destroying our earliest cities. We still gravitate toward rivers for opportunity, as well as for recreation and spiritual renewal. Despite our efforts to tame rivers using modern technology, episodic floods still bring great destruction to cities and farms along their banks. Our reverence for rivers runs deep.

Just as cultures change and evolve, so too do rivers. Almost no ecosystem on Earth matches the physical dynamism of rivers because of how frequently and rapidly their flows shift. A gentle, perfectly clear brook can become a strong torrent of muddy water and debris in a matter of hours, or even minutes, following a strong storm. Such events can also cause a river to breach its banks and entirely reshape a path across the landscape. A few months later, drought might reduce the same river to a narrow trickle of vital habitat barely capable of supporting aquatic life. Organisms that make rivers their home have adapted to these natural, wholescale habitat transitions by evolving impressive coping strategies. Many fishes deposit their eggs in inundated floodplains during high flows so that their young can feed on the abundant insects of the temporary habitat while the shallow water keeps predators away. One species of desert stream–inhabiting bug (order Hemiptera) climbs out of water toward high ground if rain clouds appear overhead to avoid the impending flash flood.

Consistent change in rivers also explains why they are so biodiverse. The fish, invertebrates, plants, and single-celled microbes inhabiting rivers persist in narrow habitat ribbons winding through the landscape. Organisms living in two streams separated by less than a mile of straight-line geographic distance but between a mountain range will likely never meet. A fish population might become split into two for thousands of years if a flood creates a waterfall barrier. Such physical isolation accelerates evolution by isolating genes, resulting in habitats that support a dizzyingly large proportion of global biodiversity. Although oceans cover about 70 percent of the Earth and rivers far less than 1 percent, scientists have catalogued over 13,000 species of freshwater fishes (mostly from rivers) but only 16,000 marine fishes. Five to ten new species of freshwater crayfish are described every year.

The best efforts of scientists are challenged by the ever-present change that epitomizes rivers and streams. Floods wash away expensive monitoring equipment and essential data stored within. Lessons learned from carefully executed experiments conducted during tranquil conditions may not at all apply during high or low flows. Studying river-dwelling animals often demands a deep understanding of distant ecosystems because of complex migration patterns. Some of the most important fish migrate to oceans while nearly all aquatic insects emerge from water to feed and mate in nearby forests.

Despite these challenges, more than a century of science across many disciplines has greatly expanded our understanding of flowing water ecosystems. Advancements in ecology and hydrology have revealed that rivers and streams are inextricably connected to lands upslope that deliver water, nutrients, and energy. Therefore, rivers and streams are considerably impacted by how humans change the landscape. Experiments show that removing top predators can send ripple effects through aquatic food webs by causing herbivorous prey populations to grow unchecked, consequently diminishing algae abundance. Conservation biologists highlight the disproportionate importance of rivers, which house more threatened animal species than any other ecosystem. The importance of river dynamism represents a common thread running through each subdiscipline. Without ever-changing flows and constant change, rivers could not support the many plants and animals that find a home within them.

Nearly all advances in river science have conveyed lessons of connectivity across ecosystems in all directions: upstream, downstream, onto land, and into oceans. Forests and grasslands not only affect how much water ultimately flows through rivers, but also provide the key molecular building blocks for life when they shed leaves that fall into

A quick terminology lesson will help clarify information in subsequent chapters. Flowing waterbodies have many names: Ribbons of blue on a map appear as a hollow, brook, creek, stream, wash, run, or river, among other obscure titles. Although these monikers might imply differences in size, the terms do not offer any technical utility for scientists. Use among terms also varies by regional differences in water availability. For example, the Cache de Poudre River flowing west from the Front Range mountains in water-scarce Colorado would be labeled a brook or creek in a water-rich state like New York or Pennsylvania. Scientists do, however, refer to all bodies of flowing water as **lotic systems** regardless of size. Lakes, ponds, and wetlands with still water are termed **lentic**. Another common term is **headwater stream**, which refers to the farthest upstream, smallest waterways in a river network. Many key ecological patterns and processes in lotic ecosystems are consistent regardless of size; thus subsequent chapters will refer to lotic systems whenever the topic is relevant from the smallest brooks to the largest rivers.

Scientists do apply a network geography approach to convey the size of a flowing water body known as **stream order**, a system that assigns a number corresponding to how many tributaries converge upstream. The smallest headwater reaches where water flows year-round are considered first-order streams. When two first-order streams meet, the order downstream rises to two. A third-order stream forms when two second-order streams meet, and so on. Large rivers such as the Mississippi might reach the tenth order. The system allows scientists to convey an approximate size, and this book will occasionally refer to stream order when size is important.

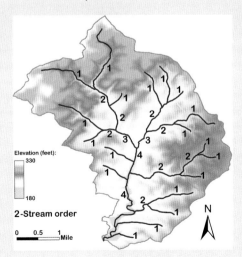

Elevation (feet):
330

180

2-Stream order

0   0.5   1
Mile

N

Figure 1.1. The stream network for the East Branch North Branch Patapsco River watershed northeast of Washington, DC, in Maryland. Stream order is labeled on each tributary and mainstem. At the outlet, this lotic system is a fourth-order stream.

channels. If maintained in a pristine state, river ecosystems effectively process this organic matter to sustain healthy estuaries and coasts. Oceans return the favor when massive populations of fish born in rivers transition into seas, grow large, then return to breed, carrying energy from marine ecosystems with them in their tissues. Rivers also support immense aquatic insect populations that take flight into surrounding forests and grasslands to spawn. Such insects provide a feast for countless terrestrial animals, including birds, bats, and spiders. Therefore, life-supporting energy may travel thousands of miles from the ocean depths to a mountain forest thanks to many of the species that comprise a functioning river ecosystem.

The purpose of this book is to reveal the wonderful stories of aquatic science to a mainstream audience and convey a deeper understanding of rivers. Learning science always works best with an interactive, hands-on approach. Thus this book also aims to enable interactive lotic science. Unprecedented advances in data technology are driving novel innovations in every branch of science, especially environmental sciences. For example, devices smaller than a fist can track temperature, oxygen concentrations, or salinity levels every minute and send data to scientists over wireless networks in real time. Although such tools might not prove useful to most non-scientists, others are fun, informative, and accessible to river aficionados willing to explore tools online. Agencies tasked with managing ecosystems support web applications that allow anyone to map a watershed, track flow levels, or identify organisms living within just about any lotic system, large or small. Wherever possible, this book briefly introduces such tools in instructional sidebars.

CHAPTER 1
WATERSHEDS

Lotic systems move water downhill, but where does all the water originate? Answering that question requires an understanding of the watershed concept. A **watershed** includes all land upstream that contributes water to a specific point in a lotic system. Water gets delivered to the surface of Earth via rain and snow and, beholden to the inflexible rules of gravity, begins a tireless journey toward the lowest point it can possibly reach. The typical water molecule will begin that journey by passing through empty pores in soil and bedrock, but gravity will eventually deliver this **groundwater** to the bottom of a valley where it contributes to lotic flow. Defining watershed boundaries and exploring land attributes explains much about how lotic systems behave. Several terms are synonymous with watershed, including **basin**, **catchment**, and **drainage**.

In most cases, defining a watershed boundary involves nothing more than following elevation contours. Walking from the edge of a channel and following a path traversing the highest elevations that contribute water to the river until reaching the starting location on the opposite bank constitutes navigating the watershed boundary for that specific point. Such journeys are rarely feasible and can be thousands of miles long for large rivers, so scientists typically use elevation to delineate watersheds. Because demarcating watershed boundaries represents such a crucial part of lotic science, watershed delineation tools have become very sophisticated and widespread, so much so that anyone can define and explore the watershed of a favorite lotic system.

Figure 2.1 shows the boundaries for the five largest watersheds in the continental United States. The greatest among these, the Mississippi River, represents the fourth-largest watershed in the world. Watershed sizes do not necessarily correspond to river size by other metrics. For example, the Mississippi would be the thirteenth-largest river in the world if ranked by flow volume. The Colorado River currently dries up completely before reaching its terminus in the Gulf of California.

Identifying the watershed boundary for any river or stream is possible using a sophisticated online tool developed by the United States Geological Survey (USGS): StreamStats. To create a watershed map for any point along a lotic system in the lower 48 United States and generate a report of key watershed attributes, execute the following steps:

1. Navigate to the StreamStats website at https://streamstats.usgs.gov.
2. Click the StreamStats application and use the map tool to zoom to the stream reach targeted for watershed mapping.
3. Zooming in will lead to an option to choose the state or region of interest on the left menu. Select the most appropriate state for the reach.
4. Continue zooming in until dark blue lines appear as waterways.
5. Click on the blue *Delineate* button on the left menu, then on the blue line of the reach location. Delineation may take a few moments and larger rivers will take more time, but most will finish within a minute.
6. The watershed area will appear in yellow. All precipitation that falls in this area and is not evaporated or transpired by plants eventually flows through the stream or river.
7. To learn more, click on the blue *Continue* button on the left menu for further information about the watershed. For example, the *Annual Flow Statistics* will calculate the average flow rate.
8. Farther down in the left menu is a menu for *Basin Characteristics*: watershed attributes that shape the character of a river or stream, such as the percentage of forested land, annual precipitation, and elevation. Click on the blue *Continue* button once variables are selected.
9. The USGS will now build a watershed report. Click again on the blue *Continue* button and a report will appear with a watershed map and all metrics. Scroll down to the bottom of the report for the option to save the document.

Major watershed boundaries constitute **continental divides** (Figure 2.1). Such boundaries demarcate the fate of rain or snowmelt by the ulti mate ocean where the rivers downslope of the divides terminate. North America features two major continental divides whose boundaries determine if rivers flow toward the Atlantic, Pacific, or Arctic Oceans. Eastern North America also features minor continental divides that parse river flow toward the Gulf of St. Lawrence, the Atlantic coast, or the Gulf of Mexico. In rare instances, precipitation may also fall in a **terminal** or

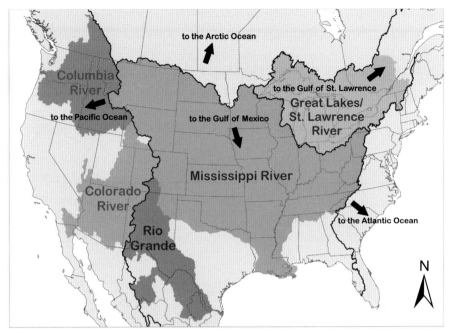

Figure 2.1. Boundaries of the five largest watersheds in the continental United States. Dark lines show major continental drainage divides and arrows illustrate flow direction.

USGS hydrologists created a tool to identify the watershed for any location or the path a raindrop will traverse on its journey to the sea.

1. Navigate to the StreamStats website at https://streamstats.usgs.gov.
2. Click on the *Exploration Tools* button that appears in the upper-left corner of the map.
3. Choose the *Flow (Raindrop) Path* option.
4. A window will appear with a button labeled *Select Point On Map*. Click on this button to return to the map application.
5. Zoom in on the map and click on the location of interest. The point does not need to be on or near a stream.
6. A similar window will appear. The raindrop path length can be adjusted using the *Limit* on the right side of the window. Be sure to both click on the circle button and adjust the distance to lengthen or shorten the raindrop path. Click the green *Go* button.
7. The hypothetical raindrop path appears as a red line on the map. Zoom in to see the names of the streams and rivers the raindrop will eventually contribute water to. To see the larger rivers farther downstream, adjust the *Limit* to a longer distance.

endorheic basin: a watershed boundary where water evaporates into the atmosphere after settling in an inland lake. The best-known North American terminal basin is the Great Basin, where water flows into the Great Salt Lake and ultimately evaporates.

Any land attribute within a watershed, including vegetation, geologic features, and human activities, significantly shapes lotic ecosystems downstream. Some consider water flowing through a river or stream to be **watershed tea**, a concept fully realized by aquatic scientists during the mid-twentieth century. However, the many features of a watershed that influence flowing water occur simultaneously, and landscapes continuously change. Thus there is still very much to learn in the field of watershed science. The attributes listed below represent major watershed features whose influence on rivers and streams are reasonably well understood.

CLIMATE

Lotic systems are inexorably linked to watershed climate. Storms or droughts within watershed boundaries obviously lead to floods and low flows. But climatic (long-term weather) attributes also shape the physical and biological character of rivers by influencing terrestrial ecosystems. Higher precipitation levels support more terrestrial vegetation, and decaying plants build soils that act as watershed-scale sponges. Therefore, watersheds with thick forests absorb far more rainfall during a storm compared to those in desert environments, where floods occur very quickly.

Atmospheric temperatures in a watershed are also key to understanding lotic systems. In very cold climates, much of the water delivered to watersheds remains locked on land as ice and snow. As a result, groundwater delivery to rivers significantly diminishes over winter but predictably floods annually once the spring snowmelt ensues. Rivers in tropical, humid climates with rainforests pulse with wet and dry seasons. The largest river on Earth by flow volume, the Amazon, flows at an average of 31.2 million gallons per second at the end of the dry season in November but more than doubles to about 65 million gallons per second by the end of the wet season in May. Sailors encounter water fresh enough to drink in the Atlantic Ocean over 100 miles offshore from the Amazon River mouth during the wet season.

MOUNTAINS

Lotic systems that flow from mountain watersheds exhibit distinctly different flow patterns relative to the lowlands. Mountain ranges where most of the precipitation falls as snow and remains frozen most of the year, such as the Rocky Mountain and Sierra Nevada ranges of western North America, prevent water from melting into rivers until spring or summer. Annual flow patterns in mountain settings follow the melt seasonality very closely, with the lowest flows occurring in winter when freezing temperatures lock water at the surface and the highest flows corresponding with peak snowmelt in late spring. Water originating as snowmelt also means very cold water temperatures year-round; thus cold-loving species such as trout thrive in montane watersheds.

LIMESTONE

Watersheds with large **limestone** deposits offer excellent examples of how environments from the deep geologic past influence modern-day lotic systems. The presence of limestone means that the environmental setting millions of years ago was oceanic, perhaps a shallow inland sea. Microscopic marine life known as plankton living in the water column created shells of **calcium carbonate**, the same chemical found in chalk and antacid medicines, to help stay afloat. When these organisms died, the shells sank and accumulated over time. If geologic forces eventually uplift such layers above sea level and the calcium carbonate shells harden under pressure from layers of rock above, limestone forms. Rainwater is naturally acidic and calcium carbonate dissolves in acid. Consequently, long-term exposure of limestone to water flowing underfoot causes cavities to form that often grow to form caves. Cavities in limestone near the land surface also cause sinkholes to form.

Lotic systems draining watersheds with large limestone deposits (Figure 2.2) are greatly affected by water flowing through the rock. Limestone results in lotic systems with the following attributes:

- *Chemical:* Water flowing through limestone has high levels of dissolved calcium and magnesium. These chemicals are not harmful to life. However, high concentrations can cause problems by reforming solid deposits in pipes—a process called **scaling**.

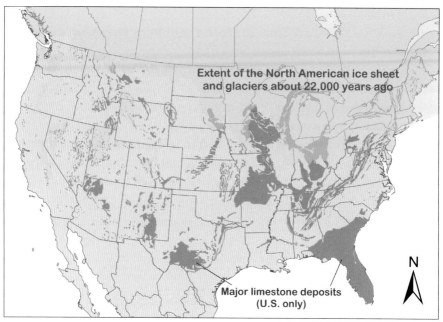

Extent of the North American ice sheet and glaciers about 22,000 years ago

Major limestone deposits (U.S. only)

N

Figure 2.2. The extent of major limestone deposits (in purple) and glacial ice during the most recent ice age (in blue) in the continental United States.

- *Thermal:* Waters draining limestone watersheds tend to be very well buffered from temperature shifts. They are unlikely to freeze during winter in cold environments and stay cooler in the summer. Thermal buffering occurs because of the large volume of groundwater running through pores in the limestone, which keeps stream temperatures stable.

- *Biological:* Most anglers know well that trout love lotic ecosystems with limestone environments. As coldwater species, trout appreciate the water temperatures kept consistent by water flowing through underground limestone. Mussels, snails, and any organisms that build a shell thrive in rivers with limestone in their watersheds because the extra dissolved calcium eases their task of building a home. Large limestone caves with abundant water flowing through them, such as Mammoth Cave in Kentucky, can result in very strange aquatic organisms, called **stygobites**, found exclusively within their native subterranean ecosystems.

- *Hydrological:* Lotic system flows draining many limestone watersheds are hydrologically buffered in a similar way to the thermal buffering described above. Flows in limestone environments tend to experience fewer floods or very low flow periods because the large groundwater stores in the limestone pores help stabilize water delivery.

Abundant limestone can also distort watershed boundaries thanks to complex patterns of subterranean water flow. Flow paths created by tunnels formed by dissolved limestone can route water across boundaries defined by topography at the surface. Therefore, defining a watershed boundary for a river with plentiful porous limestone can prove difficult or impossible unless the cave network underground is well mapped.

GLACIAL HISTORY

Earth looked and felt like a very different planet over most of the past 2.5 million years. Ice ages dominated during this period, during which continent-sized glaciers geologists call **ice sheets** up to a mile thick covered much of the Northern Hemisphere (see Figure 2.2). The ice age climate was also very different from what we experience today: During ice ages, the Sahara Desert was a lush savanna and about one-fourth of modern-day Utah was submerged under a freshwater sea called Lake Bonneville (the remnants of which comprise modern-day Great Salt Lake). Our last ice age ended about 11,500 years ago, which is a very slight period by geologic standards. We currently live during an **interglacial** period.

The ancient ice masses shaped the Earth in ways that greatly affect lotic systems flowing today. Glaciers are moving ice masses that churn up the land they flow over, carving valleys out of bedrock and depositing boulders, gravel, and sand where they terminate. Consequently, rivers draining watersheds in post-glaciated landscapes tend to flow in and out of many lakes because glacier movements created depressions in the land. The Great Lakes and tens of thousands of smaller lakes, ponds, and wetland sloughs from Maine to Alaska exist thanks to the North American ice sheet churning the land beneath it for tens of thousands of years. Ice masses also leave behind large volumes of sediment where they terminate, which helped create the fertile soils of the upper Midwest. Post-glacial soils are also highly capable of absorbing water during storms. Therefore, in watersheds that were formerly covered by an ice sheet, water easily percolates into the ground and therefore reduces the intensity of floods.

VEGETATION

Although the shape of a watershed is defined by its geologic and topographic boundaries, it also lives and breathes very much like a living organism thanks to plants. The major ingredients of **photosynthesis**, the process of synthesizing tissues and storing energy by plants (plus many single-celled organisms), are sunlight, carbon dioxide, and water. A photosynthesizing plant builds energy-storing carbohydrates by harnessing energy from the sun to chemically break apart carbon dioxide and water molecules. However, especially when the sun is down, plants also **respire** just like humans do, which means that they consume some of the carbohydrates generated during photosynthesis. Respiration results in the release of carbon dioxide and water as byproducts. Terrestrial plants release oxygen during photosynthesis and water vapor during respiration to the atmosphere via microscopic pores in their leaves called **stomata** (singular: stoma), a process called **transpiration**. Therefore, terrestrial plants are water-consuming engines, especially during periods of growth when they soak up water to support both photosynthesis and respiration.

Transpiration profoundly affects the quantity of water flowing from watersheds to lotic systems. Plants acquire the water they need for photosynthesis and respiration by tapping groundwater with their roots, thereby consuming water that would otherwise eventually flow through the ground to a stream channel. All water transpired by plants ends up exported from the watershed to the atmosphere. When plants are abundant in a watershed and actively growing, the amount of groundwater delivered to a stream can diminish greatly. In places where plant growth accelerates and slows with predictable seasonal changes, water levels in streams and rivers will rise and fall based on plant growth. Water vapor released by plant stomata is invisible, which masks the impressive volume of water plants export to the air on a bright summer day. Scientists estimate that more than half of all water that falls as precipitation annually is absorbed and transpired back to the atmosphere by plants. In cold climates, winter causes leaves to fall and vegetation slows down or entirely shuts off photosynthesis and respiration. When that occurs, transpiration also greatly diminishes and most water delivered to a watershed will find its way to a stream channel.

One group of trees imparts a profound impact on the chemical and aesthetic properties of lotic systems. The needles that fall from cone-bearing trees, or conifers (pine, spruce, fir, hemlock, and larch), release

tannins when they decompose. Tannins are acidic compounds that were historically used to cure leather by tanning the hides. When a watershed has abundant conifers, tannins leach from the decomposing needles and will stain the water in lotic systems a caramel color that resembles weak coffee or black tea. The term **blackwater** is applied to such lotic systems with high concentrations of tannins. High acidity in blackwater rivers is natural, and while they may be somewhat less biodiverse as a result, many animals have adapted to life in the acidic, tea-colored water and thrive in it. Blackwater rivers are also somewhat less prone to carrying waterborne pathogens. Though unaware of why such water was moderately safer to drink than other streams, the first waves of European colonists in North America realized this early and would cache blackwater in barrels for drinking.

HUMAN IMPRINTS ON THE LANDSCAPE

Lotic systems also carry many signatures of human activities in watersheds. Agricultural and urban lands represent the most common changes to watersheds that scientists use to determine how much rivers may have been altered by human changes on the landscape. Excess fertilizer not consumed by crops or lawns will eventually travel through the watershed and into streams, where algae consume plant-supporting nutrients just as eagerly as terrestrial plants. When such changes cause algae populations to grow very large, respiring cells can cause water oxygen levels to become depleted enough to threaten fish and invertebrates. Activities that disturb soils like tilling and construction, when not conducted with care, can cause silt to wash from watersheds to streams. When this occurs, the extra silt fills in spaces between rocks on river and stream bottoms where many organisms make their homes.

However, the most severe changes in lotic systems occur when landscape development prevents rain and snow from soaking into the watershed. Roofs, roads, sidewalks, and streets are collectively termed **impervious surfaces** by hydrologists because water cannot permeate into them. Instead, during rainfall or snowmelt, water rapidly flows downhill across these surfaces and typically gets quickly routed to a river or stream channel. Urban watersheds with extensive impervious surfaces therefore have streams that flood more rapidly, and with less rainfall, compared to similar watersheds without urban land. Stream channels physically change following watershed urbanization because of the increased flood activity. Eroded banks, loss of sand and gravel, and widened channels all typify urban streams. Impervious surfaces also effectively wash pollutants (such as oil leaked from cars) directly from pavement to stream channels. Even water temperatures change in urban streams, as rain that falls on pavement warmed by the summer sun sends a pulse of hot water to the channel. All these impacts can cause local extinction of aquatic species that are sensitive to environmental changes.

The annual **hydrograph**, a plot that shows seasonal changes of flow rates, offers perhaps the clearest expression of interactions between lotic systems and their watersheds. Figure 2.3 shows how the flow patterns of four streams change over four years, with many lessons illustrating how watersheds shape river behavior. All four lotic systems have similar watershed sizes yet show very distinct seasonal flow patterns.

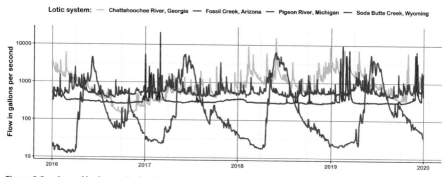

Figure 2.3. Annual hydrographs for four lotic systems in the continental United States with very different watersheds and, by extension, very different annual flow patterns. Lines depict the flow rates from January 1, 2016, to December 31, 2019. Note that the scale on the vertical axis is nonlinear: Each major gridline represents an increase in flow by a factor of ten.

In the *Chattahoochee River*, a 44.7-square-mile watershed at the point where these data come from in northern Georgia, rain (and some snow) occurs year-round and the most important plant life are deciduous forests with trees that shed their leaves in winter. The upper watershed is moderately mountainous and was never covered by a glacier during ice ages. Thus we see some evidence of seasonal changes in transpiration, with flow tending to be highest in late winter or spring and lowest in summer. But storms large enough to cause minor flooding (indicated by the spikes in flow) can occur year-round, as the watershed can only store so much water after a storm.

Fossil Creek in Arizona (68.5 square miles) is famous for its beautiful swimming holes with impressive waterfalls. The watershed has abundant limestone deposits that help keep flow extremely consistent year-round by creating springs with large water reserves. However, winter storms can quickly lead to floods on Fossil Creek because the desert watershed is very poor at retaining stormwater. Instead, the desert floor acts almost like pavement, delivering water very quickly to the stream channel and potentially threatening the safety of swimmers cooling off in the stream. Limestone in the watershed dissolves and reforms in the river, creating structures formed of calcium carbonate **travertine** that form waterfalls.

The watershed of the *Pigeon River* (57.7 square miles) in Michigan's lower peninsula was entirely under an ice sheet during the last ice age. When the ice sheet retreated it left behind many natural lakes and deep, porous soils. Consequently, although the watershed receives relatively even precipitation year-round like the Chattahoochee, flow levels remain quite stable throughout the year. The highest flows occur during spring when snowmelt delivers a predictable annual pulse of water.

Finally, the world-renowned trout stream *Soda Butte Creek* (30.9 square miles) in the northeastern corner of Yellowstone National Park shows the strongest seasonal shift in flows between seasons. Winter in Yellowstone is bitterly cold and most of the annual water delivered to Soda Butte's watershed arrives as snow that remains frozen over winter. Temperatures are so cold in winter that flow in Soda Butte gets very low throughout this season as the groundwater drains from its watershed. But snow rapidly melts once temperatures warm up enough in late spring or early summer, and flow increases by more than two orders of magnitude. Yellowstone was covered in glaciers during the last ice age, and watersheds there do have some limestone deposits. Both attributes help to slowly store and deliver water throughout the warm season, when rainfall is rarely strong enough to cause flooding.

The next chapter continues the use of hydrographs to explore how and why flows change over time in greater detail. But doing so requires keeping the watershed concept close in mind, as the physical, chemical, and biological properties of lotic systems cannot be understood without considering the landscapes they drain. All rivers and streams are intimately connected to the lands that provide them with water.

CHAPTER 2
HYDROLOGY

Hydrology is the science of how water moves through the Earth. A central tenet in the field is the **hydrologic cycle**, or the transition of water from oceans to the surface of Earth and back. Lotic systems orchestrate the hydrologic cycle finale by delivering water to its oceanic origin. The dynamics of the many complex stages throughout the hydrologic cycle, from precipitation to groundwater flow, are key toward structuring how lotic systems behave.

Before exploring water movement, however, an account of how much water exists among Earth systems reveals the rarity and value of lotic freshwater as a natural resource (Figure 3.1). Although water covers 70 percent of Earth's surface, 96.5 percent of all global water is saltwater. Permanently frozen ice and snow, with the largest volumes found in the Antarctic and Greenland ice sheets, constitute more than two-thirds of global freshwater reserves. Water flowing through lotic systems represents only 0.006 percent of global freshwater, or 0.0002 percent of all water on Earth. The Earth is therefore truly an oceanic planet, and our rivers and streams reflect the rarest representatives of global aquatic systems.

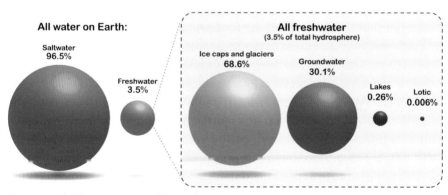

Figure 3.1. Global water proportionally quantified by marine versus freshwater and major stocks of freshwater. Note that water amounts are represented by sphere volume, not circle area. CULLEN HANES

All water traveling through lotic systems started the journey as rain or snow (precipitation). Most precipitation begins as water evaporating from a distant, oceanic source, but water vapor released by plants and evaporating from land can also contribute significantly to the clouds. As discussed in the previous chapter, the amount of precipitation that falls on a watershed directly determines how much water ultimately flows through the lotic system. Annual precipitation levels vary substantially throughout North America (Figure 3.2). By extension, the size of a lotic system relative to its watershed will be directly determined by regional precipitation. For example, if comparing flows, the Missouri and Ohio Rivers draining the two watersheds as highlighted in Figure 3.2 are approximately the same size, with both rivers flowing at an annual average of about 90,000 cubic feet per second. However, the Missouri River watershed is 7.5 times larger than the portion of the Ohio River watershed shown on the map (522,500 square miles compared to 70,130). By extension, this means that one will encounter far more permanently flowing lotic systems in wet climates relative to deserts.

Not all the water delivered as precipitation remains near the surface of Earth, however. A very large fraction of rainwater and melted snow can quickly evaporate or transpire through plants directly back into the atmosphere given the right conditions. Warm temperatures, low humidity, plenty of sunlight, and strong winds all promote physical evaporation,

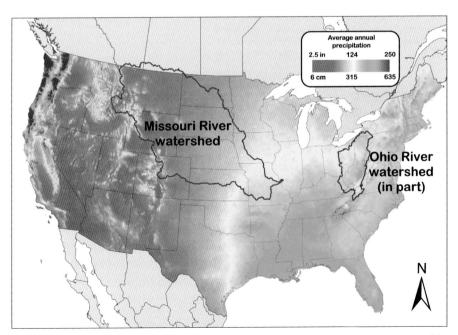

Figure 3.2. Average annual precipitation in the continental United States. In terms of flow rates, the sizes of the Missouri and Ohio Rivers draining the watersheds shown are equal.

and photosynthesizing plants serve as very effective pumps that move water from soil to the atmosphere. Both processes return an estimated 60 percent of all global precipitation that falls on land right back into the atmosphere within hours. If conditions are just right, such as in desert with low humidity and abundant sun, over 95 percent of precipitation that falls on a watershed might return to the atmosphere without ever reaching a lotic system. In other words, effectively all water that falls on a desert watershed will very quickly return to the atmosphere, as if the storm represented a pit stop on a road trip. Seasonal changes in precipitation, evaporation, and transpiration profoundly affect rivers, as only the water that arrives as precipitation and remains below or on the surface of Earth becomes flow in a lotic system. However, evaporated or transpired water does not necessarily travel far and may fall to Earth again within short periods of time or at close distance. For example, in the Amazon River watershed, more than 50 percent of all rainwater may come from water transpired by the towering rainforest trees growing within the system. A water molecule in the Amazon watershed may theoretically transition from the atmosphere to the forest trees multiple times before contributing to the mighty river, if it ever does.

Most of the water that avoids evapotranspiration will travel to a lotic system as slowly moving, subterranean flow called **groundwater**. Rainfall delivered to a watershed percolates into the soil under typical conditions, as water flows into and through pore spaces between the soil particles. The amount of water that soils can accommodate in these tiny spaces can be quite large. For instance, up to 40 percent of space in a jar of sand may be empty space, ready for water to fill. Water that travels below the depths where roots reach may contribute to flow through an **aquifer,** defined as a geologic layer with high permeability to water. The depth below ground where all pore spaces are entirely filled by water, or the point at which you will strike water if you are digging a well, is termed the **water table**. Seasonal changes in precipitation and evaporation will cause the water table to rise and fall; thus water tables can be as topographically variable as a hilly landscape. The elevation of a water table can be estimated without using a shovel by walking to the nearest lotic system, as the elevation where the water table is shallow enough that it reaches the surface of Earth marks the edge of a river or stream. The amount of time required for water to flow through soils and aquifers before it reaches a lotic system is highly variable. Ten- to one-hundred-year periods for a water molecule to flow as groundwater before reaching a lotic channel are very common, while aquifers with water that last fell as precipitation millions of years ago can be found around the world. The oldest groundwater discovered to date, extracted from a South African gold mine, was dated to 2.6 billion years ago using stable isotopes of chemicals dissolved in the water. Although such groundwater clearly was not about to contribute water to a lotic system, the situation illustrates how water can stay in the ground a very, very long time before bubbling to the surface.

The position of the water table relative to a valley channel will also determine how a lotic system changes in size as it flows downhill. Most lotic systems grow larger as they move downstream because the water table in the surrounding landscape is at least somewhat higher in elevation relative to the channel. However, if a channel is perched well above the water table, then water in the lotic system will percolate into the ground and become progressively smaller as it flows. Such scenarios are termed **gaining streams** and **losing streams**, respectively. Losing streams are most often encountered in desert settings, as lotic systems originating in higher elevations receive more precipitation then flow into drier settings.

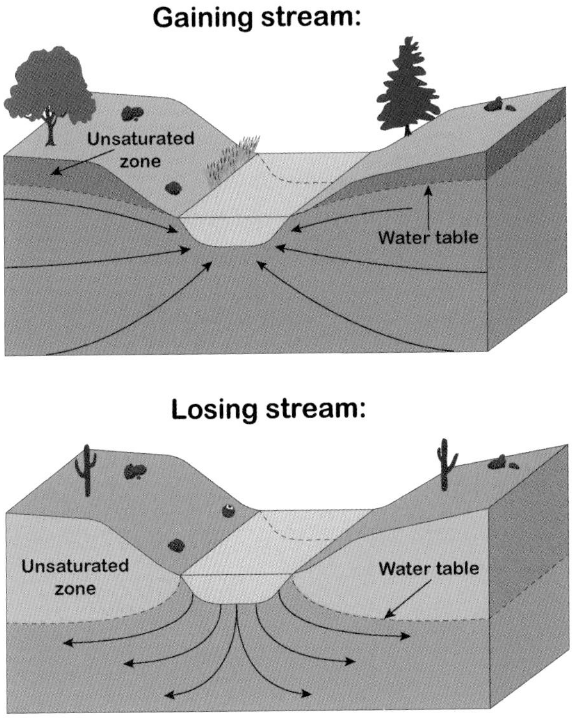

Gaining stream:

Losing stream:

Figure 3.3. The water table elevation relative to a stream channel will determine if a lotic system grows larger (gaining stream) or smaller (losing stream) as it flows downstream. CULLEN HANES

But not all water flowing through lotic systems necessarily got there by first journeying through soils and aquifers. If soil pore spaces at the surface are already completely saturated with water, and if rainfall during a storm exceeds the rate at which water can percolate into the ground, the new water will instead travel over the land surface toward the lowest point it can find, which is typically the channel of a lotic system. Therefore, a storm delivering rain to soils already fully saturated by water can rapidly lead to flooding. Water levels therefore rise and fall based on the recent weather history within the watersheds they are inexorably linked to.

A sponge serves as a useful metaphor for how water moves from a watershed to a lotic system. Soils and permeable rock layers act as a sponge, soaking up water during rain or snowmelt and then slowly releasing it over time as gravity pulls downward. Just like a sponge remains damp after squeezing it, watersheds retain some water even after gravity extracts all that it can because residual water clings to surfaces within tight soil pores. The same force that holds a suction cup to a smooth surface will retain water within soil and rock. Holding a fully saturated sponge under a faucet will result in immediate overflow, just as watersheds with soils fully saturated by water will route water quickly to a channel. Even if a sponge does have the ability to hold water, placing it under a faucet with too much flow will cause some of that flow to run off because it takes a bit of time for a sponge to absorb water. Similarly, if rainfall during a heavy storm exceeds the rate at which a watershed can soak up water, excess flow will immediately run off into the stream. On the other end of the spectrum, if a sponge really dries out, it might not instantly absorb water when placed under a faucet because the pore spaces have contracted so much. Similarly, very dry soils may become compacted and temporarily lose some absorbency.

To show how a lotic system typically responds to a storm, Figure 3.4 illustrates flow in Cataloochee Creek, a pristine mountain stream that runs east out of Great Smoky Mountains National Park, responding to two summer storms in August 2020. About three-quarters of an inch of rain fell on August 3, causing flows in the Cataloochee to rise more than threefold in five hours. The rapid increase in flow likely occurred because soils in the watershed became quickly saturated after receiving so much rain; thus some of the water that fell during the later stages of the storm flowed over land directly to the channel.

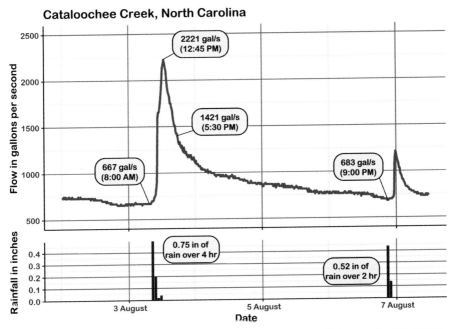

Figure 3.4. Cataloochee Creek, North Carolina, responding to two storm events that occurred in early August 2020.

Figure 3.5. Cataloochee Creek, North Carolina is a pristine mountain stream that flows east out of Great Smoky Mountains National Park. RON WELCH

If you would like to know how high your favorite waterway in the United States is currently flowing, chances are you can find real-time information on it or a nearby lotic system using the impressively large USGS network of flow monitoring stations. All hydrographs shown in this book were made using data made freely available by the USGS. But the lotic systems shown here are by no means the extent of systems they monitor. Hundreds of stations report data in real time, allowing one to check if flows are running safely for a planned activity just about anywhere water is flowing within the United States.

1. Start at the USGS National Water Information System at https://dashboard. waterdata.usgs.gov/

2. Zoom in to the lotic system of interest on the map.

3. All actively running flow monitoring gages are shown as circles with color indicating if they are running high (cool colors) or low (warm colors). Click on the dot to access the in-depth data.

4. You will see a new window appear with figures showing current and recent conditions in your lotic system (or one flowing nearby). Some USGS stations report water temperatures, for instance, and this figure may appear first. You open or close all plots using the menu on the top ribbon.

5. Data for the past seven days will appear by default. However, you can explore all data the USGS collected by selecting *Data* on the top ribbon. Doing so opens a more in-depth interface for the site. You can quickly choose to view the past 7, 30, or 365 days automatically, or choose *Change Time Span* to enter specific dates.

Flows dropped once the rain ceased, but not as quickly as they rose. More than five hours after the river peaked and the rain stopped, flow was still twice as high as it was before the storm. The tendency for water to rise much faster in response to a storm than it recedes after the peak flow is very typical in headwater lotic systems and is termed **hysteresis**. Just like a sponge, the soil and permeable rocks in the Cataloochee watershed absorbed plenty of water during the storm and then released it at a rate that gradually slowed down over time. Many predatory fish, including native brook trout that inhabit the Cataloochee, take advantage of slowly declining but still elevated flow during this period because their prey organisms are easily dislodged by turbulence. More than three days after the first storm, the Cataloochee was still flowing at a higher rate than before the first pulse of rain. Within a day, though, most water comprising flow had already been filtered by soil and rock. By the morning of August 4, the water flowing through the Cataloochee was probably crystal clear.

As discussed earlier, watershed characteristics determine flood frequency and severity. Comparing long-term hydrographs of the Cataloochee and the upper Colorado River (Figure 3.6) reveals how climate attributes determine annual peak flows. The average flow of these two lotic systems (at the points where USGS gauges that provided these data are located) are similar, but land upstream on the Colorado River consists of montane forests and alpine tundra of Rocky Mountain National Park, where most water arrives as snow and remains frozen all winter. In contrast, the Cataloochee drains a pristine deciduous forest watershed at a much lower elevation that receives more precipitation year-round. Consequently, the highest annual flows on the Cataloochee typically occur during winter or early spring, when vegetation is dormant and strong early season storms cause the creek to easily flood. Peak flow on the Colorado *always* occurs in late spring or early summer when snowmelt in the high country reaches a maximum. Although predicting the maximum flood each year is impossible, the likelihood of annual peak floods can be calculated if decades of flow data are available.

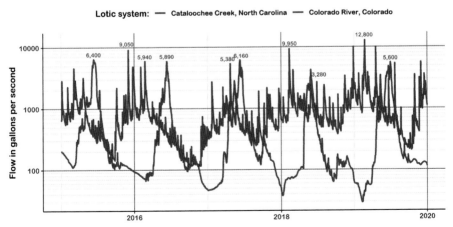

Figure 3.6. Hydrographs of Cataloochee Creek, North Carolina, and the Colorado River outside Grand Lake, Colorado, between 2015 and 2020. The highest daily average flows for each year and lotic system are noted.

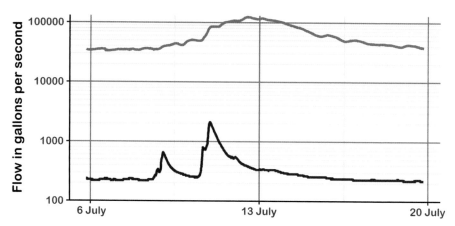

Figure 3.7. Hydrographs of the Delaware River and Pohatcong Creek, a tributary of the Delaware, responding to two summer storms in 2020.

Although all lotic systems rise after a storm, the larger the watershed, the more slowly flows rise and fall. Figure 3.7 shows two hydrographs from the Delaware River watershed: Pohatcong Creek flows west into the Delaware River from a 56-square-mile watershed in New Jersey, while the watershed of the Delaware River just downstream of Pohatcong Creek is more than one hundred times larger (6,328 square miles). Two summer storms respectively delivered 0.1 and 0.4 inch of rain on July 10 and 11, 2020, to the region. Just like the Cataloochee in Figure 3.4, flow rose sharply to a peak about ten times higher than prior to the storms and then gradually declined in the Pohatcong. However, flow gradually rose in the Delaware River and peaked a few days later than the Pohatcong peak. The Delaware River hydrograph does not even suggest that two storms occurred. As the Delaware reached peak flow in response to the storms, Pohatcong Creek was probably running clear at baseflow. The different responses to the same storms reflect a difference in watershed sizes. Like all large rivers, the Delaware would not exist without tens or hundreds of thousands of first-order streams that contribute flow to the mainstem. Pulses of water traveling through the watersheds of large rivers must travel through the network tributaries before reaching large rivers. Such dynamics explain how hydrologists can predict severe floods on the mainstem of the Mississippi River caused by snowmelt hundreds of miles upstream in Minnesota days or even weeks in advance of peak flow.

Hydrologists use long-term flow records to create what is called a **flood recurrence interval** graph to predict the annual highest flow event. To do so, one first tabulates the maximum peak flow for each year of record and subsequently rank-orders them, with the highest annual flow on record receiving a rank of one and the lowest flow ranked the highest. Next, the total number of years on record (plus one) are divided by the annual flood ranks to calculate the recurrence interval, which is a best estimate of how many years will elapse before the flood occurs again. Graphing recurrence intervals with their associated annual peak flows and fitting a straight line to the pattern (Figure 3.6) reveals the likely magnitude of annual maximum flooding. For example, the Cataloochee will *likely* reach an annual high of about 15,000 gallons per second at least every ten years, while a very high annual flood of 25,000 gallons per second would be *expected* to occur once in a century. Although the upper Colorado River watershed is about 30 percent larger, annual peak flows are significantly smaller than on the Cataloochee: The expected 10- and 100-year floods are approximately 7,500 and 13,000 gallons per second, respectively.

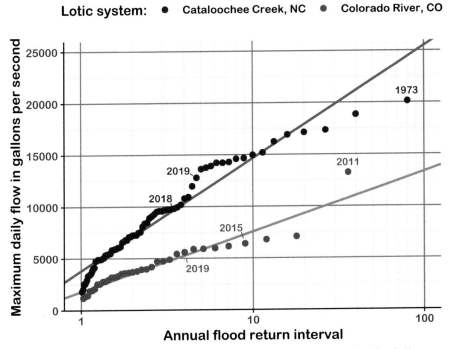

Figure 3.8. Flood recurrence interval plots for Cataloochee Creek, North Carolina, and the Colorado River outside Grand Lake, Colorado. Flows represent daily average values.

Although flood recurrence interval graphs represent useful tools, the information they convey can be easily misinterpreted. News coverage of floods that take lives and damage property often reports recurrence intervals to communicate the rarity of such events. But one should not take comfort believing that a 100-year flood will occur exactly every century. Rather, the estimated 100-year flood is what hydrologists *expect* will be the annual high flow in a lotic system every century based on the data they have to work with. Therefore, although unlikely, a 100-year flood could occur two or three years in a row simply due to chance. Longer data records create more reliable flood recurrence graphs. However, as climate change causes new patterns of rain and snow timing and magnitude, historic flow records will prove less representative of how lotic systems behave in modern times. More frequent return intervals for catastrophic floods linked to climate change have already been detected. Earlier annual peak flow dates have been discovered in the lotic systems of western North America fed primarily by melting alpine snow.

Nearly every feature in a lotic system, from the chemical concentrations in the water, to the valley shape, to the organisms that live within, are structured by ever-changing flows. High flows allow rivers to deliver sediment from the watershed that builds land downstream, such as the Mississippi River and Nile Deltas. Although floods can bring devastation to some species, they also allow many organisms to breed and feed in nutrient-rich valley-bottom floodplains. Salmon rely on seasonal cues in flow patterns to time their migration. Many species of rare wildflowers specialize in scoured riverbank habitat, where less hardy plants get easily swept away. Such repeatedly observed close relationships between organisms and flow patterns has led river ecologists to declare the **natural flow regime**, or the timing, magnitude, and duration of flow events, as a prime force shaping lotic ecosystems. Consequently, analyzing a hydrograph can lead to a deeper understanding of rivers in many ways.

CHAPTER 3
CHANNEL GEOMORPHOLOGY

The constant movement of water in lotic systems represents a powerful geologic force. Wherever they flow, lotic systems act as a buzz saw on the landscape, as water constantly erodes bedrock and sediment from channels. But lotic systems also serve as a constructive force. A piece of rock dislodged from the channel could move tens of miles downstream during a flood. Such particles eventually become deposited, thereby creating new land adjacent to the channel. The study of how flowing waters shape the surface of Earth is termed **fluvial geomorphology**, a discipline that blends geology, physics, and lotic science.

A fundamental concept of counterbalancing forces forms the core of fluvial geomorphology. Flowing water constitutes a force breaking apart rock and moving particles downstream. But rocks tend to be difficult to erode and sediment is heavy; thus channel banks and bottoms resist this force. Water overcomes this resistance and dislodges or moves sediment only when it becomes powerful enough to do so, typically when flow increases. The balance of forces means that water pulled downstream by gravity finds the path downslope that represents the least amount of energy possible needed to ultimately reach the ocean. When the force of flow matches the resistance of channel sediments, the channel itself remains stable and the path of water consistent. However, flow constantly shifts, and large volumes of sediment move downstream during floods. After a flood recedes it may reveal a changed channel, with new masses of sediment in some places and freshly eroded banks in others. The calmed flow settles into a new route that represents the path of least resistance.

Fluvial geomorphologists call this balance of forces **dynamic equilibrium**: dynamic because the channel inevitably changes with flow, and equilibrium because the destructive and resistive forces remain balanced over time. The concept does not mean an absence of channel evolution. Even under equilibrium conditions, a large flood might cause a channel to reroute itself. Instead, basic channel dimensions such as the width, depth, and frequency of meander bends remain constant. However, if key watershed attributes change, the dynamic equilibrium shifts, causing substantial evolution of channel shape. For example, climate change resulting in more precipitation will lead to accelerated erosion and deposition until a new equilibrium between the counterbalancing forces emerges.

THE VALLEY, DEPOSITION, AND EROSION

One primary means of explaining how the path of a lotic system came to be is to consider the geologic features of the valley it flows through. Watersheds in mountainous settings where hard bedrock forms most of the channel bottom tend to be confined by the canyons created by the erosive force of water. A mountain headwater stream flowing through hard granite might require millions of years to erode the channel a few feet. Therefore, lotic systems in mountainous settings tend to be straight, single-channeled, and composed of large particles that have washed down from steep slopes. Follow a river downstream in most regions and the topography becomes much gentler. Hard bedrock often gives way to earth that a shovel might break through, with most inorganic particles at the surface of Earth consisting of gravel, sand, or silt. Lotic channels in these settings are more likely to meander and periodically change course. Land adjacent to lowland channels, termed the **floodplain**, is often flat and prone to regular flooding. When lotic systems flow through floodplains, predictable rules of deposition and erosion help explain the path that emerges.

The capacity for sediment movement in a lotic system can be predicted by two simple variables: water speed and particle size. Water moving against a channel bank is more likely to erode a particle from the bank if it is moving fast. Rapidly moving flow is also more capable of moving larger-sized particles suspended in the water column, thereby transporting sediment some distance downstream after dislodging it from a channel bank. When water slows down, sediment will fall out of the water column and become deposited on the channel bottom or banks. Because larger particles require rapid water speeds to remain in motion, particle transport can be largely predicted by the size of sediment being moved.

SEDIMENT TRANSPORT

Constant channel evolution and bank erosion in lotic systems means that they are not just conduits for water, but also sediment. The amount of sediment moving through a channel is directly related to channel size because the two variables that dictate sediment movement in water—flow speed and particle size—change predictably throughout a river network.

Flow speed consistently increases from headwater reaches to the river mouth. Although the cascades and turbulence characteristic of small, headwater streams may suggest to the eye that water is moving very rapidly, shallow depths and large particles exert significant drag on flowing water. At the opposite end of the size spectrum, few mid-channel physical impediments and very deep water mean that large river flow speeds are the fastest within a river network. The human circulatory system serves as an analogy to river network flow speeds. Blood moving through our body moves fastest within the large vessels near the heart and slowest in the tiny capillary vessels connected to muscles.

In contrast, the typical particle size in a lotic channel decreases from the headwaters to the river mouth. Channel bottoms in small, headwater streams typically consist of boulders or cobbles that rolled down the adjacent hillsides and settled in the channel. Such particles require an immense degree of force to move, and flow in headwater streams rarely rises enough to do so. In large rivers, channel bottoms are largely composed of easily moved sand or silt. Channel bottoms in rivers with consistent sources of sand, such as the Amazon, often consist of undulating dunes reminiscent of the Sahara.

Sediment movement rates in a river network therefore increase as lotic systems grow. Slow water speeds and large particles mean that headwater streams transport *relatively* little sediment. Erosion and deposition in headwater reaches does occur, but only during floods. However, the rapid flow speeds and small particles in large rivers mean that they transport more sediment, even during baseflow, at rates that can be a true geologic force. For example, as it nears the Gulf of Mexico, sand and silt rolling along the channel bottom (called **bedload**) in the Mississippi River might exceed more than 100,000 tons per day. Impressive as that value may be, up to 1.5 million tons of fine sediment in the water column might move through the Mississippi during a high-flow day, a value equivalent to the weight of 130,000 school buses. New land is born where massive sediment loads moved by large rivers settle out of the water. Coastal Louisiana, including New Orleans, exists thanks to constant replenishment of sediment that originated thousands of miles upstream delivered by the Mississippi River.

CHANNEL EVOLUTION

Lotic systems moving through floodplains erode and deposit sediment in consistent patterns determined by water speed. As a lotic system moves around a meander, the fastest flows occur at the outer edge of the bend. The channel bank therefore represents a zone of erosion at this position, with the force of water gradually causing land comprising the channel bank to fall into its flow. Geomorphologists refer to this side of the channel as a **cutbank**. In contrast, the water speed at the inner edge of the meander bend is slow, near zero, or possibly even moving in the upstream direction as an eddy. Therefore, particles moving in the water column will typically fall out of suspension in the inner edge of the meander bend, and land composed of freshly delivered particles will gradually grow on this side of the channel. The bar deposit of sediment is termed a **point bar**. Cutbanks and point bars tend to be consistently positioned on opposite sides of lotic system channels wherever the system travels through a meander bend, as water speed across a meander bend almost always varies from slow on the inner edge to rapid on the outer edge (see Figure 4.1).

The erosion and deposition processes will subtly continue until reaching a threshold that causes the flow of the entire lotic system to change course. As the point bar grows over time, it pushes the water farther and laterally into the meander bend. Simultaneously, flow heading toward the meander bend meets a separate cutbank upstream and gradually erodes the bank. If enough erosion occurs at this upstream cutbank *and* enough of the point bar grows to counter the force of water flowing downstream, the entire lotic system will cut a new channel that bypasses the meander altogether. Water typically encounters less resistance in this new channel and therefore routes all flow through it. Close examination of elevation profiles adjacent to lowland rivers reveals signatures of old river channels that may not be evident on the ground, as nutrient-rich floodplain soils tend to support towering trees that mask subtle topographic changes. A former meander may become a dry channel, wetted only during high flow. Old meander bends of some large rivers flowing through very flat terrain may form an **oxbow lake**: an isolated body of water entirely cut off from lotic water but a short distance from a channel that once flowed through it (see Figure 4.2).

The size and quantity of mobile sediment in the watershed strongly influences channel evolution. Single-channeled, meandering lotic systems described above tend to have a relatively low sediment supply upstream, most often because thick vegetation like forests help prevent

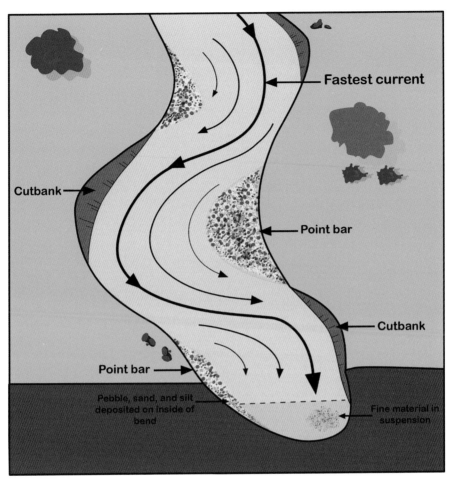

Figure 4.1. Erosion and deposition of sediment throughout lotic system meanders. NICOLE LOSKOCH-FLAHERTY

erosion. Watersheds with large quantities of loose sediment, however, usually drain to lotic systems that form multiple channels with small islands dissecting the flow, a channel form that geomorphologists refer to as **braided**. Lotic systems formed by meltwater at the terminus of glaciers always form braided channels. Although they appear immobile to the eye, glaciers constantly flow as snow and ice accumulating upslope pushes the mass of ice down their valleys. The force of moving ice grinds rock underneath glaciers, thereby creating massive volumes of loose sediment that mix with meltwater to create the streams where they terminate. Glaciers churn out so much sediment from their valleys that the lotic systems forming downstream often consist of many channels flowing around countless, short-lived islands.

Rivers can create very peculiar political boundaries when they cut off meanders and change their flow path. Two inland states, Iowa and Kentucky, include tiny parcels of land that one cannot reach unless they leave and reenter the state or swim across a river. Both geographic oddities exist thanks to lotic channel evolution associated with deposition and erosion of meander bends.

Travel to the northern suburbs of Omaha, Nebraska, and you will encounter a 2-square-mile patch of Iowa that is entirely cut off from the rest of the state by the Missouri River. The exclave, where just under 4,000 residents live in the Omaha suburb of Carter Lake, was created when a flood on the Missouri in March 1877 cut off a meander bend. An oxbow lake isolated from the Missouri mainstem by about four-fifths of a mile, also called Carter Lake, was created during the flood. Carter Lake, which was contiguous with the rest of Iowa prior to the river-shifting flood, represents the only land in Iowa lying west of the Missouri River.

At the farthest western point of Kentucky, in Fulton County, a very severe meander bend in the Mississippi River wraps around a 30-square-mile patch of the state that cannot be reached on dry land unless one traverses Tennessee. The Kentucky Bend, as it is known today, may have been created when a series of strong earthquakes that occurred in 1811 and 1812 caused the Mississippi to radically shift course in several places near the bend. The quickly changing river course likely caused a fair amount of confusion for land surveyors marking the boundary of what was then a frontier region to European settlers.

Figure 4.2. The town of Carter Lake, Iowa, a suburb of Omaha, Nebraska, that is entirely cut off from the rest of Iowa by the Missouri River. Deposition and erosion during an 1877 flood cut off a former meander bend of the Missouri that became Carter Lake, an oxbow lake.

Lotic system channels have always evolved, set new courses, and changed shape over multiple time scales. A meander bend may transition into an oxbow lake following a single storm. However, geomorphic processes also respond to major events that adjust watershed precipitation patterns or sediment supplies. Transitions between ice ages and warm periods radically alter how lotic system channels evolve over millennia. Although such long-term channel evolution may evade the eye, topographic data readily reveal river channels of a more distant past. The elevation profile of Pittsburgh, Pennsylvania (Figure 4.3) illustrates long-term channel evolution. Two rivers, the Allegheny and Monongahela, converge in Pittsburgh to form the Ohio River. Although the hills of Pittsburgh rise about 700 feet above the rivers, major pulses of sediment delivered from the Allegheny after the end of ice ages caused

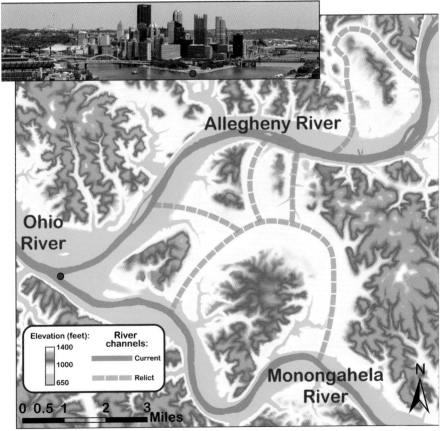

Figure 4.3. Topography of Pittsburgh, Pennsylvania, with former river channels shown as dotted lines. Modern rivers appear in solid blue. The red dots represent where the Ohio River forms from the Allegheny and Monongahela Rivers on the map and image. RYAN UTZ/PAUL WASNEKI

major channel rerouting events many times. Relict, long-abandoned river channels where city neighborhoods now exist reveal themselves in topographic maps. Today, dams and locks on the rivers prevent such large-scale changes from occurring.

POOLS AND RIFFLES

Most medium-sized lotic systems feature distinguishable habitat types that are regularly repeated along the channel. The two most easily recognized are **riffles** and **pools**. Riffles are topographic high points in the channel bottom. Flow moving through a riffle travels not just over the relatively coarse sediment but through it as well. During baseflow, water depth in riffles is shallow and the water surface is rough. In contrast, pools are depressions in the channel bottom where depths are greater than riffles, the water surface at baseflow is smooth, and the particles settling at the bottom of the channel tend to be fine, like sand or silt. Pool-riffle sequences often repeat themselves with predictable regularity. One can expect a new riffle to begin at a distance downstream of about five to seven times the channel width.

The question of why riffles and pools form with regularity remains a subject of debate for fluvial geomorphologists, though one defensible theory involves flow speed and sediment moving during floods. Perhaps somewhat counterintuitive to the eye, water moves faster in a pool than it does a riffle during baseflow. The difference occurs because the coarse, shallow sediments in a riffle offer strong resistance and therefore reduce flow speed, while the greater water depth in a pool allows water to move unimpeded near the surface. However, when a flood occurs, the elevation of water over the entire channel rises and the difference in flow speed between riffles and pools diminishes. Pulses of sediment move downstream during floods, and the fine sediments at the bottom of a pool will more likely be swept into the current. As flow begins to recede after the storm passes, water speeds decline first over a riffle. Therefore, large particles will more likely settle to the bottom of the channel in a riffle during the waning stages of floods, while flow through pools continues to transport sediment downstream. Consequently, pool-riffle sequences can be viewed as signatures of sediment waves moving through the channel, especially during floods.

Channel habitat diversity created by riffles and pools is ecologically important. A portion of flow moving through a riffle is forced through sediments because riffles are relatively higher in elevation. Thanks to constantly replenished flow from the surface, water in the pore spaces between riffle sediments contains high oxygen levels. The combination of well-oxygenated water and small spaces to hide from predators makes riffles prime habitat for invertebrates. Such favorable conditions cause larval aquatic insects to typically be far more abundant in riffles compared to pools. Spawning salmon prefer to dig their nests in riffle heads for the same reasons. A lack of flow through the fine sediment at the bottom of pools typically means low oxygen in water between pore spaces. However, plenty of larval insects can tolerate depressed oxygen levels and like to burrow in sand or silt; thus they often make pool sediments their home. Furthermore, as anglers can attest, many fish species use the slow flow speed at the bottom of pools for a place to rest while they scan the faster-moving water above for drifting invertebrates.

Lotic system size determines if pool-riffle sequences exist as the dominant geomorphic channel pattern. In the smallest headwater streams with the steepest slopes, distinguishable riffles and pools may not exist at all because channel sediments are dominated by coarse particles eroded from adjacent hillsides. Boulders, bedrock, and erratic changes in slope create a series of what geomorphologists call **step-pools**. At the other end of the spectrum, large rivers also tend to lack pool-riffle sequences because they are simply too deep for riffles to form.

TREES SHAPING THE CHANNEL

Trees growing adjacent to channels represent another example of how watershed ecosystems are intricately connected to the streams that drain them. **Large woody debris**, the term lotic scientists apply to any substantive mass of wood that falls from a bank and embeds in the channel, exerts a strong geomorphic force. Live trees growing on the channel edge also influence channel geometry by buffering the banks from the force of water.

Many geomorphic, ecological, and possibly even hydrologic effects ensue whenever a sizable tree trunk or crown falls into a lotic system. Wood spanning the entire wetted section of a channel retains sediment, smaller pieces of wood, and leaves that might otherwise be quickly carried downstream. The snag of wood and debris might also slow the speed of water locally, thereby allowing it to settle and reducing the total amount of sediment flowing downstream. Flow speed during a storm could even be slowed considerably in a headwater stream with an abundance of large woody debris distributed throughout the channel. Therefore, floods in a river might be less severe if the headwater streams flowing into it feature plenty of large woody debris. Woody snags often create small waterfalls if they trap enough sediment to redirect flow over the top of the natural dam. When this occurs, the force of flow immediately downstream will scour away sediment and create a small pool. Instream habitat diversity is thus the ecological effect created by large woody debris. Tangles of wood and leaves within the snag allows small invertebrates to feed, while the pool just downstream gives a place for predatory fish to lurk for prey. Large woody debris might be the only force creating habitat complexity for creatures inhabiting lowland streams where channel sediment consists entirely of sand.

Live trees growing on channel banks also play important geomorphic roles for streams. The roots of trees growing in the nutrient-rich soils adjacent to stream channels help anchor bank sediments in place and can greatly reduce erosion. Watersheds with agricultural activity right at the edge of channels reveal just how important trees are for preventing bank erosion. For example, when scientists planted eucalyptus trees in land adjacent to a stream in western Australia that had been

Figure 4.4. A snag of large woody debris retains a mass of sediment and organic matter across the channel of a headwater stream in the mountains of central Pennsylvania. The pool below the wood creates habitat for native brook trout.

When it comes to influencing river geomorphology, no aquatic organism matches that of the beaver (*Castor canadensis*), an amphibious rodent. Ecologists refer to organisms that reshape their physical environment as **ecosystem engineers**. Beavers might be the ultimate ecosystem engineers of nature because of their dam building, a strategy that helps them avoid predators because they can build a protective lodge in the middle of a pond. A beaver dam that spans an entire lotic channel dramatically reduces flow speed, which allows sediment to settle out of water and accumulate in great quantities. Dam ponds can grow large enough to exceed the volume of an Olympic-sized swimming pool. The effect can convert a tiny headwater stream channel surrounded by forest into a broad series of tiered pools with wetland plants growing along the margins. A beaver diet consists mostly of live bark and young tree shoots; thus most trees adjacent to beaver ponds are felled to the tooth. Beavers typically abandon their lodge and dam after about ten years or whenever they exhaust local food sources.

Lotic systems are profoundly affected by beaver dams in countless ways. Sediment that would otherwise be transported downstream slowly accumulates behind beaver dams throughout the dammed pond. High flows following a storm are mitigated by the wetland meadows adjacent to the ponds and by the dams themselves; thus a large river watershed with healthy beaver populations in the headwaters will experience less severe floods. Ponding raises the water table in land adjacent to the channel, allowing wetland vegetation to thrive far from the pond shoreline. Water temperature downstream of a beaver dam tends to be substantially higher than the flow coming into it because solar radiation warms the

Figure 4.5. A fully formed beaver pond on a headwater stream in Pennsylvania. The channel upstream of this water body is just a few feet wide.

surface of the pond. Many plant and animal species, including waterfowl, newts, frogs, and wetland plants that typically fail to set in flowing water, thrive in beaver ponds. The most profound impact from a geomorphic perspective is sediment retention in the watershed that would be otherwise washed downstream. When beavers abandon their lodge and the dam fails, a narrow channel quickly forms, allowing the accumulated sediment in the lateral margins of the former pond to remain in place. The pond transitions into a broad meadow with rich soil and a shallow water table, conditions perfect for plants requiring abundant sunlight and water.

cleared for cattle grazing, the volume of sediment eroded from the banks was reduced to just 6.7 percent of the level observed prior to planting. Trees growing on floodplains also help build land adjacent to channels. Lotic systems carry the most sediment during floods when floodplains become flooded. Flow speeds of floodwater over floodplains with thick stands of trees are much slower relative to those lacking trees. As a result, more sediment sinks out of the water column and deposits on the floodplain when trees are present.

CHAPTER 4
ECOLOGY OF LOTIC ECOSYSTEMS

The plants and animals inhabiting flowing water encounter challenges and opportunities not found in any other ecosystems on Earth. A forest bird or a turtle on a coral reef can maneuver through three dimensions, but stream-dwelling fish must navigate through a narrow, linear habitat network, one possibly limited by impassable waterfalls or dry reaches. The physical disturbances of lotic ecosystems are also unparalleled in nature. Organisms must contend with severe, regularly occurring floods that could entirely reshape habitat in hours. A few months later drought could shrink the same lotic ecosystem into isolated pools. Such regularly occurring, wholescale physical changes have no equivalent on land. Yet healthy lotic ecosystems are highly biodiverse and maintain many critical processes that benefit humans, from supporting massive salmon runs to filtering impurities from water. Many animals evolved to use flowing water as a free ride to disperse genes or collect food. Seemingly catastrophic floods deliver nutrients and create fresh habitat.

All ecosystems, including those in flowing waters, support very complex food webs. Older references in ecology might refer to a food chain, but this term makes less sense because of multidirectional feeding pathways. Some lotic food web bases consist of photosynthesizing organisms like algae and plants. Large rivers support populations of microscopic single-celled photosynthetic organisms suspended in the water column called **phytoplankton**, but only where flows do not regularly sweep populations downstream. In most settings, however, lotic ecosystems truly begin on land, where terrestrial plants shed leaves that enter headwater stream channels and decompose. Just like on land, lotic ecosystems also support fungal and microbial decomposers that recycle the biological waste from all corners of the food web. A diverse array of tiny invertebrates too small to see without aid of a microscope, the **meiofauna**, feed on algal, bacterial, and fungal cells. Larger-bodied invertebrates prey on meiofauna but also graze algal cells. Insects and crustaceans dominate this group, which ecologists collectively refer to as **macroinvertebrates**. Many fish species feast on macroinvertebrates, including trout, bass, and perch. Vertebrate carnivores like otters, pike, and gar complete the food webs by maintaining diverse diets of large-bodied prey.

Yet the ever-changing flow of water looms over all ecological processes and every organism. The downstream movement of water not only delivers energy and nutrients from headwater streams to large rivers but also transforms life-supporting organic matter both physically and chemically. Crucially, the growth in channel size also affects all ecological properties in flowing waters, from energy sources supporting food webs to the cast of animal species. An overview of energy sources that build ecosystems throughout the river network is a good place to start.

ENERGY ORIGINS

Every ecosystem on Earth requires fundamental sources of energy and molecular building blocks. Life at the lowest tier of an ecological food pyramid combines solar energy and essential elements (carbon, nitrogen, and phosphorus) to create life that all other organisms depend on. Growth in the food web base, termed **primary production** by ecologists, is driven by plants or algae capable of photosynthesis. In every ecosystem on Earth, primary production is limited by whatever fundamental resource required for photosynthesis is in shortest supply, either water, sunlight, and/or key molecules depending on the setting.

Supplies of two critical elements—nitrogen and phosphorus—typically limit primary production in terrestrial and aquatic ecosystems alike. Although gaseous N_2 nitrogen is the most common atmospheric molecule, biologically accessible nitrogen is a precious and rare resource. Yet all organisms require nitrogen to build proteins. All cells also require phosphorus to build DNA and store energy, but biologically available phosphorus is also very rare. Consequently, nitrogen and/or phosphorus often limit biological productivity, and the exchange of these critical elements among organisms often shapes energy flow through ecosystems.

Although lotic systems often support plenty of photosynthesizing organisms, those in first-order headwater streams are challenged by too much shade. Land next to a channel is termed the **riparian zone** and represents an important interface between aquatic and terrestrial ecosystems. Here, roots access limitless freshwater, creating prime habitat for terrestrial plants uniquely adapted to endure regularly occurring floods. As a result, small stream channels are typically surrounded by towering trees that block sunlight and energy driving photosynthesis. The resource that typically limits primary production in headwater streams is therefore not nitrogen or phosphorus, but sunlight. Exceptions to this rule occur during brief periods when leaf cover overhead is minimal and water temperatures are warm enough for growth, such as during early spring and late autumn in watersheds with deciduous forests.

Because only limited solar energy reaches the water, small stream ecosystems tend to have food webs built upon decomposing terrestrial vegetation. Leaves and logs that drop into channels offer a feast to aquatic microbes and fungi, which release the energy captured by the terrestrial vegetation and the organic molecules required for building new life. Decomposition also releases precious nitrogen and phosphorus, though these elements also can arrive from groundwater. Flowing water also physically breaks down the material. Therefore, dead vegetation from land surrounding small streams provides both the energy and molecular building blocks for aquatic food webs—further evidence that the lotic ecosystem is inseparable from the watershed. Aquatic scientists have assigned a special name to the terrestrial biological matter in lotic ecosystems: **allochthonous** organic matter. Stream ecosystems primarily built upon decomposing terrestrial vegetation are termed **heterotrophic**.

Microbes consuming submerged allochthonous matter form a complex, biodiverse, and forest-like miniature ecosystem. Any firm surface submerged in a lotic system for just a few hours develops a thin film of biological activity, while logs or leaves inundated for days or weeks accumulate a thick matrix of the same organisms, perhaps comprising cells in the millions per leaf. Scientists call this biological matrix a **biofilm**, a mat consisting of bacteria, cyanobacteria, algae, and fungi feeding on decaying plants that fell into the water (Figure 5.1). Biofilms form the base of small stream food webs in the same way that plants are the pillars on land. Countless species of meiofauna, including tiny crustaceans, young insect larvae, nematode worms, tardigrades, and copepods, feed on biofilms. Larger consumers then feed on both meiofauna and biofilms to support the higher food web tiers.

But the scene changes when the channel widens. As lotic systems grow, more light reaches the water surface to drive photosynthesis. Therefore, in third- through sixth-order streams not fully shaded by surrounding trees and with depths shallow enough for sunlight to reach the channel bottom, photosynthesis becomes a fundamental food web pillar. In medium-sized lotic systems, the biomass created by aquatic plants and light-loving algae matches or exceeds that derived from

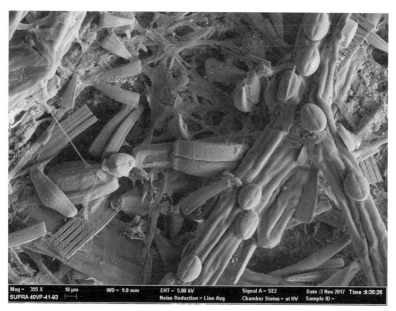

Figure 5.1.   A scanning electron microscope image of lotic biofilm from Fossil Creek, Arizona. Organisms shown include diatoms, filamentous algae, and fungi. JANE MARKS

decomposing land plants. In these larger reaches, vegetarian fish species like suckers appear in large numbers. Scientists consider these stream reaches to be **autotrophic**—built upon solar energy rather than decomposition. Because sunlight is readily available, the resource that limits primary production here is usually biologically accessible nitrogen or phosphorus.

As the system becomes a large river, the fundamental energy source shifts yet again. The food web here transitions to one partially based on phytoplankton, but only in the largest rivers where backwater channels prevent populations from being carried downstream. Deep, broad rivers like the Mississippi are too murky for light to penetrate. A lack of light limits photosynthesis, except at the channel edges and near the water surface. Just like in small, headwater streams, decomposition represents an important base of the food web, as decaying organic material from farther upstream in the river network provides a feast for microbes.

Regardless of the ecological transitions that occur as a river grows, small streams dominate river networks by number. As described above, no large river would exist without the contributing water from countless headwater streams. Biological processes extend this concept: Flow

Some lotic systems and their watersheds receive massive energy pulses from an unlikely source: oceans. Many fish species are born in small streams then migrate into the ocean to grow, a phenomenon termed **anadromy**. Salmon represent the most celebrated and ecologically important anadromous fish in North America. When salmon are ready to breed, they swim upstream in the same river networks where they were born. The drive leads to herculean migrations. For example, Chinook Salmon (*Oncorhynchus tshawytscha*) in the Yukon River travel over 2,000 miles into the Canadian Yukon territory from coastal Alaska, equivalent to the distance between New York and Phoenix. Most salmon inevitably die after breeding in their ancestral streams, where their bodies are left to decompose (although all salmon species in the Pacific Rim die after breeding, a lucky few Atlantic Salmon may live to spawn another day). The decomposing salmon tissue provides a nutritional and energetic boost to the entire aquatic food web. However, many terrestrial animals also eagerly consume salmon carcasses, including meat-eaters like bears, foxes, and eagles. Waste from these animals is terrific fertilizer for terrestrial plants.

Energy and molecules allowing salmon to grow large originates in the ocean, where adults feed on krill and small fish. Therefore, migrating salmon deliver a massive pulse of energy and nutrients to the watershed from the ocean. When

Figure 5.2. Coho Salmon carcasses in Eagle Creek, a tributary of the Columbia River in Oregon. Many organisms, both aquatic and terrestrial, will feast on the decomposing carcass. Because this salmon grew large in the Pacific Ocean, energy that originated in a marine ecosystem now becomes part of the forest and stream food webs. COURTNEY MEIER

terrestrial scavengers consume salmon carcasses, they release waste in the forest, creating energy sources termed **marine-derived nutrients**. Scientists can tell if nitrogen from tissue came from the ocean or the atmosphere by measuring atomic weights, allowing ecologists to measure the extent of marine-derived nutrients in watersheds supporting salmon runs. One analysis showed that about 25 percent of nitrogen in the wine grapes of California near rivers where Chinook Salmon return to spawn came from the ocean via salmon tissues. Results from another study tracing nutrients in trees of coastal Alaska found a quarter of the nitrogen in Sitka spruce came from salmon. Marine-derived nutrients were detected in trees growing up to 330 feet away from stream channels. Trees in watersheds receiving the salmon-derived energy pulse grew four times faster than their counterparts in watersheds lacking a salmon run. Therefore, in the land of salmon, lotic systems allow the ocean to feed forests and fields.

moves organic materials and the energy stored within their chemical bonds downstream. However, any material of biological origin composed of carbon, collectively referred to as **organic matter**, is continuously processed by many organisms along the journey. Molecules of a tree leaf that fell into a small, headwater stream are consumed, processed, and released as waste repeatedly along a downstream journey. Phytoplankton in the Mississippi River water column depend on the nutrients processed from trees hundreds or thousands of miles upstream.

THE BREATHING, FLOWING ECOSYSTEM

Ecosystems breathe in a sense by exchanging carbon dioxide and oxygen molecules with water or the atmosphere in sync with the sun. When the sun is up, photosynthesizing cells produce more oxygen as a bioproduct than the amount collectively consumed by all other non-photosynthesizing organisms. Overnight, though, the cellular respiration of *all* organisms, including those that were photosynthesizing earlier in the day, consumes plenty of oxygen. Solar radiation–driven cycling also occurs annually at the global scale. Atmospheric CO_2 concentrations are rising due to fossil fuel burning. But a very close look at carbon dioxide levels over time reveals a cyclic decline in levels during the Northern Hemisphere summer and a corresponding uptick during winter. The annual cyclic pattern occurs because the great expanse of boreal forest in Siberia and North America consumes massive amounts of carbon dioxide during the summer growing season, a process that halts in winter. Corresponding oxygen cycling does not occur because oxygen is so abundant in our atmosphere.

Lotic ecosystems also cyclically exchange life-supporting molecules as the sun rises and sets. Atmospheric gases such as nitrogen, oxygen, and carbon dioxide dissolve into water. If the concentration of a gas in our atmosphere increases, so too does the level of that gas in water, as the atmospheric weight of the gas pushes molecules to dissolve. Animals attain oxygen from dissolved molecules in the water and release dissolved carbon dioxide in return, a process called **respiration**. When enough sunlight reaches the stream, photosynthesizing microbes and plants consume carbon dioxide and release oxygen, thereby acting as a molecular counterweight to respiration. As a result, water in lotic systems where photosynthesis comprises a major source of energy shows strong cyclic patterns of rising oxygen concentrations during the day and falling concentrations overnight, such as in the Greenbrier River (blue line in Figure 5.3), a medium-sized river with a 1,360-square-mile

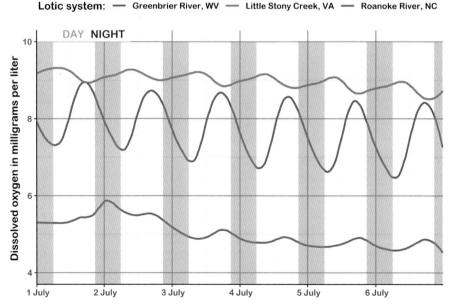

Figure 5.3. Dissolved oxygen cycling in three lotic systems of the southeastern United States during July 2020. All three sites are located within a 120-mile radius of one another and therefore experience similar weather and sunlight. Day and night periods are illustrated by vertical bands.

watershed in West Virginia. The more photosynthesis that occurs during the day, the greater the daily swing in oxygen. Oxygen is easier to attain when concentrations are high, so animals and microbes breathe easier during the day.

However, channel size strongly shapes oxygen cycling. Photosynthesis is limited in headwater streams because trees shade solar radiation. Therefore, oxygen-depleting respiration is the primary biological process influencing concentrations in decomposition-driven ecosystems. Yet other forces can help prevent oxygen depletion. Oxygen solubility is directly related to water temperature, with colder water able to retain a much higher concentration of oxygen molecules in solution. Small, headwater streams are mostly fed by groundwater with minimal sun exposure; thus water temperatures tend to be cold. Additionally, turbulence at the water surface helps oxygen dissolve into water, sometimes at levels higher than the water temperature would otherwise allow. A small waterfall may completely replenish oxygen depleted by respiring organisms. Therefore, because small, headwater streams tend to be cold and feature plenty of turbulence, oxygen levels typically remain very high. The oxygen patterns shown in Little Stony Creek (green line in Figure 5.3), a headwater stream draining a 20.2-square-mile watershed, clearly show such cycling. In contrast to the nearby Greenbrier River, oxygen levels *decrease* during the day when relatively warm air temperatures make oxygen less soluble and *increase* overnight as the air cools. Daily oxygen variation is much less dramatic than in the Greenbrier River because shading keeps water consistently cool. The combined physical forces of high surface turbulence and cooler water temperatures easily outweigh oxygen depletion by respiring animals and microbes.

Farther downstream, oxygen levels in large rivers tend to be relatively low and stable. If phytoplankton and aquatic plants in a large river are abundant, they elevate levels during the day via photosynthesis. However, cloudy water in larger rivers prevents photosynthesis by blocking sunlight and limits daily oxygen cycling. Turbulence in larger rivers is uncommon; thus water surface oxygen replenishment tends to be low. Large rivers also have warmer water compared to upstream, further contributing to low oxygen levels. All such factors combined mean that oxygen in large rivers remains low and exhibits minimal daily cycling. Oxygen data from a lower reach of the Roanoke River in North Carolina (tan line in Figure 5.3), a river draining a 9,250-square-mile watershed, illustrate patterns typical of large rivers. Roanoke River oxygen concentrations are overall much lower than smaller, nearby lotic systems and the daily cycle is muted, with perhaps some photosynthesis driving a moderate rise during the day.

Such differences in oxygen concentrations throughout a river network drive physiological adaptations. Oxygen requirements are best known among fishes, although thresholds extend to other aquatic organisms. All fish species thrive in dissolved oxygen levels above 9 mg/L (milligrams per liter), and none can survive below about 3 mg/L. Between these extreme values, tolerance to low oxygen levels varies significantly. Headwater stream fishes, such as trout and sculpin, rarely coped with low dissolved oxygen in their evolutionary history. As a result, these cold-adapted species can become stressed when levels dip below about 8 mg/L. In contrast, animals making a home farthest downstream in a river network cope with persistently low dissolved oxygen. Most large river fishes tolerate oxygen levels that would stress or kill headwater species. During prolonged hot temperatures, however, fish remain near the water surface to attain the precious little oxygen dissolving into the river from the atmosphere. Some large river fishes, including gar, bowfin, and some catfishes, gulp air at the water surface to extract oxygen from air via their swim bladders when water concentrations get dangerously low. Burrowing mayfly larvae grow long, feathery abdominal gills to efficiently extract what little oxygen persists in water within sand grains.

THE RIVER CONTINUUM CONCEPT

Tracing energy sources and food web foundations in lotic ecosystems as outlined above reveals why organisms are found where they are within a river network. Downstream transitions in the fundamental energy sources supporting lotic food webs, from decomposing terrestrial plant matter in headwater streams to photosynthesis in medium-sized streams to decomposing material washed from upstream in large rivers, means that the feeding opportunities change predictably with channel size. Patterns in dissolved oxygen and temperature as channels enlarge also impact the animal distributions. Ecologists studying such dynamics developed a fundamental theory explaining biodiversity in river networks: the **River Continuum Concept**. The underlying idea behind the RCC is that lotic system size and energy sources explain distributions of aquatic plants, invertebrates, and fishes.

Heterotrophic biofilms feeding on decomposing vegetation in head-water streams provide fodder for a diverse cast of large organisms. Many species of aquatic invertebrates, such as the juvenile stages of giant stoneflies (*Pteronarcys*), amphipods, and crayfish, chew dead leaves that fall into the streams to consume biofilms growing on them. Although both leaf and biofilm get digested, a nutritional analog to human diets would be energy-rich peanut butter (biofilm) on a cracker (the dead leaf). In other words, microbes provide the bulk of nutrition to leaf-consuming inverte-brates, while the leaf itself constitutes a delivery vessel. Lotic ecologists refer to these invertebrates as **shredders** because they physically process allochthonous material. Other invertebrates called **collectors** feed on bio-films by crawling around the channel bottom or filtering organisms from the water column. However, few organisms specialize in photosynthesiz-ing organisms because they simply do not exist in abundance. Fish spe-cies are limited to invertebrate predators like trout and sculpin.

New feeding opportunities emerge as water from tributaries cause lotic systems to grow wider and sunlight reaches the stream channel. Photosynthesizing microbes and aquatic plants basking in the light of wide channels provide something to eat for vegetarian invertebrate spe-cialists called **grazers**, like snails and specialized aquatic insects. Fish species that forage algae, such as suckers and some minnows, become common. Larger filter-feeding invertebrates like mussels derive their diet by filtering microscopic organisms from the water column. Despite this new source of energy, most medium-sized streams still feature abun-dant leaf packs and logs from terrestrial plants in the watershed; thus shredding insects and organisms that thrive in small streams endure. For this reason, medium-sized streams often reflect peak biodiversity in the river network.

Water clarity decreases downstream as the channel deepens. Pho-tosynthesis becomes limited to channel margins and the uppermost water column where phytoplankton can grow. Yet the consistent supply of nutrients and decomposing material from upstream feeds plenty of organisms. Invertebrates in large rivers mostly feed by filtering prey from the water column while others collect such material as they bur-row through sediments. Large river feeding opportunities also support goliath fish species. Paddlefish grow up to 185 pounds by filter-feeding plankton and small invertebrates from the water using their massive gape. Their cousins the sturgeon cruise channel bottoms to feast on invertebrates residing in the silt and reach jaw-dropping lengths: The river-breeding White Sturgeon of western North America can live for over a century and grow up to 20 feet long.

The River Continuum Concept describes how channel size, energy sources, temperature, and photosynthesis shape plant and animal

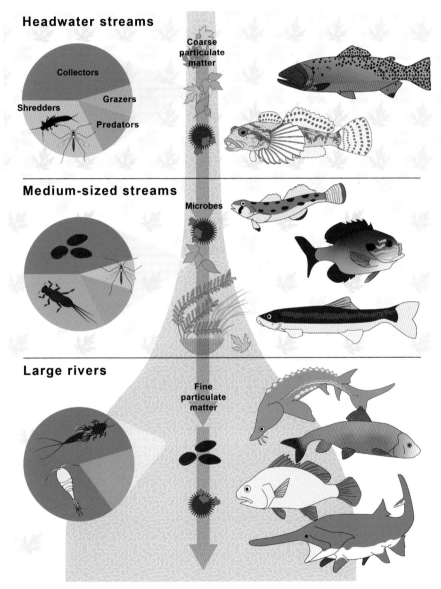

Figure 5.4. The River Continuum Concept. As rivers grow, the energy and carbon that supports ecosystems shifts from coarse terrestrial plant matter in the headwaters to fine organic matter in large rivers. Invertebrate and fish communities change as well, with medium-sized rivers representing the most biodiverse reaches.
HANNAH LUONI GARRISON

distributions. Many experiments in relatively pristine settings have shown that the theory holds up well. For example, invertebrates of the Salmon River in Idaho attain peak diversity in medium-sized streams. Fish biodiversity in the Seine River watershed, the river that flows through Paris, is also highest in medium-sized streams, although pollution in the Seine might limit biodiversity farthest downstream. The River Continuum Concept message reinforces the idea that rivers are intricately connected to tributaries and their watersheds through water, energy, and nutrients. Consequently, keeping large river ecosystems healthy requires that the many thousands of tiny streams contributing water and energy to create them remain healthy, too.

EXCHANGING ENERGY THROUGH INSECT PREDATION

Mobile organisms effectively transfer energy and nutrients throughout the ecosystems they navigate. Most of the above discussion on energy emphasizes immobile, microscopic organisms because they numerically and ecologically dominate food webs. But larger-bodied animals are also incredibly important conduits for moving energy and nutrients throughout river networks and across ecosystems. Perhaps most important among such transferences are those created by insects.

Most of the tens of thousands of insects in lotic ecosystems spend their juvenile life underwater and emerge to terrestrial surroundings in adulthood. By doing so, insects switch from swimming and breathing underwater to taking flight, allowing them to find mates and deposit eggs in locations upstream that may be safer from predators. Individuals emerge from water synchronously to maximize the likelihood of successful reproduction in events that anglers and scientists alike call a **hatch**. When insect hatches with very dense populations in large rivers occur, the resulting swarms of adults in terrestrial ecosystems surrounding the channels can be spectacular. For example, annually occurring mayfly hatches on the upper Mississippi River near La Crosse, Wisconsin, are so thick that they trick weather-tracking radar into reporting severe thunderstorms. While most hatches are not quite so dramatic, they occur throughout a river network and year-round, with some stonefly species emerging in mid-winter to find mates on the snow. The consistent emergence of insects from lotic ecosystems provides a rich source of prey for many terrestrial animals, including birds, bats, and spiders.

Scientists go to heroic lengths to quantify the importance of aquatic insects in terrestrial ecosystems. Ecologists working in the mountainous headwater streams of Hokkaido, the heavily forested northernmost main island of Japan, built greenhouse structures that entirely covered headwater stream channels in a famous experiment measuring energy exchanges between land and water. Doing so prevented the emerging aquatic insects from mingling with the surrounding forest ecosystem, allowing ecologists to track how forest-dwelling predators responded

Figure 5.5. A mesh greenhouse over a headwater stream in Hokkaido, Japan, in an experiment testing how aquatic insects interact with the surrounding forest. COLDEN BAXTER

to the lack of emerging aquatic prey. Results revealed that headwater streams provide a critical prey source to many terrestrial animals. Experimentally turning off the flow of aquatic insects reduced spider densities by over 80 percent. In spring, the season when aquatic insect hatches peak in temperate-climate streams, bat detections were thirty-three times greater above control streams without a greenhouse compared to those where the aquatic insects were prevented from emerging. Emerging aquatic insects also comprised more than 50 percent of the diets for insect-eating birds such as tits and warblers. Such interactions between predator and prey truly blur the line dividing aquatic and terrestrial ecosystems.

The direct exchange of insect prey between land and water occurs in the opposite direction as well. Ecologists working in New Zealand headwater streams during the mid-twentieth century found that there were far more (nonnative) trout than would be expected based on available underwater prey. Trout are primarily insect predators, but there simply were not enough juvenile aquatic insects to support observed trout densities found in these streams. Subsequent studies in similar headwater streams around the world revealed that trout (and other insectivorous fishes) feast on terrestrial insects that fall onto the water surface from surrounding vegetation. In the Hokkaido greenhouse experiments, physically separating the forest from the stream reduced terrestrial insects in trout diets by over 50 percent. Such experiments further reinforced the idea that forest and headwater stream ecosystems are intricately linked. Forests feed headwater streams the energy powering aquatic food webs by shedding not only leaves into the water but also insect prey for carnivorous fishes at the top of the food web. In return, the stream returns energy to the forest when aquatic insects emerge to breed.

ENVIRONMENTAL FLOWS

Ever-changing flows in lotic ecosystems maintain aquatic biodiversity as well. Viewed from the safe vantage point on a streambank, a flooding lotic system rapidly moving torrents of muddy water downstream seems a thoroughly inhospitable place for life. But such catastrophic events are vital for all aquatic organisms. Naturally rising and receding flows in lotic systems, what scientists refer to as the **natural flow regime**, help organisms in countless and sometimes surprising ways.

Floods move many ecologically important materials beyond water. During floods, large pulses of both inorganic (rocks, sand, and silt) and organic material move downstream. Such events effectively clean channels of fine sediment because water more easily moves small particles. When this occurs, the many organisms that use spaces between boulders, cobbles, and pebbles (termed interstitial spaces), including insects, crustaceans, and small fishes, get a habitat housecleaning. Too much fine sediment accruing in interstitial spaces results in diminished oxygen; thus floods help many aquatic animals breathe easier long after they recede. Floods also sweep biofilm mats downstream, thereby creating fresh habitat for fast-growing algae and microbe species that would otherwise be overgrown by long-lived species. Fresh wood from logs moved intro channels during floods provides new fodder for microbes and creates refuge habitat for many fish species by creating pools. High flows also create temporary opportunities for fish to move upstream, as side channels create new migration conduits.

Floods in large rivers produce vast ecological opportunities for countless species by flooding lands adjacent to channels. Floodplains are ecologically vital for many plants and animals as an interface between land and water, where the boundary between aquatic and terrestrial habitat becomes entirely blurred. Receding floodwaters leave behind fresh nutrients (carbon, nitrogen, and phosphorus) delivered as organic matter from upstream. Plants greatly benefit from this pulse of nutrition, allowing floodplains to sustain towering trees. Flooding causes obvious physical stress to smaller plants, but floodplain specialist species are adapted to endure. As a result, floodplains support plant species found nowhere else. Aquatic organisms also thrive in the temporary aquatic habitat of a flooded floodplain. Primary production in water tends to be very high in flooded floodplains because nutrients are released with the rising water. Excess plant and algae growth feeds herbivorous animals, which then feed predators. Shallow water and high primary production in inundated floodplains maintain high dissolved oxygen levels. Smaller-bodied fishes also find shelter from predators lurking in mainstem channels. For all these reasons, countless organisms feed and exclusively breed in large river floodplains, including multiple species of catfish, sunfish, and minnows.

Perhaps the most dramatic and ecologically significant seasonal floodplain flooding of any river occurs annually on the Amazon. The Amazon watershed has a climate dominated by cycling between wet (December through May) and dry (late July through November) seasons, a climate pattern termed **monsoonal**. Wet season rainfall causes the Amazon River to rise about 50 feet from the minimal level observed in the dry season. Because much of the Amazon watershed consists of low-elevation land, massive tracts of forest land transition into flooded wetlands annually. About 57,000 square miles (the size of Michigan) of the Amazon watershed is flooded during the dry season, but this area grows to 96,000 square miles (adding an area the size of Virginia) at the peak of the wet season. The weight of water associated with this massive annual fluctuation causes the land itself to rise and fall. Using high-resolution global positioning equipment, geologists detected the Earth's surface in Manaus, Brazil (near the center of the Amazon basin), fluctuating annually up to 3 inches because the water weight pushes the South American continental plate down during the wet season.

Organisms of the Amazon River ecosystem time life history strategies with monsoonal seasonal changes. Forests along river channels that reliably flood each year, known locally as **várzeas**, are composed of water-loving trees that are ecologically just as much aquatic as they are terrestrial. The onset of the wet season allows aquatic microbes to feast on várzea leaf litter and soil nutrients that accumulated during the dry season, thereby supporting the entire aquatic food web. Countless fish species breed in tangles of inundated wood to provide shelter from predators to their offspring. Predators, including the pink Amazon River dolphin, are aware of this strategy and prowl the flooded forest. Towering várzea trees easily survive the annual flood, and many species time reproductive cycles to ensure

Figure 5.6. A seasonally flooded forest (várzea) adjacent to the Juma River, an Amazon River tributary. ALEXEY YAKOVLEV

fruits drop on flooded lands. Although some fishes possess powerful jaws to crush seeds, many distribute viable seeds throughout the watershed by consuming the fruit. In doing so, lotic fishes fulfill the ecological role of seed dispersal for terrestrial plants, a task usually completed by birds or mammals. Flooded várzeas also support floating meadows: patches of buoyant aquatic vegetation that cover water surfaces for up to hundreds of acres. Many species of fish and aquatic invertebrates specialize on floating meadow habitat to hunt, hide, and breed.

CLEANING FRESHWATER FOR THE COASTS

Ecologically exchanging nutrients and energy throughout a river network can be vital for maintaining healthy coastal ecosystems. Most rivers end when waters flow into the ocean or an **estuary**—an inland coastal ecosystem where salt- and freshwater mix, such as the Chesapeake and San Francisco Bays. If river water entering coasts or estuaries is pristine, all intricately linked ecosystems in the network thrive.

Perhaps the most important factor determining how rivers shape the ecological health of coastal ecosystems involves two critical nutrients that most often limit photosynthesis: nitrogen and phosphorus. In coastal ecosystems, sunlight and water are plentiful and do not limit photosynthesis except in water too deep for light to penetrate. Instead, low nitrogen and/or phosphorus availability is what most often keeps plant and phytoplankton populations in check. Add more of these two key nutrients to a pristine coastal ecosystem and extra photosynthesis inevitably ensues. Such an idea may sound harmless or even beneficial, as plants and phytoplankton provide food for other organisms. However, when photosynthesizing organisms grow without limit, excessively large populations inevitably die and decompose. When this occurs, decomposition consumes so much dissolved oxygen that concentrations plummet to dangerous lows. Catastrophic fish-kills occur if oxygen concentrations remain low for prolonged periods.

Many coastal ecosystems, especially estuaries, get most or all nitrogen and phosphorus from inflowing rivers. Higher concentrations of these nutrients in rivers elevate the likelihood of fish-kill events in the receiving coastal waters. Each of these nutrients is typically in short supply within lotic systems as well, so organisms often assimilate them into tissues, which slows their transport downstream. Both elements are taken up in plant or animal tissues and therefore periodically stored before being released again when those organisms decompose or release waste. Lotic scientists use the term **nutrient spiraling** to describe uneven molecular transport downstream: A nutrient molecule briefly travels with the water before being biologically integrated into the ecosystem, where a living organism stores it until death. Retaining nitrogen and phosphorus in organisms means that these ecologically precious nutrients remain in the watershed. The transition of aquatic insects into adulthood described above also exports some of the nitrogen and phosphorus back to land. Such processes help slow or decrease the rate of nutrient delivery downstream toward coasts.

Yet lotic ecosystems can also permanently export nitrogen, thereby decreasing how much gets sent downstream. If a nitrate molecule (NO_3) dissolved in lotic water flows through sediments with naturally low oxygen levels, a special class of microbes known as **anaerobic** (living without oxygen) consumes the nitrate and releases harmless N_2 gas that bubbles into the atmosphere. The **denitrification** process means that nitrogen permanently leaves the ecosystem and never reaches the coast. Some lotic ecosystems are denitrification superstars, with fully 100 percent of received nitrogen exported to the atmosphere as N_2 gas. Denitrification rates vary wildly, but the process occurs throughout river networks, from small, headwater streams to large rivers. Pristine lotic ecosystems with high biodiversity tend to be exceptionally efficient at denitrification. Therefore, rivers delivering water to coasts from a network of healthy streams support thriving coastal ecosystems by keeping photosynthesis in check.

Thanks to human actions, coastal ecosystems suffer when river networks cannot maintain denitrification rates high enough to keep conditions pristine. Nitrogen and phosphorus typically limit photosynthesis in agriculture; thus fertilizers for crops include these two key nutrients. However, excess fertilizer not consumed by crops percolates into groundwater that flows into lotic channels. Lotic ecosystems draining agricultural watersheds therefore tend to have nitrogen and phosphorus concentrations elevated far beyond natural levels. Denitrification in lotic systems increases to some degree with increasing nutrients, but too much inevitably results in excess nitrogen export from rivers to coasts, with significant consequences for marine ecosystems. For example, a persistent patch of ocean with dissolved oxygen levels far below what can sustain most marine life (popularly termed a *dead zone*) lurks offshore of where the Mississippi River terminates in the Gulf of Mexico. The Gulf dead zone seasonally fluctuates but in some years grows larger than the size of Massachusetts. Agriculture in the Mississippi River watershed sending excess nutrients to the Gulf via the river allows the dead zone to persist. Cities in the watershed also contribute nutrients but to a lesser degree. Recent technological advances in agriculture can allow farmers to reduce excess fertilizer application. Unfortunately, the slow speed of groundwater flows means that helpful changes in agricultural practices applied today may not benefit the Gulf for decades or centuries, and the dead zone may endure just as long.

CHAPTER 5
A PRIMER ON IDENTIFYING ORGANISMS

Identifying the animals can be a rewarding and enlightening experience. Simultaneously, the sheer diversity of organisms found in any ecosystem, the technical jargon associated with scientifically oriented field guides, and the challenge of finding important anatomical features can discourage amateur naturalists. Some species are obvious and identifiable without taking the organism from water, while many others are indistinguishable without the use of a microscope or DNA.

THE LINNAEAN SYSTEM

All organisms on Earth evolved from a single ancestorial spark of life that occurred billions of years ago. Evolution subsequently led biological diversity to blossom into countless species. The single ancestral source of life means that every species is part of one enormous family. But species that evolutionarily diverged more recently share more genetic material with one another, meaning that they are more closely related. Understanding this evolutionary relatedness helps to organize groups of organisms and can explain why certain traits appear among species.

Scientists use a system invented by an eighteenth-century Swedish naturalist, Carl Linnaeus, to classify organisms by evolutionary lineage. Linnaeus organized species that most resembled one another into a genus (plural: genera). Genera that were most like one another were placed into the same family, similar families were organized into classes, and additional tiers in the system were added up to the highest tier, the kingdom. Linneaus developed his system about a century before Charles Darwin outlinod the process of evolution, yet the hierarchical approach works very well within the evolutionary framework. All species are organized into the Linnaean system in modern-day **taxonomy**, or the science of classifying organisms. The system constantly revises, including at the uppermost levels, as biologists unfold the evolution story and learn that groups with very similar appearances are distantly related. For example, the highest classification level is now the domain (Figure 6.1).

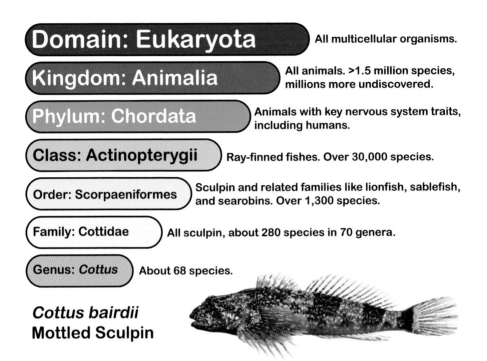

Domain: Eukaryota — All multicellular organisms.

Kingdom: Animalia — All animals. >1.5 million species, millions more undiscovered.

Phylum: Chordata — Animals with key nervous system traits, including humans.

Class: Actinopterygii — Ray-finned fishes. Over 30,000 species.

Order: Scorpaeniformes — Sculpin and related families like lionfish, sablefish, and searobins. Over 1,300 species.

Family: Cottidae — All sculpin, about 280 species in 70 genera.

Genus: *Cottus* — About 68 species.

Cottus bairdii
Mottled Sculpin

Figure 6.1.   Taxonomy of the Mottled Sculpin (*Cottus bairdii*).

Although scientific names often intimidate amateur naturalists, gaining familiarity with the basics results in deeper understanding. Characteristics consistently found within key taxonomic levels, such as families of fishes or orders of insects, leads to easier field identification because such attributes are found in *every* species within the group. Common names often mislead and neglect key identifying attributes. For example, the mudminnow (family Umbridae, genus *Umbra*) is very distantly related to the minnow family and possesses unique anatomical attributes that minnows lack. Species in the family Percopsidae are commonly referred to as trout-perches, but these fishes are neither trout nor perches. Unlike common names, the Linnaean system is globally applied: In Spain, a brown trout is called a *trucha marrón* and in France it is a *truite brune*, but in *all* countries the scientific name is *Salmo trutta*.

Etymological rules applied to each level in the Linnaean system also help ease learning. For example, all animal taxonomic family names end in the suffix *idae*. The fish family that includes all species of trout, salmon, and white fish is Salmon*idae* and the family for perches is Per*cidae*. Thus, to remember these two scientific family names, one only needs to recall the relatively easy first parts, Salmon- and Perc-. Every name in the Linnaean hierarchy is capitalized except the species. Genus and species names are italicized while every other level does not receive a special font type.

THE SCALE OF BIODIVERSITY

Lotic systems are so biodiverse that identifying aquatic animal species often proves very challenging. For example, up to 923 fish species occur in freshwater across North America, some of which are found only within a single, small watershed. Other groups are far more biodiverse: At least 13,000 aquatic Coleoptera (beetle) species occur globally. Because this book covers multiple aquatic animals, only a portion of species are described in detail, with an emphasis on those more likely to be encountered by amateur naturalists in North America. Furthermore, some groups, including most insects, simply cannot be identified to species or even genus by the amateur naturalist because they are so biodiverse and/or difficult to distinguish without a microscope. In these instances, this book provides guidance on how to identify organisms to higher tiers of the Linnaean system.

Another challenge when identifying organisms involves how rapidly our understanding of biodiversity patterns change as science progresses. The family tree of life began by comparing anatomical features to infer relationships among organisms. Although such methods often prove accurate, this approach sometimes misleads because evolution can cause structures to disappear. The best way to decipher which species are most closely related is by investigating DNA. Because DNA processing technologies have recently become very inexpensive, scientists are constantly learning new surprises in the tree of life, and taxonomic relationships are continually being updated. Therefore, be aware that some taxonomic groupings outlined in subsequent chapters could soon change

DICHOTOMOUS KEYS

Biologists use systems of questions framed with two possible outcomes, known as **dichotomous keys**. With a bit of patience and willingness to learn anatomical terms, amateur natural history enthusiasts can also use dichotomous keys. Each key question refers to important body parts that consistently distinguish organisms and posits two description options. Choosing an option leads to additional questions, each with another two outcomes, until the identity of the organism is revealed.

For example, the pair of options below starts off the dichotomous key for fish families:

A) Pairs of fins absent; mouth consists of a disc aimed downward rather than a jaw; seven gill slits; eel-like body	**Petromyzontidae (lampreys)**, page 122
B) At least one pair of fins present; mouth includes a jaw; one gill slit	2

If the fish matches descriptors in part A), the node (in boldface) suggests the fish is a lamprey. But if part B) better describes the fish, identification requires moving to question 2 and continuing to choose among pairs until reaching a node. Although the list of attributes provided in each choice are those that best describe the organism in question, certain features could appear in both choices. For example, all lampreys possess a distinctly eel-like body, but so too do eels. Therefore, allusion to an eel-like body (or lack thereof) does not appear in part B) of question 1.

Because the rules structuring dichotomous keys are based off anatomical structures linked to evolutionary lineages, they are far more reliable than the pictorial identification tools employed by some field guides. Therefore, dichotomous keys tailored for the novice appear in each subsequent chapter. The taxonomic level for each key varies by organism: family for fishes, order for insects and crustaceans, and variable levels for bivalve mollusks.

Important anatomical structures for identifying animals to lower tiers than the dichotomous keys operate are underlined in the text and highlighted within accompanying images. Common names are emphasized only among fishes because the relatively low numbers of species allow for the use of common names, which in this book are capitalized following American Fisheries Society guidelines.

CHAPTER 6
INSECTS

Although insects might not first come to mind with the mention of rivers, lotic insects are enormously ecologically important and wildly biodiverse. Flowing waters support more species of insects than any other multicellular aquatic animal. Nearly 100,000 insect species spend at least one life stage dependent on water and are therefore considered aquatic, a number that grossly underestimates the true value as new species are discovered regularly. Many species consume coarse organic matter or algae then fall prey to larger organisms, thereby transferring energy from basal to higher levels of food webs. Countless freshwater fish species directly rely on insects as prey. Finally, most aquatic insects migrate to terrestrial ecosystems as adults and transfer energy from lotic ecosystems back to the land, thereby creating a biologically rich riparian zone. Without insects, aquatic ecosystems would simply cease to be.

AQUATIC INSECT DIVERSITY AND ORIGINS

Insect biodiversity dominates the multicellular animal world, both in land and in freshwater. Scientists have catalogued about one million insect species worldwide as of 2020. However, up to seven million additional species await discovery, as the biodiversity-rich tropics remain relatively understudied. Furthermore, modern genetic techniques routinely reveal two or more distinct species from what was previously considered a single species. Aquatic insects inhabit every freshwater environment capable of supporting life, from lakes and lotic systems in the Arctic and Antarctic to the tropics. Insect species outnumber other multicellular animals by a factor of 10 to 100 in nearly all lotic ecosystems. Oceans represent the only major ecosystem on Earth where insects are effectively absent, with only a few dozen species worldwide inhabiting the water surface or beaches.

The most useful level in the Linnaean hierarchy for insect taxonomy is the order, as insect orders are easily identified without a microscope. Furthermore, anatomical, behavioral, and life history strategy differences among insect orders are very distinct. Most insect order names end in the suffix *-ptera*, which is Latin for wing. Therefore, learning

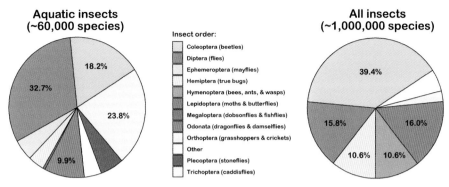

Figure 7.1. Proportions of insect species among taxonomic orders in total and in freshwater. Gray circles also relatively depict the total number of species.

scientific names of most insect orders usually only requires familiarity with the prefix.

Dominant insect orders in terms of biodiversity differ moderately between aquatic and terrestrial environments. Orders Diptera (flies) and Coleoptera (beetles) are the biodiversity heavyweights, with both combined comprising more than half of all insect species on land or in water. Differences in major species surface beyond these two hyper-biodiverse groups. Trichoptera (caddisflies), Ephemeroptera (mayflies), Plecoptera (stoneflies), and Odonata (dragonflies and damselflies) are orders of exclusively aquatic insects that comprise about half of all aquatic insect species, yet these represent relatively small groups with respect to total insect diversity. Lepidoptera (butterflies and moths) and Hymenoptera (bees, ants, and wasps) contribute a quarter of total insect biodiversity, but aquatic species within these orders are rare.

Fossils and genetic data suggest that insects adapted to life in freshwater many times over 400 million years. The earliest insects appeared about 450 million years ago. Modern-day representatives of the most ancient insects, including Protura (coneheads), Zygentoma (silverfish), and Diplura (bristletails), are entirely terrestrial, strongly suggesting that insects first evolved on land. Odonata and Ephemeroptera, both entirely aquatic orders, appear in the fossil record and/or branched off from other insects around 350 million years ago. High atmospheric oxygen levels plus a lack of competitors allowed close relatives of dragonflies to attain 28-inch wingspans during this period. Other modern-day aquatic insects are not necessarily closely related to Odonata or Ephemeroptera. Instead, other aquatic orders evolved from terrestrial ancestors on multiple occasions separated by tens or hundreds of million years.

INSECT LIFE STAGES

All insects transition through life stages with distinct appearances. Although some insects give birth to live young, most start life as an egg. Juvenile insects are known as **nymphs** or **larvae** depending on what comes next: nymphs transition directly to adults, while larvae first become **pupae** before the adult stage. Insects that pupate bear no resemblance to their larval stage form, while those that metamorphose from nymphs to adults look somewhat similar between stages. Insects with a three-stage life history lacking a pupal stage are termed **hemimetabolous**, while four-stage insects are called **holometabolous**. Pupal insects do not feed and have limited or zero mobility during the pupal stage, although a few crudely swim and chew.

Physiologic transitions help insects serve multiple biological needs. Insects feed primarily, and sometimes exclusively, during larval or nymph stages. Rapidly growing nymphs and larvae shed outgrown exoskeletons multiple times in a process called molting. Juvenile insect stages among molts are called **instars**. Insects with five to seven instars are common, though some molt fifty or more times before transitioning to adulthood. Nearly all holometabolous insects cease feeding during the pupal stage. Pupation allows insects to metamorphose into an adulthood that looks radically different from the larval stage. In hemimetabolous insects, the final instar will crawl onto land and molt into adulthood. Breeding occurs during the adult stage of both hemi- and holometabolous insects. Some adult insects feed as adults, but a large proportion ingest only water, nectar, or nothing at all. Those that cease feeding altogether, such as Ephemeroptera, tend to live a few days to several hours as adults.

Entomologists consider an insect to be aquatic if it spends at least one life stage in freshwater. Most freshwater insects have an aquatic juvenile (larval or nymph) stage, then emerge from the water to spawn. However, some may spend their entire lives in aquatic habitat, while others hatch from eggs laid on vegetation overhanging water and have only a juvenile aquatic life stage. Each insect order profile in the following pages specifies which life stages are aquatic.

INSECT ANATOMY

Identifying insects often involves careful examination of their body parts under a microscope. However, key anatomical parts that are visible with limited to no magnification and that do not require sacrificial collection can be used to distinguish orders. The fundamental insect body plan involves three primary sections: the **head**, **thorax**, and **abdomen**. Thoraxes are further divided into three sections, each with a pair of segmented legs, which may be difficult to distinguish in some groups. Fleshy, delicate **gills** for extracting dissolved oxygen from the water often project from thoracic or abdominal segments of juvenile insects. The terminal leg

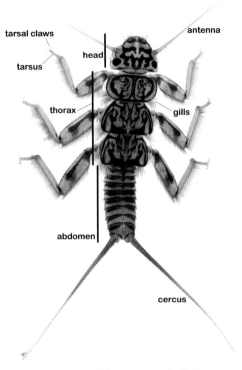

Figure 7.2. A nymph of the genus *Agnetina* (order Plecoptera, family Perlidae) with key insect anatomical features highlighted.

segment is called a **tarsus,** and an attribute that distinguishes some groups is whether the insect has one or two **tarsal claws** at the end of this segment. Two **antennae** project from the head; in some groups these are very short and indiscernible without magnification. The end of the abdomen might have long, segmented filaments called **cerci** (singular: cercus).

Although the anatomy described above can be discerned in all adults, some holometabolous insects may conceal or lack key parts during the larval stage. For example, most aquatic Diptera larvae bear little resemblance to the typical insect, as they lack segmented legs and their head may be concealed within fleshy extensions of thoracic segments.

A KEY TO NORTH AMERICAN AQUATIC INSECT ORDERS

The dichotomous key below is written for amateur naturalists to identify insects collected from water to order in the field. Adult insects are covered in the key but *only* if adults live within or on the surface of water. Exceedingly rare lotic insect groups are also omitted from this key and book. For example, some Lepidoptera (moth and butterfly) larvae are aquatic, but in North American lotic systems they are uncommon. Aquatic Neuroptera (lacewing) larvae parasitize rare freshwater sponges and are therefore unlikely to turn up unless specifically targeted.

Identification beyond taxonomic order typically requires the use of a microscope. Even in a laboratory, determining the genus can be challenging or impossible, while identifying species may require a careful look at both adult sexes and/or DNA analysis. However, some aquatic insect families are conspicuous enough for successful field identification. Therefore, the following pages emphasize insect order identification and highlight anatomical traits useful for identification in common families. Traits used to distinguish orders and families are underlined in narrative text. While some terrestrial stage attributes are noted, emphasis is placed on aquatic life stages.

A few simple items facilitate insect field identification. Hand lenses are inexpensive, portable, and greatly enhance the ability to spot important traits of all small aquatic organisms. Placing an insect in a small container filled with water from the ecosystem where it was collected and viewing it with a hand lens will reveal most traits highlighted below.

Brief accounts of select families are included in each order. Absent in this chapter are range maps because, unlike fishes or mussels, insects are very rarely identified to species and scientists often lack detailed distributional information. However, representative species of most families discussed below range throughout North America.

1. A) Segmented legs absent, head visible or hidden
   .... **Diptera (flies)**, page 89
   B) Thorax with three pairs of segmented legs; head visible............. 2

2. A) Two pairs of fully developed wings present, although
   hindwings fully or partially concealed by hardened forewings .. 3
   B) Wings absent or undeveloped and embedded within wingpads.... 4

3. A) Hardened forewings homogeneous and entirely hardened; mouthparts designed for chewing
....**Coleoptera (beetles)** adult stage, page 87

   B) Only upper half of forewings hardened, back half membranous; mouth consists of a sucking tube
....**Hemiptera (true bugs)**, page 78

4. A) Two or three long, slender cerci with more than ten segments at end of abdomen...5

   B) Cerci absent, singular, very short, or long but unsegmented and paddle-like...6

5. A) One claw per tarsus; gills commonly on abdominal segments; almost always with three cerci (rarely with two, see image for 4A) ....**Ephemeroptera (mayflies)**, page 72

   B) Two claws per tarsus; gills rarely on abdomen and never past the second abdominal segment; always with two cerci (see image for 2B)................................**Plecoptera (stoneflies)**, page 75

6. A) Mouth positioned under head and composed of large, folded but extendable organ used for grasping prey
...........................**Odonata (dragonflies and damselflies)**, page 69

   B) Mouth consists of a tube or several parts for chewing (see image for 3B) 7

7. A) Mouth consists of a sucking tube (see image for 3A)
....**Hemiptera (true bugs)**, page 78

   B) Mouth consists of several parts for chewing (see image for 3B)....8

8. A) Antennae extremely small, usually impossible to see without a microscope; two hooks on the last abdominal segment; individuals often (but not always) concealed within cases made of sand or organic material
.... **Trichoptera (caddisflies)**, page 83

   B) Antennae visible; individuals never embedded within constructed case...9

9. A) One claw per tarsus *or* abdomen without lateral filaments *or* abdomen ending in two slender filaments
....**Coleoptera (beetles)** larval stage, page 86

   B) Two claws per tarsus *and* lateral filaments on abdominal segments present *and* abdomen ending in one long, slender segment *or* two false legs with large hooks
.......**Megaloptera (alderflies, dobsonflies, and fishflies)**, page 81

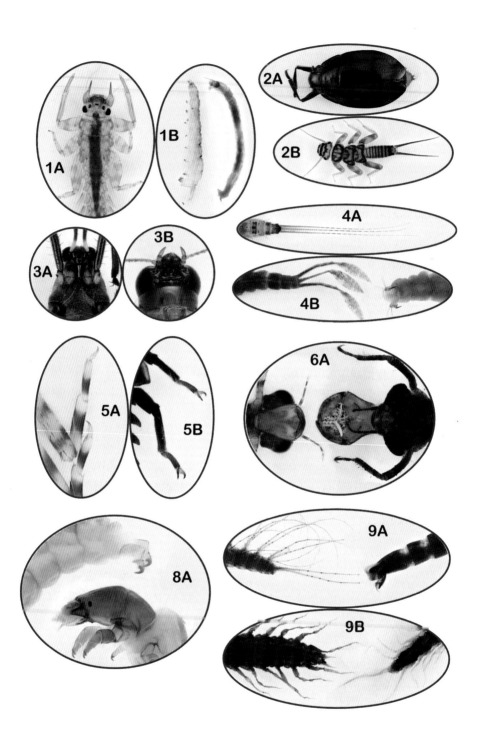

ODONATA (DRAGONFLIES AND DAMSELFLIES)

Diversity and distribution: Odonata consist of about 5,950 species divided into two sub-orders that can be easily distinguished by amateur naturalists: the Zygoptera (damselflies) and Anisoptera (dragonflies). North America north of Mexico supports about 440 species in 73 genera. Odonata are found in a diverse range of aquatic habitats from the Arctic to the tropics. Lentic habitats (ponds, lakes, and wetlands) and slow-moving, large rivers tend to support greater Odonata diversity relative to lotic systems, but several families or genera are lotic specialists. Impressive flight abilities also allow for heroic migrations and very broad distributions. For example, the Anisopteran *Pantala flavescens* (globe skimmer) has a native range that includes most of North and South America, all of Australia and Africa, Southeast Asia, western Europe, and Hawaii thanks to an ability to migrate over oceans.

Ecology and life history: Odonata are top predators of the insect world underwater and on land. Nymphs possess projectile mouthparts that impale prey then hold victims close to the mouth. Observing such mouthparts is difficult in the field, as they are contracted at rest and held on the underside of the head. One can observe underwater feeding by capturing live nymphs, placing them in a container with standing water plus a few sticks to climb on, and offering live mosquito larvae as prey. Juvenile aquatic insects are common Odonata prey, but large Anisopteran nymphs also consume tadpoles and small fish. Adults capture other insect adults in the air using their legs. Prey items in the adult stage include flies, mosquitoes, bees, and moths.

Female Odonata deposit fertilized eggs underwater by placing them into pierced vegetation or selectively depositing them on hard surfaces with plenty of oxygen. Such strategies mean that adult females temporarily dive into water. Copulating adults are often observed flying as one unit with abdomens linked together.

Odonata are unmatched in aerial speed and maneuverability, with two fully formed wings allowing them to hover in place, fly backward, and charge at speeds over 30 miles per hour. Several Odonata species undergo impressive migrations, often in large swarms. For example, *Anax junius* (green darter) migrates between Canada and Mexico over a few generations. Such behaviors presumably evolved to exploit changing food and reproduction resources among seasons. *Pantala flavescens* adults travel over the ocean from India to east Africa following monsoonal winds.

Most of the images shown in this chapter were generously provided by Macroinvertebrates.org: *Atlas of Common Freshwater Macroinvertebrates of the Eastern United States*. The online resource is a visually rich teaching and learning collection for freshwater macroinvertebrate identification with a strong emphasis on insects, which complements information presented in this chapter. High-resolution, zoomable images are annotated with close-up views of key diagnostic characters marked down to family and genus for the 150 commonly encountered taxa. A fully downloadable mobile app with an identification guide and practice flashcards is available for use in the field, even without internet access.

Key Traits

Nymphs: The two Odonata suborders, Zygoptera (damselflies) and Anisoptera (dragonflies), possess both similar and divergent attributes, but their overall appearances are distinct enough to warrant separate discussion. An attribute that both possess, and therefore one that identifies the entire order, is the projectile mouthparts that impale prey positioned at the bottom or front of the head. Such weaponized mouthparts stay retracted except when hunting (Figure 7.3 shows them extended). Both orders also always have prominent wingpads.

The two suborders can be readily distinguished in the field. Anisoptera have very short, sharp cerci at the end of the abdomen while Zygoptera have cerci consisting of three long, broad gills that they also use for propulsion. Zygoptera also tend to be smaller and slenderer than Anisoptera.

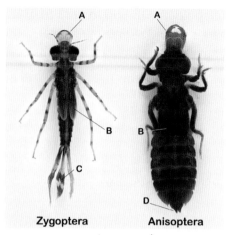

Zygoptera   **Anisoptera**

Figure 7.3. Traits of the two major Odonata suborders during the nymph stage. On the left is Argia (suborder Zygoptera, family Coenagrionidae) and on the right is Lanthus (suborder Anisoptera, family Gomphidae. Traits for identifying Odonata to order include A) projectile mouthparts and B) wingpads held parallel. The suborder Zygoptera can be identified by the C) three long, broad gills as cerci, while Anisoptera have D) three short, sharp cerci. MACROINVERTEBRATES.ORG/ ANDREA KAUTZ

Adults: All adult-stage Odonata are terrestrial. Adult Odonata have two pairs of wings that are about the same size and large eyes, are often brightly colored, and possess impressive flight skills. Zygoptera adults hold their wings overlapping and Anisoptera position wings laterally and not overlapping (such that you can see all four) while at rest.

Figure 7.4. A Zygoptera adult in the genus *Enallagma* (family: Coenagrionidae). Traits to identify adults in the suborder include A) two wing pairs that are about the same size held overlapping while at rest.

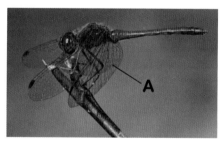

Figure 7.5. An Anisoptera adult in the genus *Sympetrum* (family: Libellulidae). Traits to identify adults in the suborder include A) two wing pairs that are about the same size held laterally and non-overlapping while at rest. SUZANNE THORNTON

Select Families (nymphs)

Odonata tend to be more common and diverse in lentic habitat. However, a few families are lotic specialists.

Calopterygidae (jewelwings) can be identified by their very long first antennae segments, which are longer than the rest of the antennae segments combined. Most Calopterygidae damselflies are lotic.

Cordulegastridae (spiketails) are mostly lotic species whose nymphs have abundant hairs throughout their body and legs that collect fine sediment, giving them a dirty appearance. They have relatively long, thin antennae.

Gomphidae (clubtails) are very common in lotic environments. Gomphidae nymphs also have sediment-collecting hairs, but unlike Cordulegastridae their antennae are short and stubby.

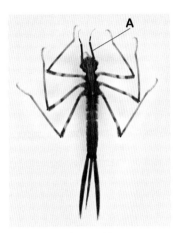

Figure 7.6. Calopterygidae: Calopteryx nymph. A trait to identify the family Calopterygidae is the A) very long first segment of antennae.
MACROINVERTEBRATES.ORG/ANDREA KAUTZ

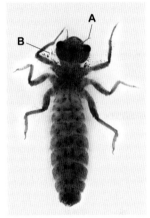

Figure 7.7. Cordulegastridae: Cordulegaster nymph. Traits identifying the family Cordulegastridae include A) long, narrow antennae and B) hairs that collect sediment and give nymphs a dirty appearance.
MACROINVERTEBRATES.ORG/ANDREA KAUTZ

Figure 7.8. Gomphidae: Ophiogomphus nymph. Traits identifying the family Gomphidae include A) short, stubby antennae and B) hairs that collect sediment and give nymphs a dirty appearance.
MACROINVERTEBRATES.ORG/ANDREA KAUTZ

EPHEMEROPTERA (MAYFLIES)

Diversity and distribution: Over 3,000 species comprise Ephemeroptera, an ancient order of exclusively aquatic insects. About 650 species in 94 genera occur in North America north of Mexico. Ephemeroptera nymphs can be found in all aquatic habitats, from small, headwater streams to large rivers and lakes. Some species burrow in soft sediments while others crawl over the surface of rocks in fast-flowing water. A few large river or lentic specialists swim through the water column. Ephemeroptera biodiversity tends to increase toward the tropics, where many species remain undiscovered. The southern Appalachians harbor the densest concentration of North American Ephemeroptera biodiversity. Most Ephemeroptera species are very sensitive to environmental degradation and are therefore most abundant and diverse in pristine ecosystems.

Ecology and life history: Ephemeroptera represent the vegetarians of the aquatic insect community, as the nymphs of most species feed exclusively on algae and detritus. Feeding strategies include scraping living periphyton from hard surfaces, burrowing to collect detritus in sand and silt, gathering soft algae from surfaces, and capturing phytoplankton from the water column.

A popular misconception of Ephemeroptera is that they possess lifespans lasting only a few days. Such is the case for the adult stage, which is solely for spawning and may only span three days to a few hours. However, Ephemeroptera nymphs grow underwater for several months to over a year. Some species have several generations per year, with more in warmer conditions. Most species emerge during spring, when abundant algae promote rapid nymph growth and atmospheric conditions minimize the risk of desiccation. Females release eggs (sometimes in the thousands) on the water surface that sink and may hatch within minutes. Adult Ephemeroptera lack a functional mouth and do not feed or drink water. Both sexes die on the water surface after spawning, resulting in an abundant feast for fish.

Ephemeroptera emergence events can be a spectacle to behold. Each species possesses a narrow time window to emerge as adults that may last only a few days. Extremely large swarms of Ephemeroptera adults might emerge from pristine lotic systems, a strategy that serves to overwhelm their many aerial predators including birds, bats, and predatory insects. Unlike any other insect, Ephemeroptera undergo a single molt as adults.

Figure 7.0. An Ephemeroptera nymph in the genus *Neoleptophlebia* (family: Leptophlebiidae). Traits to identify Ephemeroptera to order include A) one claw per tarsus, B) wingpads in mature nymphs, C) gills present on most abdominal segments, and D) usually three but sometimes two long, segmented cerci. MACROINVERTEBRATES.ORG/ ANDREA KAUTZ

Key Traits

Nymphs: A little practice will allow the amateur naturalist to readily identify Ephemeroptera nymphs in the field, although initially they can be confused with immature Plecoptera (stoneflies) or Coleoptera (beetles).

All Ephemeroptera have <u>one claw per tarsal claw</u>. Most species possess flexible, partially transparent <u>gills held laterally on several abdominal segments</u>. Gills may be quite small and/or easily fall off in some families. Nearly all Ephemeroptera have <u>three long, many-segmented cerci</u>, although a minority have only two. Finally, most Ephemeroptera nymphs have easily visible <u>wingpads</u> by the second or third instar.

Adults: Adult Ephemeroptera possess <u>two to three long cerci</u>; <u>two pairs of transparent wings</u> with the <u>hindwing being smaller than the forewing</u>; <u>large, round eyes</u>; and are often <u>colored shades of brown to orange or yellow</u>. Distinguishing among Ephemeroptera in the adult stage is much more difficult than nymphs. However, local naturalists and anglers often know the species identity for those with massive annual hatches.

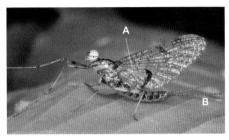

Figure 7.10. An Ephemeroptera adult in the genus *Neoleptophlebia* (family: Leptophlebiidae) with key order traits highlighted. CHRISTINA BUTLER

Select Families (nymphs):

Ephemeroptera are found in all types of lotic systems, from lowland blackwater rivers to mountain headwater streams. North America hosts twenty families.

Baetidae are common, small-bodied, delicate Ephemeroptera that often attain very dense populations. Nymphs possess <u>long antennae</u>, <u>small and fragile gills</u>, and <u>sometimes have only two cerci</u>.

Caenidae (small square-gilled mayflies) nymphs can be readily identified by their <u>large, square-shaped gills</u> that cover much of the abdomen. Abdomen edges often also have conspicuous <u>lateral spikes</u>.

Ephemerellidae (spiny crawlers) are very widespread and often extremely abundant in headwater streams. <u>An abdomen with lateral spikes</u> characterize nymphs, though the most reliable attribute is a <u>lack of gills on the first two abdominal segments</u>, which can be hard to spot without magnification because the gills are so small in this family.

Ephemeridae (burrowing mayflies) are found in lotic systems with soft sediment, including large rivers where hatches create immense swarms. Identifying traits reflect their habitat: <u>Large tusks</u> help them burrow through sand, and <u>long, fingered gills</u> help attain the limited oxygen in their benthic habitat.

Heptageniidae (flat-headed mayflies) can be easily identified by their <u>flattened head</u>, which along with a compressed body allows them to crawl over surfaces in fast-moving water without being swept downstream. One can observe rapidly pulsating gills by closely examining live nymphs. They are most common in lotic systems with rapids. The genus *Epeorus* has <u>only two cerci</u>.

Isonychiidae (brush-legged mayflies) includes only one genus, *Isonychia*. Nymphs of this genus have <u>long, brush-like hairs on the forelegs</u> and a <u>broad stripe</u> running down the thorax and abdomen. The foreleg hairs are used for filter-feeding from water. All *Isonychia* species occur east of the continental divide.

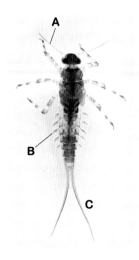

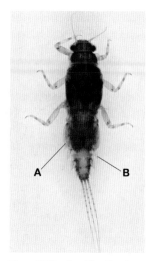

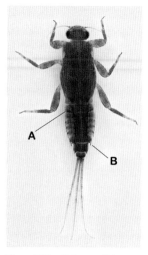

Figure 7.11. Baetidae: Heterocloeon nymph. Traits identifying the family Baetidae include A) long, conspicuous antennae, B) small, delicate gills, and C) some genera with only two cerci. MACROINVERTEBRATES.ORG/ ANDREA KAUTZ

Figure 7.12. Caenidae: Caenis nymph. Traits identifying the family Caenidae include A) large, square-shaped gills that cover much of the abdomen and B) backward-facing spikes on the visible abdominal segments. MACROINVERTEBRATES.ORG/ ANDREA KAUTZ

Figure 7.13. Ephemerellidae: Ephemerella nymph. Traits identifying the family Ephemerellidae include A) gills absent on the first two abdominal segments and B) backward-facing spikes on the abdominal segments. MACROINVERTEBRATES. ORG/ANDREA KAUTZ

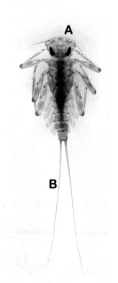

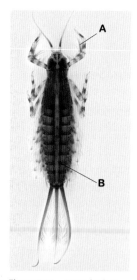

Figure 7.14. Ephemeridae: Hexagenia nymph. Traits identifying the family Ephemeridae include A) large tusks on the head for burrowing through sand and B) long, fingered gills. MACRO INVERTEBRATES.ORG/ANDREA KAUTZ

Figure 7.15. Heptageniidae: Epeorus nymph. A trait to identify the family Heptageniidae is A) the flattened, wide head. The genus Epeorus B) has just two cerci. MACROINVERTEBRATES.ORG/ ANDREA KAUTZ

Figure 7.16. Isonychiidae: Isonychia nymph. Traits identifying the family Isonychiidae and genus Isonychia include A) long, brush-like hairs on the forelegs and B) a broad stripe on the back of the thorax and abdomen. MACROINVERTEBRATES .ORG/ANDREA KAUTZ

PLECOPTERA (STONEFLIES)

Diversity and distribution: Any angler targeting trout will immediately recognize nymphs of Plecoptera, an order of hemimetabolous insects that specialize in cold lotic habitat. About 3,700 Plecoptera species occur globally, with 750 found in North America north of Mexico. North American species are organized into 9 families and about 90 genera. Unlike most organisms, Plecoptera biodiversity increases with distance from the equator and as waters transition from warm to cold, with the greatest species diversity found in temperate lotic systems draining mountainous watersheds. A few species have become lake specialists and adapted unique life histories, such as *Capnia lacustra* (family: Capniidae), which lives in Lake Tahoe at depths up to 300 feet, gives birth to live young, and never exits water in adulthood.

Ecology and life history: Plecoptera feeding strategies fall into two categories: leaf shredders or predators of other insects. Leaf-shredding Plecoptera play a vital ecological role in lotic food webs as agents of converting coarse organic matter from the surrounding forest into fine or dissolved organic matter that can be more easily integrated into the aquatic food web. Although they directly ingest the leaves, leaf-shredding Plecoptera derive their nutrition from biofilms growing on leaf surfaces. Predatory Plecoptera consume other aquatic insects. Mouth anatomy reveals which feeding strategy a Plecoptera nymph employs, but viewing distinguishing parts requires a dissecting microscope. The nymphs of some species transition from vegetarianism to predation as they mature.

Plecoptera emerge as adults that feed for a few weeks to a month before spawning. Terrestrial food sources include vegetation, fungi, pollen, nectar, and algae. Although most adult stages occur between winter and summer, Plecoptera adults emerge year-round. A surprisingly large fraction of Plecoptera species emerge in winter and can be found cheerily crawling over snow when air temperatures are below freezing. The antifreeze proteins allowing stoneflies to defy an icy death greatly reduces predation risk, as nearly all terrestrial stonefly predators are in a state of diapause during winter.

No other aquatic insect order is as environmentally sensitive as the Plecoptera, as nymphs can be impacted by the slightest pollution or pulse of warm water. Environmental scientists therefore closely monitor Plecoptera diversity and populations to assess water quality.

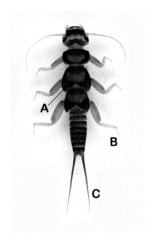

Key Traits

Nymphs: Plecoptera nymphs can usually be field identified, although some species remain very small even during late instars and will require a hand lens to view attributes. All Plecoptera nymphs possess <u>two long cerci</u> at the abdomen tip, and each leg ends in <u>two tarsal claws</u>. Mature nymphs have <u>conspicuous wingpads</u>. Many Plecoptera nymphs have <u>conspicuous gills on the thorax bottom</u> while only one family has gills on the abdomen, and these are limited to the first two segments. Plecoptera nymphs most

Figure 7.17. A Plecoptera nymph in the genus *Neoperla* (family: Perlidae). Key traits to identify the order Plecoptera include A) visible wingpads in mature nymphs, B) two claws per tarsus, and C) always with two long cerci. MACROINVERTEBRATES .ORG/ANDREA KAUTZ

Figure 7.18. A Plecoptera adult in the genus *Pteronarcys* (family: Pteronarcyidae) with key order traits highlighted. A) Wings are usually held overlapping at rest, but B) when extended two pairs of wings with thick veins become visible.

resemble Ephemeroptera, but the latter most often has three cerci, always has just one tarsal claw, and gills line most of the abdomen.

Adults: Adult Plecoptera tend to be small and dark-colored insects, although notable exceptions exist. All Plecoptera adults have two sets of wings that are about the same size and tend to have thick veins. The wings overlap and are held close to the body at rest.

Select Families (nymphs)

The nine North American Plecoptera families include some that are easily distinguished in the field and others that cannot be identified from one another unless placed under a microscope. Important traits include gill attributes, body size, and wingpad shape.

Leuctridae (rolled-winged stoneflies) are small, slender nymphs with parallel wingpads and an elongate body. Leuctridae nymphs shred leaves and can be very locally abundant in cold lotic systems.

Peltoperlidae (roach-like stoneflies) have a roach-like appearance and stout body. Most of the head is concealed under the thorax, and the wingpad plates are thicker than the exposed abdomen. Peltoperlidae nymphs are leaf shredders.

Perlidae (common stoneflies) nymphs are insect predators that have elaborate gold and dark brown patterns on their backs and many-fingered gill tufts on their undersides.

Perlodidae (stripetails) also have patterns on their backs but lack fingered gill tufts and often exhibit abdominal stripes. Perlodidae nymphs are insect predators.

Pteronarcyidae (giant stoneflies) are difficult to mistake in the field due to their large size, which can approach 1.5 inches. These leaf-shredding stoneflies also have gills on the bottom of the first two abdominal segments.

Taeniopterygidae (broadbacks) are leaf-shredding nymphs with large wingpads that diverge from the body.

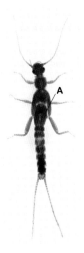

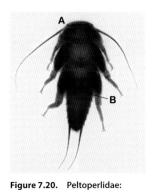

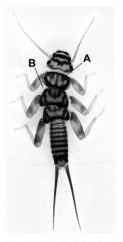

Figure 7.19. Leuctridae: Leuctra nymph. Traits identifying the family Leuctridae include A) parallel wingpads and an elongate body. MACROINVERTEBRATES.ORG/ ANDREA KAUTZ

Figure 7.20. Peltoperlidae: Tallaperla nymph. Traits identifying the family Peltoperlidae include A) a head that is largely covered by the thorax, B) wingpad plates that are much wider than the abdomen (shown here as transparent but often opaque), and a roach-like appearance. MACROINVERTEBRATES .ORG/ANDREA KAUTZ

Figure 7.21. Perlidae: Agnetina nymph. Traits identifying the family Perlidae include A) gold and brown patterning on the head and thorax and B) gill tufts. MACROINVERTEBRATES.ORG/ ANDREA KAUTZ

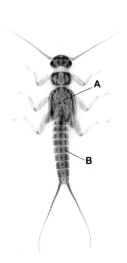

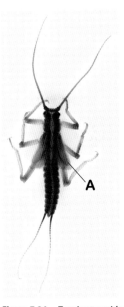

Figure 7.22. Perlodidae: Isoperla nymph. Traits identifying the family Perlodidae include A) gold and dark patterns on the back and head, B) stripe patterns on the abdomen, and a lack of gills tufts. MACROINVERTEBRATES.ORG/ ANDREA KAUTZ

Figure 7.23. Pteronarcyidae: Peteronarcys nymph viewed from the top (left) and bottom (right). Traits identifying the family Pteronarcyidae include A) gill tufts on each thoracic and the first two abdominal segments and a large body size (approaching 1.5 inches). MACROINVERTEBRATES.ORG/ ANDREA KAUTZ

Figure 7.24. Taeniopterygidae: Taeniopteryx nymph. Traits identifying the family Taeniopterygidae include A) large wingpads that diverge away from the body. MACROINVERTEBRATES .ORG/ANDREA KAUTZ

HEMIPTERA (TRUE BUGS)

Diversity and distribution: Hemiptera represent a substantially diverse order of insects on land and in water. Most of the nearly 100,000 Hemiptera species are terrestrial, but some families within the order are entirely aquatic. About 4,700 aquatic Hemiptera species exist globally with over 400 described from North America, a small proportion because Hemiptera biodiversity increases toward the equator. Aquatic Hemiptera tend to occupy either the water column or skim the water surface in search of prey. Hemiptera can be found in lotic, lentic, hot spring, and estuarine aquatic environments.

Ecology and life history: Hemiptera are hemimetabolous and are the only other aquatic insect order aside from Coleoptera where the adult stage is found in water. Some aquatic Hemiptera have aquatic nymphs while others transition to water in adulthood. Adult and nymph-stage Hemiptera are very similar in appearance, with the primary difference being a lack of wings during the nymph stage. Most aquatic Hemiptera can fly but only do so briefly to disperse into new aquatic environments.

The anatomy of the Hemipteran mouth reveals their predatory role in aquatic food webs. Hemipterans possess piercing mouthparts that resemble a pointed, elongate tube or arrowhead that punctures prey. The primary feeding strategy of Hemiptera involves capturing prey with their forelegs, injecting digestive enzymes into the victim, and extracting the partially digested slurry. Invertebrates dominate the prey items of Hemipterans, but a few large species target fish and tadpoles. A popular online video documents a battle between a water snake and a giant water bug (*Lethocerus* spp.)—the latter won the contest. Some species in Belostomatidae and Corixidae can inflict a painful puncture to humans.

A significant proportion of aquatic Hemiptera inhabit the water surface. Members of these skimming families, Gerridae and Veliidae, ambush prey on or just below the water surface. The feet of these insects support very dense mats of water-resistant hairs that prevent sinking and provide propulsion.

Adult Hemiptera that spend long periods of time underwater carry a bubble of air trapped between the wings and body to extract oxygen from. Once depleted of oxygen, the bubble is released and the individual returns to the surface for a fresh reserve.

Key Traits

Adults: Although only adult-stage Hemiptera are covered in depth here, nymphs and adults retain all anatomical traits between stages except for wings, which occur only during the adult stage. Hemiptera are best identified by their piercing mouthparts that are held close to the body underneath the head when not feeding. Adults possess forewings that are hardened and leathery halfway down the length of the wing, called **hemelytra**, while the hindwings are membranous and folded underneath the hemelytra at rest.

Figure 7.25. Top and bottom view of a Hemiptera adult in the genus *Gerris* (family: Gerridae) with key order traits highlighted, including A) piercing mouthparts and B) forewings that are half hardened and leathery. MACROINVERTEBRATES.ORG/ANDREA KAUTZ

Select Families (adults)

Although sixteen aquatic Hemiptera families occur in North American freshwaters, some are exceedingly rare while others exclusively inhabit lentic habitat. The five families described below reflect those most likely to be encountered in lotic ecosystems. Distinguishing among these families in the field is relatively straightforward using body shape, size, and habitat as diagnostic characteristics.

Belostomatidae (giant water bugs) rank among the largest aquatic insects, with one genus (*Lethocerus*) growing to 3 inches. Aside from their large size, Belostomatidae males are often collected with dozens of incubating eggs affixed to their backs. Species in this family tend to favor lentic habitat and occur only in slow-moving or backwater lotic ecosystems, where they sit still underwater and ambush prey.

Corixidae (water boatmen) have an oval body, patterns of stripes on the thorax back, and short antennae concealed under the head. The mid- and hindlegs are long and flattened to enhance swimming ability. Large Corixidae species are fried and served as a delicacy called *ahautle* in Mexico.

Gerridae (water striders) have a long body, antennae, and legs. Gerridae are master predators of water surfaces but do not dive and are the largest among the water-skimming Hemiptera.

Notonectidae (backswimmers) get their common name from their upside-down swimming style. Hindlegs are long and have abundant hairs for propulsion. The antennae are very small and concealed under the head. Notonectidae resemble Corixidae but do not have striped patterns on the back.

Veliidae (riffle bugs) skim the water surface and are much smaller than Gerridae. The legs and antennae are long and easily visible. Unlike Gerridae, Veliidae favor fast-moving water.

Figure 7.26. Belostomatidae: Belostoma adult. Adults in this family are best identified by their large size (up to 3 inches) and eggs that are often found attached to the backs of males (not shown here). MACROINVERTEBRATES.ORG/ ANDREA KAUTZ

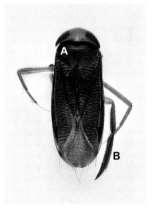

Figure 7.27. Corixidae: Hesperocorixa adult. Traits identifying the family Corixidae include an oval-shaped body, A) striped patterns on the thorax back, short antennae concealed under the head, and B) elongated and flattened mid- and hindlegs. MACROINVERTEBRATES.ORG/ANDREA KAUTZ

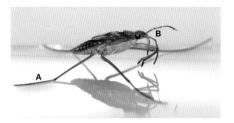

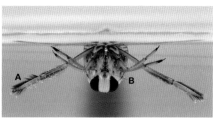

Figure 7.28. Gerridae: Gerris adult. Traits identifying the family Gerridae include A) swimming on the water surface of pools or still water; B) a long body, antennae, and legs; and a larger body size than the similar Veliidae. RYAN DOUGLAS

Figure 7.29. Notonectidae: Notonecta adult. Traits identifying the family Notonectidae include an upside-down swimming style, A) long hindlegs with abundant hairs to aid in swimming, and B) small antennae concealed under the head. RYAN DOUGLAS

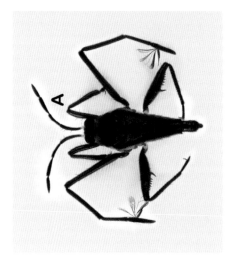

Figure 7.30. Veliidae: Rhagovelia adult. Traits identifying the family Veliidae include swimming on the water surface of riffles, A) long and easily visible antennae and legs, and a smaller body size than the similar Gerridae. MACROINVERTEBRATES.ORG/ ANDREA KAUTZ

MEGALOPTERA (ALDERFLIES, DOBSONFLIES, AND FISHFLIES)

Diversity and distribution: Megaloptera are a very small and fully aquatic order of insects, with only about 400 described species globally and 45 in North America with representative specialists of both lentic and lotic habitat. The taxonomic name comes from the large size attained by many species, including the largest aquatic insect on Earth and recordholder of the greatest wingspan among all insects (8.5 inches): the Chinese dobsonfly *Acanthacorydalis fruhstorferi*.

Ecology and life history: With Megaloptera fossils dating back to approximately 250 million years ago, the order may have been the first holometabolous insect group to evolve on Earth. Only the larvae are aquatic; all other life stages (including eggs) are terrestrial. Females deposit fertilized eggs on rocks or vegetation just above the waterline so that larvae can quickly head for the depths after hatching.

Megaloptera larvae of all species are predators of smaller invertebrates and scavengers of decomposing animal matter. Several species specialize on burrowing through soft sediments and ambushing prey. Large larvae of some species hunt tadpoles. The large and intimidating tusks found on adults should not raise alarm, as adults do not feed.

Key Traits

Larvae: Megaloptera larvae have lateral filaments extending from each abdominal segment. The fleshy abdomen terminates in two false legs (Figure 7.31) or a single, long filament (Figure 7.33). Larvae in the family Corydalidae can grow up to 1.5 inches long.

Adults: Adult Megaloptera have two pairs of equally sized wings and often possess mouthparts with tusks for fending off rivals when mating.

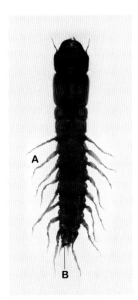

Figure 7.31. A Megaloptera larva in the genus *Nigronia* (family: Corydalidae) with key order and family traits highlighted, including A) lateral filaments extending from each abdominal segment and B) the last abdominal segment terminating in either a pair of false legs (shown here) or a single, long filament (**Figure 7.33**). MACROINVERTEBRATES.ORG/ANDREA KAUTZ

Figure 7.32. A Megaloptera adult in the genus *Corydalus* (family: Corydalidae) with key order traits highlighted, including A) large tusks used for fending off rivals while mating and B) two pairs of equally sized wings. JUDY GALLAGHER

Select Families (larvae)

North American Megaloptera are composed of just eight genera in two families, the latter of which can be easily distinguished in the field. **Corydalidae** (hellgrammites, dobsonflies, and fishflies) have eight pairs of lateral abdominal filaments and an abdomen that terminates in two false legs. Most Corydalidae larvae grow large, and some exhibit patterns on the head and hardened thoracic plates. With seven genera in the family, Corydalidae dominates North American Megaloptera biodiversity. **Sialidae** (alderflies) larvae have seven pairs of abdominal segments and the abdomen terminates in a single, long filament. The family includes only one genus, *Sialis*, which burrows in soft sediments of lotic and lentic ecosystems. *Sialis* larvae do not grow as large as those in Corydalidae.

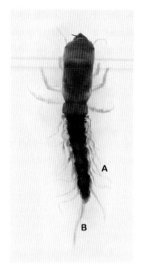

Figure 7.33. Sialidae: Sialis larva. Traits identifying the family Sialidae include A) seven pairs of lateral abdominal filaments and B) the abdomen terminating in a single, long filament. MACROINVERTEBRATES .ORG/ANDREA KAUTZ

TRICHOPTERA (CADDISFLIES)

Diversity and distribution: Trichoptera are close relatives of Lepidoptera (moths and butterflies) and dominate insect biodiversity in freshwater. With over 14,000 catalogued species worldwide and approximately 1,500 in North America, Trichoptera rank only second in biodiversity among aquatic insects and represent the largest entirely freshwater order. Trichoptera thrive in all freshwater habitats, including lentic and lotic ecosystems from the Arctic to the tropics. As is the case with most organisms, Trichoptera biodiversity increases with proximity to the equator.

Ecology and life history: Trichoptera are holometabolous, with a four-stage life cycle including a pupal stage. Eggs, larvae, and pupae are all aquatic life stages, while adults emerge to feed on nectar and spawn in terrestrial ecosystems.

The most notable attribute of Trichoptera is the portable protective case many species inhabit as larvae. Trichoptera use a substance very similar to silk to construct elaborate tube structures out of sand, pebbles, twigs, leaf fragments, or moss. Cases provide protection from predators, and some route flow through the case to help the larva feed. Many families or genera are distinguished by case material or shape thanks to the impressive diversity of construction strategies. A few clever artists with affinity for aquatic life create jewelry with help from Trichoptera. The larvae are kept in aquaria with precious stones and their cases become earrings or necklaces once abandoned.

Not all Trichoptera make cases, but species that do not also use silk in clever ways. Some caseless Trichoptera (chiefly those in the family Hydropsychidae) spin large, elaborate nets that direct flow through flexible, balloon-like structures. Fine organic matter or small animal prey get trapped by the nets, providing an easy meal to larvae. Other caseless Trichoptera create elaborate structures out of spiderweb-like silk nets and twigs to live and feed in.

Trichoptera larval feeding strategies are wildly diverse. Most filter-feed on microscopic animals or algae and fine organic matter. A few species shred leaves to digest biofilms, and others are predators of other aquatic invertebrates.

Key Traits

Larvae: Several traits help to easily distinguish Trichoptera larvae from other insects. Most obvious among these are the cases, which usually entirely conceal larvae from view. The larvae of many species, however, do not build cases. Case-building caddisflies are always depicted with their corresponding cases in the families highlighted below. Larvae completely lack wingpads because wings develop entirely during the pupal stage. The abdominal segments are entirely fleshy and often have gills in tufts or finger-like structures. Finally, the last abdominal segment features two false legs terminating with a large hook.

Figure 7.34.   A Trichoptera larva in the genus *Ironoquia* (family: Limnephilidae) and corresponding case with key order traits highlighted, including A) nearly entirely fleshy abdominal segments and B) two false legs with large hooks at the end of the abdomen. A protective case usually indicates a Trichoptera larva, although not all Trichoptera build cases.
MACROINVERTEBRATES.ORG/ANDREA KAUTZ

Adults: Adult Trichoptera closely resemble moths and are often nocturnally active. Most species are drably colored shades of brown or gray and have long antennae. The two pairs of wings are held close to the body at rest and form a tent-like structure over the abdomen. Like moths and butterflies, close examination of Trichoptera adults reveal

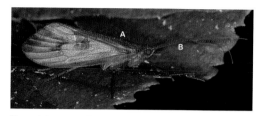

Figure 7.35. A Trichoptera adult with key order traits highlighted, including A) abundant hairs and B) long antennae. JUDY GALLAGHER

that their wings and body are covered with dense hairs that entomologists call **trichomes**, which gives the order its name.

Select Families (larvae)

North American Trichoptera are organized into 26 families and 157 genera. Some families are exceptionally rare and include less than 10 species while others exceed 200 species. A few families specialize in lentic habitat. Those covered below are widespread in lotic ecosystems. Key traits used to distinguish families in the field include case and gill structure.

Goeridae larvae can be identified by their tank-like cases flanked with large stones on the sides. Although this family includes only two genera and six species in North America, some species are very abundant in streams with clean water.

Helicopsychidae (snail casemaker caddisflies) create helical cases resembling snail shells using sand grains. The family includes only one genus in North America, *Helicopsyche*.

Hydropsychidae (net-spinning caddisflies) constitute the largest family of caseless Trichoptera in North America. Larvae can be easily identified in the field by their abundant abdominal gill tufts and dark-colored plates on each thoracic segment. Unlike most Trichoptera, several Hydropsychidae species are very pollution-tolerant.

Lepidostomatidae larvae build four-sided and symmetric cases out of leaves and are most abundant in mountainous lotic systems with cold, clear water.

Limnephilidae (northern casemaker caddisflies) represent one of the most biodiverse Trichoptera families, with more than 250 North American species that make cases with variable shapes and materials. High diversity in this family means that no single trait can firmly identify this family in the field, but most species have two humps that laterally project on the first abdominal segment. All species build cases.

Philopotamidae (finger net caddisflies) are caseless larvae that can be identified by their yellow head and first thoracic segment that ends in a black stripe. The other thoracic segment and abdomen are fleshy and white.

Phryganeidae (giant casemaker caddisflies) grow larger than any other Trichoptera larvae (up to 1.5 inches) and make large, irregularly shaped cases out of organic material.

Rhyacophilidae larvae are caseless Trichoptera that feed on other insects during late instar stages. They are often colored green when alive and have rounded, bulged abdominal segments.

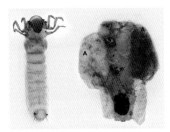

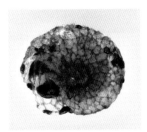

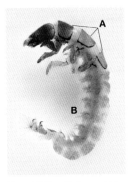

Figure 7.36. Goeridae: Goera larva and case. The trait that best identifies the family Goeridae is a tank-like case flanked with large stones on the sides. MACROINVERTEBRATES.ORG/ANDREA KAUTZ

Figure 7.37. Helicopsychidae: Helicopsyche larva. Larvae in this family are easily identified by the snail-like shape to the case made of sediment. MACROINVERTEBRATES.ORG/ANDREA KAUTZ

Figure 7.38. Hydropsychidae: Cheumatopsyche larva. Traits identifying the family Hydropsychidae include A) dark, large plates on the back of each thoracic segment and B) conspicuous gill tufts on all abdominal segments. MACROINVERTEBRATES.ORG/ANDREA KAUTZ

Figure 7.39. Lepidostomatidae: Lepidostoma larva. The family Lepidostomatidae is best identified by the four-sided, symmetrical cases made of leaves or twigs. MACROINVERTEBRATES.ORG/ANDREA KAUTZ

Figure 7.40. Limnephilidae: Pycnopsyche larva. Few reliable traits can be used to identify the family Limnephilidae in the field, although A) many species have humps on the first abdominal segment. All species build cases. MACROINVERTEBRATES.ORG/ANDREA KAUTZ

Figure 7.41. Philopotamidae: Chimarra larva. Traits identifying the family Philopotamidae include A) yellow-colored head and legs and B) black stripe on the first thoracic segment. MACROINVERTEBRATES.ORG/ANDREA KAUTZ

Figure 7.42. Phryganeidae: Ptilostomis larva. Trichoptera in the family Phryganeidae grow larger than any other Trichoptera. MACROINVERTEBRATES.ORG/ANDREA KAUTZ

Figure 7.43. Rhyacophilidae: Rhyacophila larva. Traits identifying the family Rhyacophilidae include A) rounded and bulged abdominal segments. Trichoptera in this family are usually green colored when alive; the specimen shown here is preserved and has lost the green color as a result. MACROINVERTEBRATES.ORG/ANDREA KAUTZ

COLEOPTERA (BEETLES)

Diversity and distribution: Coleoptera have long been considered the most biodiverse of any animal group on Earth. Globally about 18,000 Coleoptera have at least one aquatic life stage among the approximately 390,000 total species in the order, ranking third in aquatic insect diversity behind Diptera and Trichoptera. North American freshwater ecosystems harbor about 1,400 species. Aquatic Coleoptera inhabit lentic and lotic habitat at all latitudes and on all continents except Antarctica, with more biodiversity found toward the tropics. Unlike most other aquatic insects, Coleoptera can be found on the surface of or diving in water at all life stages, including as adults.

Ecology and life history: The life stages in which the holometabolous Coleoptera are aquatic varies wildly among species. Some remain on or in water from egg to adult, while others might have only aquatic larval and/or pupal stages. Others are terrestrial as larvae then transition to water in adulthood.

Aquatic Coleoptera feeding strategies are very diverse. A significant proportion are predators, including the impressively fast-moving Gyrinidae that skim the water surface then dive to capture prey. The Dytiscidae, another predatory family, capture small fish and tadpoles as larvae or adults. Feeding strategies may change with life stages. For example, the Hydrophilidae are predators as larvae then become omnivorous scavengers as adults. Other families shred submerged leaves or wood to feed on biofilms.

Underwater respiration strategies among adult Coleoptera are impressively creative. Many species across four families (including Dytiscidae) mimic SCUBA systems by carrying portable pouches of air with them underwater to breathe from until oxygen in the bubble becomes depleted. At that point the bubble is released and the larva returns to the water surface for a new one. Others permanently retain a single or series of small air bubbles near their body called a **plastron**. Oxygen diffuses into the plastron air from the water once the Coleoptera depletes concentrations for its own cellular respiration. The plastron allows some Coleoptera, such as those in the Elmidae, to remain permanently underwater despite the need to breathe air. Wings and elytra usually support the plastron. Although aquatic beetles do fly to disperse into new lotic systems, once plastrons develop, the ability to fly permanently ends.

Key Traits

Larvae: Generalizing aquatic Coleoptera larvae is difficult because of the high diversity in traits and form among families. Nearly all larvae possess <u>eye spots</u> in a cluster rather than a single, contiguous eye. The abdomen usually <u>terminates in gills or gill tufts</u> rather than the long cerci found in other orders, although these are sometimes small or inconspicuous. Although some larvae might resemble Trichoptera, Coleoptera larvae tend to have <u>hardened plates on abdominal segments</u> and lack large hooks on the terminal segment. Nearly all larvae have three pairs of segmented legs on the thorax.

Figure 7.44. A Coleoptera larva in the genus Tropisternus (family: Hydrophilidae) with key order traits highlighted, including A) multiple eyespots and B) hardened plates on the abdomen. MACROINVERTEBRATES.ORG/ANDREA KAUTZ

Adults: The easiest way to identify an adult Coleoptera is by the **elytra**: the hardened forewings that no longer help with flying but instead provide protection from predators and desiccation. No other insect order possesses forewings that are completely hardened. Other traits common to aquatic Coleoptera adults include an <u>oval body shape</u> and <u>shiny sheen</u>. Those that swim possess long hairs on at least one pair of legs to boost propulsion.

Figure 7.45. A Coleoptera adult in the genus Optioservus (family: Elmidae). A) The elytra, hardened forewings that characterize the order.
MACROINVERTEBRATES .ORG/ANDREA KAUTZ

Select Families (larvae and adults)

Counting the true number of North American aquatic Coleoptera is difficult because many species, genera, and families have close association with water during a life stage but may not entirely depend on it. Entomologists consider species within about one hundred genera in twenty-five families to be aquatic. Truly water-loving families commonly encountered in lotic systems are covered in detail below.

Dytiscidae (predaceous diving beetles) represent the largest family of aquatic Coleoptera and are predators of tadpoles, fish, and other insects. Most species specialize in lentic habitat, but some are found in large rivers. Larvae grow quite large (over 1.25 inches), with a <u>large head</u> and <u>pointed mandibles</u> for feeding on oversized prey. Adults are <u>rounded</u> and <u>streamlined</u> for swimming, with <u>long hairs on the hindlegs</u>. Dytiscidae adults resemble Gyrinidae but have just one pair of eyes.

Elmidae (riffle beetles) get their common name for their love of the well-oxygenated lotic riffles they inhabit as larvae and adults. Larvae are <u>small, elongate</u>, and often have an <u>orange-brown hue</u>. The <u>last abdominal segment</u> is typically covered by a <u>long, solid plate</u>. Adults look like typical land-dwelling beetles with elytra pocked with small depressions arranged in rows. Elmidae adult <u>claws are large</u> to facilitate crawling against currents.

Gyrinidae (whirligig beetles) are unmistakable thanks to their tendency to form large aggregations on the water surface of large rivers where they swim and dive at dizzying speeds in search of invertebrate prey or decomposing fish. Larvae and adults are aquatic, but pupae are terrestrial. Larvae have <u>long, filamentous gills extending from the sides of their abdominal segments</u> and <u>two pairs of hooks on the last segment</u>. Adults are <u>rounded and streamlined</u>, but most unique is their <u>two pairs of eyes</u> that allow for simultaneous sight above and below water.

Psephenidae (water pennies) are aquatic only during the egg and larval stages. Larvae are unmistakable thanks to their <u>very flattened body</u> and <u>round shape</u>. Their head, legs, and gills are all tucked under their body segments to ease movement underwater, where they scrape algae from rocks. Large Psephenidae populations often indicate good water quality.

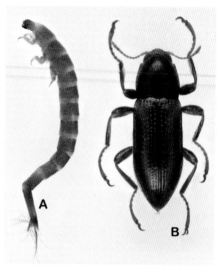

Figure 7.46. Dytiscidae: Agabus larva (left) and adult. Traits identifying the family Dytiscidae include A) pointed mandibles and B) a large head in larvae and C) long, abundant hairs on hindlegs in adults. MACROINVERTEBRATES.ORG/ANDREA KAUTZ

Figure 7.47. Elmidae: Dubiraphia larva (left) and adult. Traits identifying the family Elmidae include an orange hue, small body, and A) long, solid plate on the last abdominal segment in larvae and B) large claws for climbing through riffles in adults. MACROINVERTEBRATES.ORG/ANDREA KAUTZ

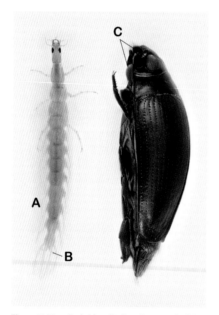

Figure 7.49. Psephenidae: Psephenus larva, viewed from above (left) and below. Larvae in the family Psephenidae are very easily identified by their round and very flattened body. MACROINVERTEBRATES.ORG/ANDREA KAUTZ

Figure 7.48. Gyrinidae: Gyrinus larva and adult. Traits identifying the family Gyrinidae include A) long, filamentous gills extending from the abdomen and B) two pairs of hooks on the last abdominal segment in larvae and C) two pairs of eyes in adults. MACROINVERTEBRATES.ORG/ANDREA KAUTZ

DIPTERA (FLIES)

Diversity and distribution: Diptera dominate biodiversity in the insect world of today on land and in water. Scientists have catalogued about 160,000 Diptera species, but some estimate that another 100,000 remain undiscovered, placing the order third behind Coleoptera and Lepidoptera. Among aquatic insects, Diptera rank first and constitute a third of all water-dependent insects, with over 46,000 species described today but plenty yet unknown to science. Diptera occupy every aquatic environment on Earth, including small, ephemeral bodies of still water and depths exceeding 4,000 feet in lakes. A large fraction of Diptera are lotic habitat specialists. The largest non-marine animal in Antarctica is a stream-dwelling aquatic Diptera in the family Chironomidae.

Ecology and life history: Despite their vast biodiversity, Diptera represent the youngest major order of insects, with an evolutionary record dating to only about 240 million years ago. The order is holometabolous, with most aquatic species possessing water-dependent egg, larval, and/or pupal stages.

Every aquatic insect feeding strategy can be found within the Diptera. The Simulidae (blackflies) filter-feed from the water column by capturing small prey and detritus using mouthparts that resemble delicate fans. Many species of Tipulidae (craneflies) shred leaves to feed on biofilms residing on leaf surfaces. The Blephaceridae are vegetarian grazers of algae and detritus. Most aquatic Diptera families include a few predatory species while others, such as the Tabanidae (horseflies), are entirely composed of invertebrate predators.

Adult aquatic Diptera often continue feeding post-emergence, including the Simulidae and Culicidae (mosquitoes) that feed on us. Large swarms of adult Empididae (dance flies) engaged in a mating dance can develop over the surface of lotic systems. Most female aquatic Diptera deposit fertilized eggs by quickly dropping them below the water surface. Some species spend adulthood and mate skating across the water surface, while a few dive underwater to deposit eggs.

Key Traits

Larvae: Unlike any other aquatic insect order, larval Diptera lack segmented legs. False legs composed of fleshy thoracic extensions with a circle of hooks called **prolegs** occur on some species. The head capsule is concealed by fleshy extensions of the thorax in many families, although the head is always clearly visible in some key aquatic families.

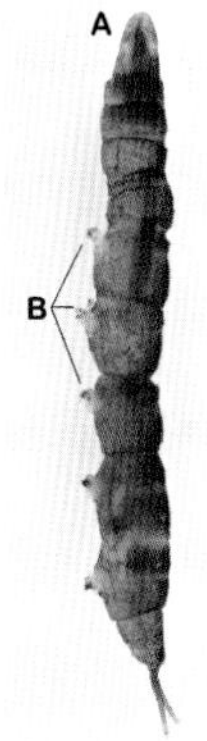

Adults: The sizable biodiversity within the family results in adults with wildly varying sizes, shapes, and key traits. However, adult Diptera are easily positively identified by having only one pair of wings. Diptera hindwings evolved into structures called **halteres** that help with balance and aerodynamics.

Figure 7.50. A Diptera larva in the genus Dicranota (family: Pediciidae) with key order traits highlighted, including A) head capsule concealed by fleshy thoracic tissue and B) prolegs. MACROINVERTEBRATES.ORG/ ANDREA KAUTZ

Figure 7.51. A Diptera adult in the family Tipulidae with key order traits highlighted, including A) one pair of wings and B) halteres evolved from hindwings. CHRIS PARKER

Select Families (larvae and adults)

Many aquatic Diptera families specialize in lentic, wetland, or ephemeral pond habitat. Large families, such as the Tipulidae, include fully terrestrial and aquatic species with some specializing on perennially waterlogged soils, thereby challenging the question of what constitutes an aquatic species. Perhaps the most important Diptera families for sustaining the well-being of humans, the Culicidae (mosquitoes), require still water and are not found in running waters. Major Diptera families of lotic ecosystems are described below.

Blephaceridae (net-winged midges) stand out from other Diptera larvae by having lateral extensions of their abdominal segments and a single suction cup on the underside of each segment. Larvae in this family crawl over hard surfaces in water with very swift current to feed on algae. Species in this family are extremely sensitive to pollution.

Chironomidae (midges) are possibly the most biodiverse family within the Diptera, with thousands of species occupying all types of aquatic habitat. Some species are very sensitive to pollution while others thrive in degraded ecosystems, allowing them to become the dominant aquatic invertebrate. The head capsule is always visible and the body is elongate in this family. Most species possess a pair of prolegs with hooks on the final abdominal segment.

Limonidae larvae have a head that is concealed within the thorax and often have a bulbous terminal abdominal segment. The last abdominal segment also has lobed structures with spiracles—structures used to acquire oxygen.

Simulidae (blackflies) are very familiar to people living in post-glacial landscapes, where swarms of adults incessantly bite during the summer. Larvae are shaped like bowling pins with a head capsule that is always visible and fanlike mouthparts that capture prey from flowing water.

Tipulidae (craneflies) are a very diverse family with over a thousand species in North America. The larvae have a head concealed within the thorax, and the abdomen lacks prolegs and ends in fleshy, fingerlike extensions with spiracles.

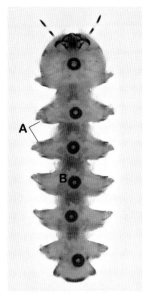

Figure 7.52. Blephaceridae: Blepharicera larva (view of underside). Traits identifying the family Blephaceridae include A) fleshy lateral extensions of abdominal segments and B) a single suction cup on the bottom of each abdominal segment.
MACROINVERTEBRATES.ORG/
ANDREA KAUTZ

Figure 7.53. Chironomidae: Chironomis larva. Traits identifying the family Chironomidae include A) a visible head, elongate body, and B) a pair of prolegs with small hooks at the end of the abdomen.
MACROINVERTEBRATES.ORG/
ANDREA KAUTZ

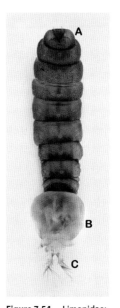

Figure 7.54. Limonidae: Hexatoma larva. Traits identifying the family Limonidae include A) a head concealed by fleshy thoracic tissue, B) a bulbous terminal abdominal segment, and C) lobed structures bearing spiracles at the end of the abdomen.
MACROINVERTEBRATES.ORG/
ANDREA KAUTZ

Figure 7.55. Simulidae: Prosimulium larva. Traits identifying the family Simulidae include a body shaped like a bowling pin, visible head, and A) fanlike mouthparts used to filter water for food.
MACROINVERTEBRATES.ORG/
ANDREA KAUTZ

Figure 7.56. Tipulidae: Tipula larva. Traits identifying the family Tipulidae include A) a head concealed by fleshy thoracic tissue, a lack of prolegs, and B) an abdomen ending in fingerlike extensions.
MACROINVERTEBRATES.ORG/
ANDREA KAUTZ

CHAPTER 7
CRUSTACEANS

Three major orders of large-bodied crustaceans—Decapoda (crayfishes), Amphipoda (amphipods), and Isopoda (isopods)—conspicuously crawl through the benthic zones of nearly all North American lotic ecosystems. Each of these three orders is included in the taxonomic class Malacostraca, a group that includes dominant marine invertebrates such as shrimp, crabs, and lobsters. Some shrimp and crab species have evolved to thrive in freshwater, particularly along coasts and in the tropics. Multiple species of migratory shrimp (also in the order Decapoda) constitute a large proportion of invertebrate fauna in small streams of Caribbean islands. Such species spend adulthood in lotic ecosystems then broadcast their fertilized eggs into the water column. A lucky few will be carried all the way to nursery marine waters along the coast. However, shrimp and crabs are rare in North American lotic systems. Small-bodied crustaceans commonly occur in freshwaters, including *Daphnia*, ostracods, and Anostraca (fairy shrimp). But these crustacean groups are either too small to see without a microscope or uncommon in flowing waters. Consequently, this chapter focuses on the three large-bodied crustacean orders commonly encountered in North American lotic ecosystems.

Although not as biodiverse as insects, the hundreds of freshwater amphipod, crayfish, and isopod species fulfill critical ecological functions in lotic systems. All three are **detritivores**: omnivorous consumers of live and decaying organic matter, including leaves that fall into water from surrounding forests and grasslands. Leaf shredding by crustaceans and some insects (mainly Plecoptera, Diptera, and some Trichoptera) makes energy that originated in terrestrial ecosystems available to aquatic food webs. Freshwater crustaceans also recycle energy and nutrients within aquatic food webs by consuming dead organisms of all sizes. Many larger organisms feed on freshwater crustaceans, including hundreds of fishes that rely on young amphipods and isopods as primary prey. Raccoons, otters, and snakes consider crayfish a delicacy.

FRESHWATER CRUSTACEAN LIFE HISTORY

All large-bodied freshwater crustaceans engage in internal fertilization followed by direct care of young by the females. Offspring broods remain in a cluster within a pouch or held by the legs under the maternal abdomen until they are large enough to survive on their own. Like insects, crustaceans grow by molting: fully shedding their hard exoskeleton multiple times until reaching adulthood. Fully grown adults typically also molt at least once per year to dislodge parasites. Unlike insects, however, crustaceans do not undergo metamorphosis and juveniles are anatomically identical to adults.

FRESHWATER CRUSTACEAN ANATOMY

Anatomical traits among freshwater crustaceans vary among taxonomic classes and orders. However, those of the Malacostraca, which includes all three common large-bodied crustaceans, share several key traits. Decapoda, Amphipoda, and Isopoda typically possess a body plan that includes a fused head and thorax called a **cephalothorax** plus a six-segmented abdomen. The thorax has eight segments, but these may be difficult or impossible to see from the back or side. Each of the thoracic segments usually includes a pair of segmented legs, although some groups lack one or more leg

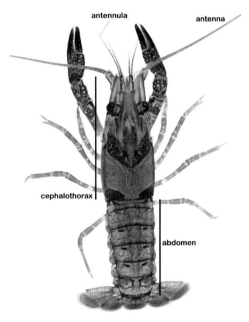

Figure 8.1. *Procambarus spiculifer* (white tubercled crayfish) with crustacean anatomical features highlighted. ALAN CRESSLER

pairs. All Malacostraca have a long pair of primary antennae and a secondary, shorter pair called **antennula**. The entire body is protected by an exoskeleton made of calcium and **chitin**, a fibrous structure that also provides structural support in insects and fungi.

A KEY TO NORTH AMERICAN FRESHWATER CRUSTACEANS

Identifying the three major freshwater Malacostraca orders can be easily performed in the field without a microscope or hand lens. Distinguishing large-bodied crustaceans to taxonomic order simply requires consideration of body shape and size. However, only the Decapoda can be further identified to family or genus in the field, with Amphipoda and Isopoda requiring magnification for detailed identification.

1. A) Body very compressed from side to side; body length less than ½ inch; legs not projecting laterally from body while at rest
    .... **Amphipoda (amphipods)**, page 95

    B) Body not compressed or compressed from top to bottom; legs project from body laterally such that they are visible from a top view while at rest 2

2. A) Body compressed top to bottom and usually less than ½ inch; legs not modified to form large claws... **Isopoda (isopods)**, page 96

    B) Body not compressed; first pair of legs modified to form large claws; adults typically grow longer than ½ inch
    .... **Decapoda (crayfishes)**, page 97

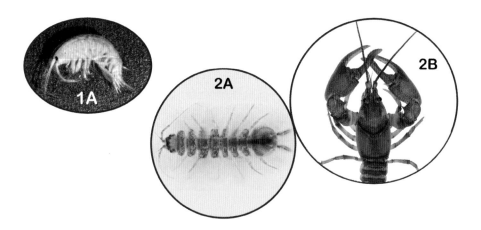

AMPHIPODA (AMPHIPODS)

Diversity and distribution: Amphipoda consist of about 8,000 species that inhabit marine, freshwater, and terrestrial ecosystems worldwide. About one-quarter are found exclusively in freshwater on all continents, including Antarctica. Approximately 240 species in 23 genera and 12 families occur in North American freshwaters, although many more remain undescribed by scientists. All freshwater habitats support Amphipoda, but nearly half of all species only occur in caves and springs, where they are often the most biodiverse animal group present.

Ecology and life history: Predatory, herbivorous, detritivorous, and omnivorous Amphipoda all occur in freshwater. Most primarily consume detritus or are omnivorous, opportunistic feeders. Amphipoda are often the key invertebrate that shreds decomposing terrestrial leaves. Although leaf-shredding Amphipoda attain most of their nutrition from the microorganisms on the leaf surface, physically breaking down leaf material is crucial for integrating energy from terrestrial ecosystems into aquatic food webs.

Female Amphipoda keep fertilized embryos near their body in a chamber supported by specialized legs on the abdomen. Most reproduce only once and complete a full life cycle within a year, but some longer-lived Amphipoda may have more than twelve broods.

Key Traits

Amphipoda can be easily identified in the field by their body shape. Nearly all freshwater species are compressed side to side and have a curved or hook-shaped profile that very few other freshwater invertebrates possess. Most common species are colored white or pink and lack patterned pigmentation. Identifying among Amphipoda families is difficult without magnification.

Figure 8.2. Gammarus, an Amphipoda in the family Gammaridae. MACROINVERTEBRATES.ORG/ANDREA KAUTZ

ISOPODA (ISOPODS)

Diversity and distribution: Crustaceans in the order Isopoda occur throughout the world in every major ecosystem, including marine, terrestrial, and freshwater habitats. Among the approximately 10,300 Isopoda species on Earth, over 6,000 occur in the oceans and nearly 950 occupy freshwater environs. Freshwater Isopoda occupy all lotic and lentic habitats, but like the Amphipoda a large proportion of species specialize in subterranean habitats like caves and springs. Over half of all freshwater Isopoda species possess native ranges in temperate to Arctic Europe and Asia. North America supports about 130 species organized into 18 genera and 23 families.

Ecology and life history: Although Isopoda adopting every major feeding strategy can be found in freshwater habitats, nearly 75 percent of all species are omnivores that primarily feed on detritus, particularly decaying leaves. Many Isopoda detritivores harbor bacteria in their guts that aid in breaking down leaves that are indigestible to other aquatic invertebrates.

Reproduction in Isopoda is typical of large-bodied freshwater crustaceans. Females keep embryos and young within a pouch under the abdomen and support their broods using foot-like structures that males do not possess. Some Isopoda species reproduce only once, while others may rear over a dozen broods in a lifetime.

Key Traits

Most Isopoda can be easily distinguished from other large-bodied crustaceans in the field based on body shape. Freshwater Isopoda tend to have a flattened body from top to bottom and their legs project laterally. The last body segment of an Isopoda, called the **telson**, is as wide or wider than the rest of the body. Unlike other large-bodied crustaceans, each major body segment supporting a pair of legs in the Isopoda is easy to distinguish.

Nearly all freshwater Isopoda families are impossible to distinguish from one another without magnification.

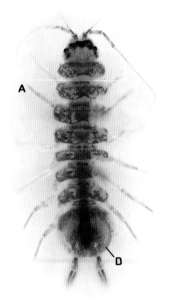

Figure 8.3. The freshwater Isopoda Asellus (family: Asellidae) with key traits highlighted, including A) legs projecting laterally and B) a widened final body segment (the telson).
MACROINVERTEBRATES.ORG/ANDREA KAUTZ

DECAPODA (CRAYFISHES)

Diversity and distribution: Decapoda represent by far the most biodiverse group of large-bodied crustaceans in North American freshwater ecosystems. Although the taxonomic order Decapoda includes crustaceans commonly recognized as shrimp, in North American lotic ecosystems two families with a lobster-like body plan (crayfishes) dominate: Astacidae and Cambaridae. Among the 650 freshwater Decapoda commonly recognized as crayfishes, around 400 species occur in North America. Therefore, North America represents the most important global hotspot of crayfish biodiversity.

Crayfishes occur in every aquatic habitat and often blur the lines between freshwater and terrestrial life. Many species thrive in lotic systems of all sizes. Some crayfishes spend most of their existence in burrows excavated in the mud immediately adjacent to stream channels, which can be spotted by the chimney-like mud structure at the surface. Burrowing species dig up to 6 feet down to reach groundwater for soaking in during the day, then venture to the land surface to forage overnight. Like their Amphipoda and Isopoda cousins, many crayfishes have evolved to thrive in cave ecosystems.

Ecology and life history: Nearly all North American crayfishes are omnivorous consumers of any organic material they can find or capture. Many species shred and ingest decaying leaves but do so to consume the biofilms growing on the surface. Although most species can survive consuming vegetation and detritus, such meals will be set aside if animal prey can be captured or scavenged. All crayfishes are active nocturnally and spend the day under rocks or resting in burrows.

Most crayfishes possess a two-year lifespan, although a few species from colder climates and in caves live for over two decades. Like other large-bodied crustaceans, crayfishes molt several times, including as adults, to accommodate new growth and shed parasites.

Key Traits

Lotic crayfishes are easily distinguished from other crustaceans by their large body size that commonly reaches or exceeds 2 inches in most species. Also conspicuous are the two foremost legs modified to very large claws. Crayfish use the enlarged foreclaws for intimidating potential predators, cutting up food, and (in some species) capturing prey. The claws on the second foremost leg pair

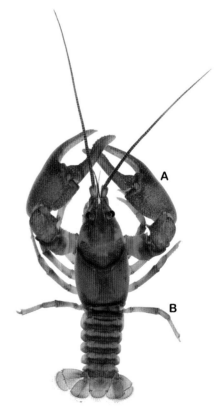

Figure 8.4. The crayfish *Cambarus fasciatus* (Etowah crayfish) in the family Cambaridae with key traits highlighted, including A) forelegs modified into large claws and B) enlarged legs for crawling. ALAN CRESSLER

may also be enlarged to a lesser degree. On the midbody, <u>four leg pairs are enlarged for crawling</u>, while the remaining, hindmost <u>legs below the abdomen are smaller and used for swimming</u>.

No field-observable traits reliably distinguish crayfish families or genera among the hundreds of North American species. However, many conservation agencies or natural history programs provide locally oriented crayfish identification guidance, as reliable identifying traits often do exist among a limited number of species.

Crayfish biodiversity is highly variable throughout the United States and concentrated in the Southeast. Depending on the location, identifying crayfish might be an obvious choice among two or three candidates or a challenge requiring careful anatomical study to select from a dizzying array of species. Taking the time to learn about the crayfish species in a favorite lotic system is worth the effort, as some invasive crayfish species are rapidly spreading and outcompeting rare, native species for resources. Therefore, distinguishing between invasive and native species might be important before using crayfish as bait or collecting for the pot.

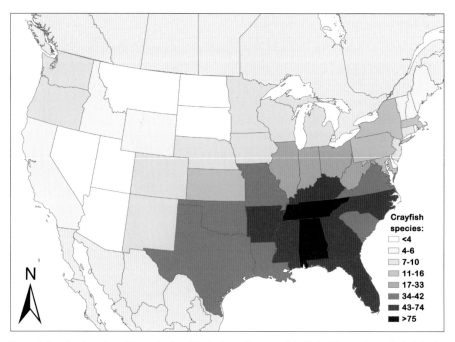

Figure 8.5.   Number of crayfish species found in the lower 48 states of the United States. Counts include both native and introduced species.

CHAPTER 8
BIVALVE MOLLUSKS

Freshwater bivalve mollusks, animals commonly known as mussels and clams, represent critically important but often overlooked organisms in lotic ecosystems. Mussels and clams comprise the taxonomic class Bivalvia (bivalves) within the phylum Mollusca (mollusks), a very large group that includes snails, slugs, squid, and octopuses. All bivalves form calcium carbonate shells that are mirror images of each other, with each shell half called a valve.

Hundreds of bivalve mollusk species occur throughout the rivers of North America, with notable biodiversity in the mussel family Unionidae, which contributes more bivalve mollusk species to lotic systems than any other group worldwide. Among the approximately 1,050 Unionidae mussel species, more than 350 are found within North American freshwater ecosystems, just over three times as many species as found in any other continent. Therefore, North America represents the global hotspot for freshwater bivalve mollusk biodiversity. Unfortunately, proportionally more species of Unionidae mussels are considered threatened or endangered than any other animal group in the United States.

Freshwater bivalve mollusks perform a diverse array of ecological functions important to lotic ecosystems and humans. All bivalve mollusks are filter feeders: They obtain food by siphoning water into their body and extracting very fine particulate organic matter. Consequently, bivalve mollusks literally clean the water by simply feeding, resulting in clearer water wherever they occur in abundance. Many Native American tribes traditionally consumed freshwater mussels and used shells to make jewelry, tools, and spoons. Freshwater mussel shells were used to make buttons during the nineteenth century before plastic became the preferred material. More recently, tiny pieces of freshwater mussel shells are polished into fine spheres and inserted into marine oysters to trick the latter bivalve into making pearls.

FRESHWATER BIVALVE MOLLUSK LIFE HISTORY
Ocean-dwelling bivalve mollusks typically reproduce by broadcasting gametes (sperm and eggs) into the water where they meet and form

a fertilized embryo. However, this approach is ineffective in flowing waters because fertilized embryos would be washed downstream. Consequently, most freshwater bivalve mollusks only broadcast sperm into the water for females to collect and fertilize eggs internally. Distribution strategies for young freshwater bivalve mollusks vary among groups and include some very clever tricks. For example, native Unionidae mussels co-opt fish into distributing their young. Some species have separate male and female individuals while others are hermaphroditic.

Once young bivalve mollusks find a suitable home by riding the current or fish gills, they settle in the benthic zone where they remain at the surface or become partially buried. All freshwater bivalve mollusks filter water for food and make meals out of phytoplankton, small zooplankton, and particulate organic matter.

FRESHWATER BIVALVE MOLLUSK ANATOMY

Most amateur naturalists encounter bivalve mollusk shells that have washed onto riverbanks. If the two shells of a bivalve mollusk are tightly held together, the animal is still alive and should not be disturbed from the sediments unless it is an invasive species. All bivalve mollusks have an **anterior** (front) end where a **foot** emerges that allows the animal to crawl across or through the substrate. On the posterior (back) end, two **siphons** emerge: one for taking in water to filter for food and the other for ejecting water. Lucky snorkelers who take care to not disturb mussels can observe filter-feeding. The shell crest is called the **umbo**.

umbo

anterior end
(foot emerges)

posterior end
(siphons emerge)

Figure 9.1. A *Cumberlandia monodonta* (spectaclecase) shell, a native mussel species in the family Margaritiferidae with anatomical features highlighted.

A KEY TO NORTH AMERICAN FRESHWATER BIVALVE MOLLUSKS

Identifying freshwater bivalve mollusks to species in North America usually requires extensive training and experience thanks to the profound biodiversity within the group. However, a few key invasive species and major groups can be identified in the field. Note that the key below is *not* meant to be comprehensive but rather offer basic guidance for commonly encountered bivalve mussels of North American lotic ecosystems.

1. A) Shell longer than wide, D-shaped with very straight edge along umbo, and often exhibiting zigzagged striped pattern; animal no larger than 1.5 inches
........................*Dreissena polymorpha* **(zebra mussel),** page 106
   B) Not as described above 2

2. A) Shell about as wide as long (shaped like a clam) and sometimes symmetric; less than 3 inches long or wide; patterns absent or consisting of consistent, smooth ridges 3
   B) Shell usually longer than wide (sometimes subtly so) and always asymmetric; many species growing much larger than 3 inches; patterns consisting of complex ridges, warts, or stripes of varying widths .... **Native mussels,** page 102

3. A) Shell much smaller than a human pinkie fingernail
   .... **Sphaeriidae (fingernail clams),** page 105
   B) Shell about as large or larger than a human fingernail, sometimes symmetric, and often with parallel ridges
   .... *Corbicula fluminea* **(Asian clam),** page 108

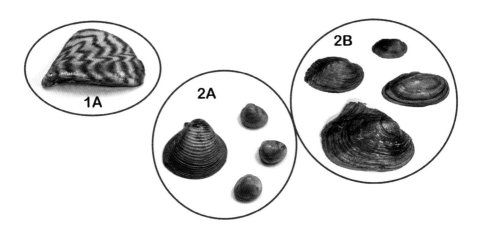

NATIVE MUSSELS

Diversity and distribution: North America represents the principal global hotspot of freshwater mussel biodiversity, with just under 300 species in the taxonomic order Unionida, commonly referred to as unionid mussels. Two taxonomic families comprise the order: Margaritiferidae (5 species) and Unionidae (293 species). Like many other animals, unionid mussel biodiversity is concentrated in the southern Appalachian region, where states like Tennessee and Alabama support well over 100 species.

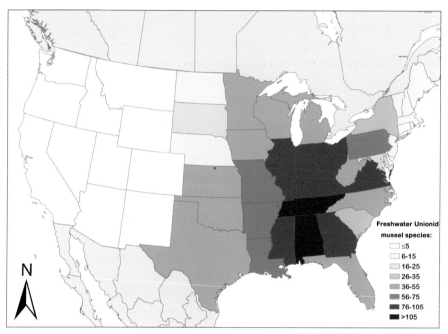

Figure 9.2. Freshwater mussel species count among US states.

Ecology and life history: Unionid mussels employ a fascinating reproductive strategy involving vertebrate parasitism. Only sperm is released into the water and fertilization occurs within mother mussels. Once young mussels are mature enough to be released, the mother mussel lures a fish in order to eject the young mussel larvae into the tissue of the unsuspecting host. Luring strategies vary among species: Some mimic prey while others resemble a potential mate complete with fake eyes and fins. Once the host gets close enough, a blast of water shoots the young mussels toward the victim. The larval, parasitic mussels are called **glochidia** and have barbed projections to anchor themselves to the host. Glochidia most often attach to host gills but can also cling to fins. Cysts usually form around the glochidia until the ride is over, at which point the young mussel ejects from the host and settles within the sediments.

Once settled, Unionid mussels behave like normal bivalve mollusks. Feeding involves filtering water through siphons to extract small plants, animals, and detritus particles. Humans have long used many native mussel species as a source of food and later for making buttons. Freshwater mussels do create pearls, and historic pearl booms severely depleted populations in many places. Today the species are valued because healthy populations clarify water and improve benthic habitat by building shells.

Unfortunately, North American native freshwater mussels proportionally included more species at risk of extinction than any other animal group in the continent. Most species are acutely sensitive to pollution and excess sedimentation, both widespread environmental problems. Some only parasitize 1 or 2 fish species; therefore, if the fish population declines, so too does the mussel. Introduced mussel species (zebra mussels and Asian clams) effectively compete for food and space. Consequently, 199 species (65 percent of all species) are considered at some risk of extinction. Already 29 species (10 percent) have gone extinct.

Key Traits

Generalizing traits among all North American Unionid mussels is difficult due to significant biodiversity within the group. Some species grow to about the size of an adult thumb while others approach the dimensions of a dinner plate. The shells of many exhibit warts, ridges, and stripes while other species possess simple, smooth shells. Technical keys to identify mussels even to genus require careful investigation of subtle shell attributes, and many species have very limited geographic ranges. The ten mussel species with the broadest distributions in North America are shown in Figure 9.3.

The best way to decipher mussel species in a favorite lotic system is to check with the state or local natural resource management agencies that are tasked with protecting native freshwater mussels. Most offer accessible guides to local native species and list the conservation status of each. Reporting a chance discovery of a rare or threatened population might help such agencies protect this important natural resource.

Figure 9.3. The ten species of native North American Unionid mussels with the broadest ranges: A) *Leptodea fragilis* (fragile papershell), B) *Lasmigona complanata* (white heelsplitter), C) *Pyganodon grandis* (giant floater), D) *Lasmigona costata* (flutedshell), E) *Utterbackia imbecillis* (paper pondshell), F) *Potamilus alatus* (pink heelsplitter), G) *Strophilus undulatus* (sloughfoot), H) *Amblema plicata* (threeridge), I) *Eurynia dilitata* (spike), and J) *Toxolasma parvum* (lilliput). All are in the family Unionidae. A quarter in the lower right corner is provided for scale.

SPHAERIIDAE (FINGERNAIL CLAMS)

Diversity and distribution: The family Sphaeriidae consists of about 230 species of very small, exclusively freshwater bivalve mollusks found on every continent except Antarctica. North America supports 41 species of Sphaeriidae, all commonly called fingernail or pea clams. Unlike most other animal groups, Sphaeriidae biodiversity is greater in northern climates, especially in regions that were covered by glaciers during the last ice age.

Ecology and life history: Sphaeriidae clams are uniformly tiny, with most species attaining a size much smaller than a human pinkie fingernail. However, their small size belies their ecological importance. Populations can grow very dense and clean the water by filter-feeding. Larger organisms, from shorebirds and bottom-feeding fishes to insects, consume large volumes of Sphaeriidae clams. However, the Sphaeriidae also serve as intermediate hosts of fish and bird parasites.

Sphaeriidae clams are hermaphroditic and can self-fertilize. Only sperm is broadcast into the water and fertilization always occurs within the mother clam. After the mother ejects juveniles, they can attach themselves to mobile organisms, including birds and insects, to disperse. Clinging to bird feet allows Sphaeriidae clams to colonize remote, isolated waters that other bivalve mollusks could not possibly reach.

Key Traits

Sphaeriidae clams are easily distinguished from other bivalve mussels by their very small size. Most species are so small that they could be mistaken for large sand grains. All assume a typical clam shape: nearly or fully symmetric with about equal width and length. Identifying Sphaeriidae to genus or species requires magnification and specialized guides. Young *Corbicula fluminea* (Asian clams) look identical to Sphaeriidae, but the former grow much larger; thus the two can be distinguished if enough specimens are detected.

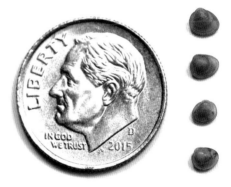

Figure 9.4. Sphaeriidae clams in the genus *Pisidium*.

DREISSENA POLYMORPHA (THE ZEBRA MUSSEL)

Distribution: The zebra mussel is an infamous invasive species rapidly spreading through North American lotic ecosystems. Originally from within the Caspian and Black Seas regions of Europe, the zebra mussel hitched a ride within boat ballasts to the Great Lakes in 1988 and quickly spread. The range in North America continues to expand as boats and anglers inadvertently move the zebra mussel. Therefore, the range map showing the North American zebra mussel's range as of 2021 (Figure 9.5) could expand further. To help arrest the spread of zebra mussels, always carefully check and thoroughly clean boat hulls or gear before traveling between waterways.

Figure 9.5. Range of *Dreissena polymorpha* (zebra mussel) in North America.

Ecology and life history: The zebra mussel is tolerant of overcrowding, resulting in mussel blankets exceeding 60,000 individuals per square foot on any available hard surface. Tiny zebra mussels even settle on other live organisms, including other mussels and dragonfly nymphs. The species becomes a filter-feeding force once populations grow to high densities. For example, dense populations in Lake Erie have filtered the water to a crystal clear blue hue resembling the Caribbean. Once food resources are exhausted, however, massive die-offs ensue that often lead to severe oxygen depletion.

Zebra mussels release eggs and sperm into the water in mass spawning events. Fertilized eggs develop into larvae called **veligers** with the ability to swim short distances, although currents carry the young mussels much farther. Juvenile mussels firmly affix themselves to hard surfaces but can also move short distances if food becomes scant. Adults live for up to five years.

The zebra mussel is in the family Dreissenidae, a globally distributed mussel family comprising about twenty species. Two species within the family in the genus *Mytilopsis* are native to estuarine waters of southern North America, but these species do not occur in freshwater.

Key Traits

The zebra mussel shell is easy to distinguish by its <u>distinct D-shape</u> and <u>zigzag stripe pattern</u>, although the latter does not occur in all individuals. Furthermore, no other North American mussel species forms the high densities on hard surfaces typical of zebra mussels.

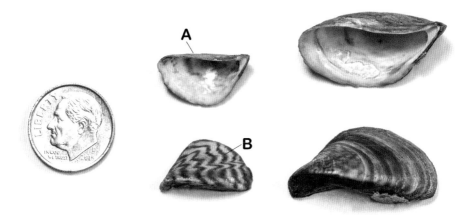

Figure 9.6. *Dreissena polymorpha* (zebra mussels) with key traits highlighted, including A) a strong D-shape caused by the straight edge below the umbo and B) zigzag stripes.

CORBICULA FLUMINEA (THE ASIAN CLAM)

Distribution: The clam *Corbicula fluminea*, commonly called the Asian clam, is a far more widespread but less well-known invasive bivalve mollusk relative to the zebra mussel. First introduced in 1938, *C. fluminea* now inhabits the waters of forty-six US states.

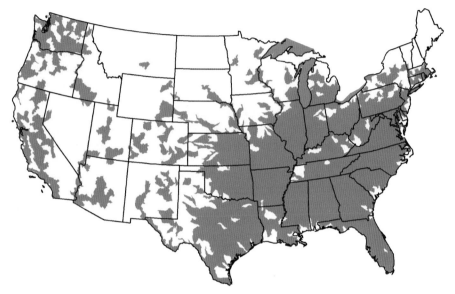

Figure 9.7. Range of *Corbicula fluminea* (Asian clam) in North America.

Ecology and life history: *C. fluminea* occurs in a wide range of aquatic habitats, from lakes to lotic systems, and can thrive in both cold and warm waters. Unlike the zebra mussel, *C. fluminea* adults typically make a home in loose substrate, especially sand. Adults often partially bury themselves in sand or silt.

Reproductive traits of *C. fluminea* help explain why it is such a successful invader. Only sperm is broadcast into the water and fertilization occurs within mother clams. A small fraction (usually less than 5 percent) of individuals are hermaphroditic. Fertilized embryos develop until old enough to feed on their own, at which point the mother releases young into the water current. Populations residing in warm water might reproduce twice annually.

Although not as ecologically damaging as the zebra mussel, *C. fluminea* often outcompetes native mussels for food and habitat. Such competition contributes to the endangered status of many native mussel species. Dense populations of *C. fluminea* diminish native mussels because they consume native mussel larvae by filter-feeding.

C. fluminea belongs to the family Cyrenidae, a family of clams comprising about 110 species. Some species within the Cyrenidae are native to North America and may resemble *C. fluminea*, but these species are not found in freshwater.

Key Traits

The *C. fluminea* shell can usually be distinguished from other mussels because the <u>width is about the same length as the height</u>. Furthermore, the shells of many individuals are <u>symmetric</u> and exhibit <u>fine, parallel ridges</u>. Shell colors range from light yellow to dark brown.

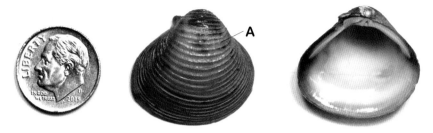

Figure 9.8. *Corbicula fluminea* (Asian clam) with A) fine, parallel ridges highlighted.

CHAPTER 9
FISHES

No other animal draws humans to lotic systems more than the beautiful fish species found within. Although large predators like trout and bass call to anglers, hundreds of species not typically attracted to bait await discovery, many of them bright and colorful enough that they would appear at home on a coral reef.

Counting fish species in lotic ecosystems can be difficult because migratory species transition among habitats. Many migrate from lotic systems into estuaries or the open ocean, while others spend part of their lives in lakes then move into running water to feed or spawn. Large river ecosystems can occasionally attract surprising marine guests. For example, bull sharks (*Carcharhinus leucas*), a large, globally distributed, and occasionally dangerous species, use rivers as nurseries and have been spotted as far upstream in the Mississippi River as Illinois. Migratory species are often very important to lotic ecosystems, as they transfer vast energy stores across ecological boundaries. Therefore, fishes requiring freshwater to complete one life cycle stage are considered freshwater species.

A quick etymological lesson will clarify passages in the following pages. *Fish* can be a singular or plural term for individuals, while the plural *fishes* refers to multiple fish species.

GEOGRAPHIC PATTERNS OF DIVERSITY

North American lotic ecosystems support exceptionally diverse fish communities. A scientific survey of all global fishes reports 923 native species occurring in freshwaters of the United States and Canada. Only a small fraction of this number, perhaps less than 5 percent, exclusively occupy lentic habitats. Although the species count north of Mexico represents only 6 percent of the 14,947 recorded globally, climatic contextualization shows that North America is a global freshwater fish biodiversity hotspot. Almost twice as many fishes occur in North American waters than in Europe and Central Asia (including Russia) combined, where 590 native species are found. Australia and New Zealand together support 618 native species. The Duck River watershed, a

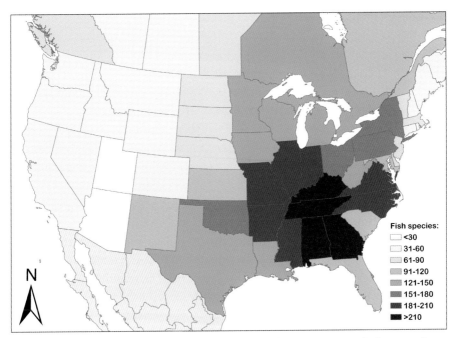

Figure 10.1. Freshwater fish species counts by state and province. Counts represent true freshwater species that commonly occur in both lotic systems and lakes, but not marine species that occasionally enter freshwater.

biodiversity gem in Tennessee, boasts 150 native fishes, a number that exceeds the freshwater fish count of the United Kingdom, France, Germany, and Spain combined (132 species).

Fish biodiversity is unevenly geographically distributed within North America, a pattern explained by climate and habitat diversity. The highest concentration of fish biodiversity north of Mexico occurs in the southeastern United States, with particularly high diversity in the southern Appalachians. North American fish biodiversity tends to decline from south to north and east to west.

In nearly all plant and animal groups, including fishes, biodiversity increases with proximity to the equator. For example, the two great tropical rivers of the world, the Amazon in South America and the Congo in Africa, support 2,268 and 1,115 species in their watersheds, respectively, although ichthyologists estimate that hundreds of fishes in the Amazon await discovery. The climate throughout most of the United States and southern Canada is temperate except for southern Texas and Florida, where the climate is subtropical. Therefore, more species are found in southern North America.

Recent geologic events also explain geographic gradients in North American fish biodiversity. Most of northern North America and much of the western half of the continent was covered by ice sheets over the past two million years, with short-lived warm periods (the climate of Earth today) intermittently disrupting the cold. Repeated advances and retreats of glacial ice meant that plants and animals had to migrate to find suitable conditions. In the southeastern United States, the north-south orientation of the Appalachian Mountains allowed fishes on the western slope to migrate throughout the Mississippi River watershed and find refuge when cold temperatures advanced. Waterfalls and rapids in the Appalachians also isolate fish populations, leading to diversification. Such geography contrasts with Europe, where the east-west orientation of the Alps prevented migration during glacial transitions, a factor that limited European freshwater fish biodiversity.

Similarly, the isolated rivers, deserts, and mountain glacial ice of the western United States limited migration. No fish habitat existed in most of Canada and the northern continental United States during glacial periods because the land was buried under a thick ice sheet. Consequently, the fishes of Canada today largely reflect those able to migrate north once ice sheets retreated. Therefore, the peculiarities of the North American climate and mountain range orientation explain why the southeastern United States is a biodiversity hotspot.

FAMILY PATTERNS OF DIVERSITY

As is the case in most organisms, freshwater fish biodiversity consists of a small number of families with many species and numerous families with few or one species. The two most biodiverse North American fish families in the United States and Canada are the Cyprinidae (minnows and carps) with 263 species and Percidae (darters and perches) with 196 species. Most North American families are far less biodiverse: Representatives of up to 65 families of fishes have been recorded in freshwaters of the continent, and 19 of these consist of just 1 species.

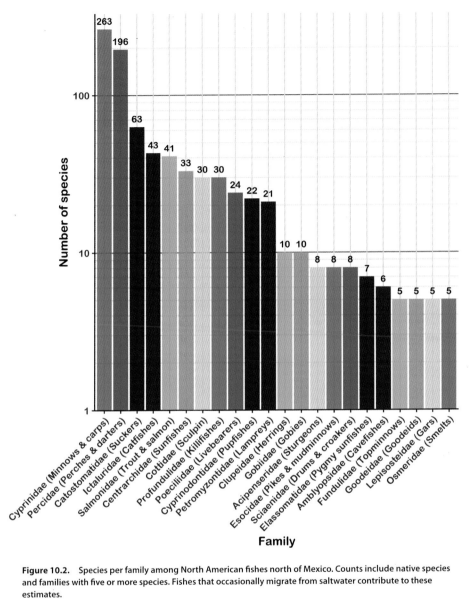

Figure 10.2. Species per family among North American fishes north of Mexico. Counts include native species and families with five or more species. Fishes that occasionally migrate from saltwater contribute to these estimates.

Most interactions between humans and lotic fishes involve anglers pursuing sportfish, yet sportfish reflect only a tiny fraction of North American freshwater fishes. A world of biodiversity awaits those willing to engage with their favorite lotic systems in unconventional and fun ways.

Lotic systems are increasingly recognized for their high potential as destinations for snorkeling. Many lotic fishes pay little heed to snorkelers, allowing close observation of brightly colored species. The minimum gear required to go snorkeling is a mask and snorkel. Because running water constantly cools the body, most destinations require a wetsuit if remaining in water for more than a few minutes.

Minnow traps offer another way to discover select smaller fish species in a favorite lotic system. Conventional minnow traps consist of a cylindrical cage with cone-shaped openings on one or both ends that allow fish to enter but prevent easy escape. Although fish can easily obtain oxygen while in a trap, the most humane way to observe fishes in this way would be to check the trap within at most a few hours after deployment so they can be released with minimal stress. Many species of madtom catfish can be caught with chicken liver or small morsels of meat as bait, while minnows can be attracted with breadcrumbs.

Anglers who appreciate fish biodiversity can also use their skills to target unconventional species. A growing number of anglers have recently gravitated to microfishing: using modified traditional angling techniques to capture, photograph, and release the many brightly colored fishes not typically caught on hook and line. Specialized gear for microfishing, including tiny hooks and line no wider than a strand of human hair, can be rigged to capture fish that would never be seen using conventional approaches. Dedicated microfishers keep records of each fish species they collect with the aim of cataloguing all species in their state or region.

Check out the North American Native Fishes Association (nanfa.org) for a wealth of resources and online forum discussions on native fishes, including capture and observation techniques.

FIN ANATOMY

A few key anatomical structures help identify fishes—most importantly, the fins. The shape, size, and position of fins distinguish many families. The **caudal fin**, used for propulsion, varies significantly among families based on habitat and feeding strategy. The **dorsal fin** sits atop the fish to help it remain upright. Dorsal fins appear as two narrowly separated fins in some families. Most fishes have two lower fin pairs for steering: the **pectoral** and **pelvic fins.** Pectoral fins also help with propulsion. Finally, the **anal fin** singularly sits at the bottom of the fish between the pelvic and caudal fins. Not shown in Figure 10.3 is the **adipose fin,** a

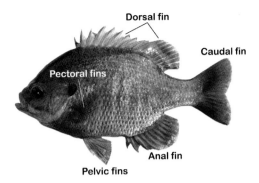

Figure 10.3. Fins on a Bluegill (Centrachidae: *Lepomis macrochirus*).

small fin between the dorsal and caudal fins in only three North American freshwater families: Salmonidae (trout and salmon), Ictaluridae (catfishes), and Percopsidae (trout-perches).

A KEY TO NORTH AMERICAN FRESHWATER FISH FAMILIES

The following dichotomous key identifies fish to taxonomic family. In-depth discussions of each family, with important structures noted on images, follow the key. The chapter is *not* meant to comprehensively cover all fishes that might be caught in North American freshwaters. Species that rarely enter freshwater from oceans and those unlikely to occur in lotic systems (such as Amblyopsidae—cave fishes) are not included.

Some families are very distinct and are easily field identified. Eels, sticklebacks, sturgeons, and lampreys are all hard to misidentify. In other cases, fishes in disparate large families might exhibit very similar appearances. Examples include the Cyprinidae (minnows) versus Catostomidae (suckers) and the Poeciliidae (livebearers) versus Fundulidae (killifish). Reliable features that can always be used to distinguish families do exist, but they often demand prior identification experience and/or use of a microscope. The key below is written for the amateur naturalist to use in the field.

1. A) Pairs of fins absent; mouth consists of a disc aimed downward rather than a jaw; seven gill slits; eel-like body
        ....**Petromyzontidae (lampreys)**, page 122
    B) At least one pair of fins present; mouth includes a jaw; one gill slit 2

2. A) Caudal fin asymmetrical, with the upper half of the fin extending further (sometimes slightly) than the lower half; adults grow to well over 3 feet long.................................3

   B) Caudal fin mostly symmetrical, with the lower half of the fin about as long as the upper half 4

3. A) Snout consists of a long, paddle-like structure that is about one-third the length of entire body; very large gape designed for filter-feeding...............**Polyodontidae (paddlefishes)**, page 135

   B) Body with rows of conspicuous and large, bony plates (scutes); mouth aimed downward; a pair of barbels present on underside of snout ....**Acipenseridae (sturgeons)**, page 128

4. A) Jaws very long, beak-like, and featuring many conspicuous teeth; dorsal fin set far back on body with length much less than one-half of body; very elongate fish found near the water surface of slower-moving lotic systems

   ....**Lepisosteidae (gars)**, page 137

   B) Not as described above.................................5

5. A) Dorsal fin very long, more than one-half the length of entire body; large, conspicuous, dark spot set at the upper base of caudal fin (Figure 10.14); head with snake-like appearance

   ....**Amiidae (bowfin)**, page 133

   B) Not as described above.................................6

6. A) Body very long and eel-like; dorsal, caudal, and anal fins all contiguous with one another; very fine scales

   ....**Anguillidae (eels)**, page 136

   B) Not as described above.................................7

7. A) Conspicuous adipose fin present, though sometimes appearing contiguous with caudal fin but not dorsal fin 8

   B) Adipose fin absent.................................10

8. A) Scales absent; two pairs of barbels located near the mouth

   ....**Ictaluridae (catfishes)**, page 140

   B) Scales present; barbels absent.................................9

9. A) Dorsal fin with two flexible spines; pelvic and anal fins with one flexible spine; adults rarely more than 4 inches long

   ....**Percopsidae (trout-perches)**, page 152

   B) No flexible spines associated with fins; adults grow much larger than 4 inches; trout or salmon-like appearance

   ....**Salmonidae (trout and salmon)**, page 164

10. A) Belly projects strongly downward and is very keel-like in cross section, often with a ridge of sharp scutes ....**Clupeidae (herrings)**, page 154

    B) Belly flat or moderately rounded, never with sharp scutes 11

11. A) Dorsal fin set far back near caudal fin; snout with duck-like appearance except in one small species restricted to the Olympic Peninsula of western Washington State .... **Esocidae (pikes)**, page 158

    B) Not as described above 12

12. A) Anus located just behind head; body stout with arched back; dark body; Atlantic and Gulf Coast drainage watersheds ....**Aphredoderidae (pirate perch)**, page 177

    B) Not as described above 13

13. A) Pelvic fin consists of a single, conspicuous spine; one to three prominent spines present on back in front of dorsal fin; adults rarely more than 2 inches long .... **Gasterosteidae (sticklebacks)**, page 178

    B) Not as described above 14

14. A) One dorsal fin present 15

    B) Two dorsal fins present, either separated or connected with a (sometimes slightly) shortened margin separating the fin into two primary sections 19

15. A) Caudal fin fully rounded 16

    B) Caudal fin forked or at least with middle indentation 18

16. A) Upper jaw joined to snout by thick tissue; prominent, dark blotch or pair of bands usually appearing at the base of caudal fin; dorsal fin always set very far back on body, usually above anal fin or farther .... **Umbridae (mudminnows)**, page 162

    B) Not as described above 17

17. A) Front of dorsal fin usually clearly set well behind the front of anal fin *or* dorsal fin is very large and conspicuously patterned; body lacking a thick, horizontal, dark stripe and orange pigmentation; anal fin of males with long extension .... **Poeciliidae (livebearers)**, page 188

    B) Front of dorsal fin set ahead of, at, or very slightly behind anal fin; dorsal fin not large and conspicuously patterned ....**Fundulidae (killifish)**, page 187

18. A) Dorsal fin with ten or more rays; mouth almost always aimed downward..............................Catostomidae (suckers), page 195

    B) Dorsal fin with nine or fewer rays (except for carp, which have a spine-like ray at the start of dorsal fin); mouth aimed upward, straight, or downward

    ....Cyprinidae (minnows and carps), page 214

19. A) Pelvic fin set far back in body; dorsal fin largely separated into two distinguished sections; very narrow-bodied fish

    .... Atherinopsidae (silversides), page 250

    B) Pelvic fin set approximately midway along body, otherwise not as described above..20

20. A) Scales too small to see without the aid of a microscope; large mouth; flattened, stout body; pectoral fins splayed for resting on bottom substrate; adults rarely more than 4 inches long

    ....Cottidae (sculpin), page 253

    B) Scales visible..21

21. A) Anal fin with one to two spines..22

    B) Anal fin with three or more spines...23

22. A) Fish of large rivers; prominent, deeply sloping head; adults commonly grow longer than 20 inches; gray/silver body lacking distinctive color patterns; only one North American freshwater species in family .... Sciaenidae (drums), page 257

    B) Fishes found in many habitats; only three species within family grow more than 9 inches long as adults; many species with bright colors and/or complex patterns; second-most diverse freshwater fish family in North America......................Percidae (perches and darters), page 259

23. A) Dorsal fins narrowly separated or very slightly joined; lateral stripe pattern usually present

    .... Moronidae (striped basses), page 276

    B) Dorsal fins moderately or broadly joined; body typically flattened side to side; patterns do not include lateral stripes

    .... Centrarchidae (sunfishes), page 279

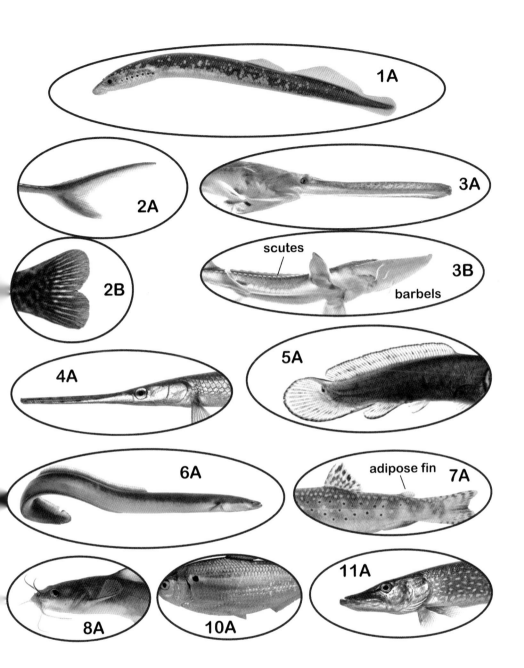

1A

2A

2B

3A

scutes

3B

barbels

4A

5A

6A

adipose fin 7A

8A

10A

11A

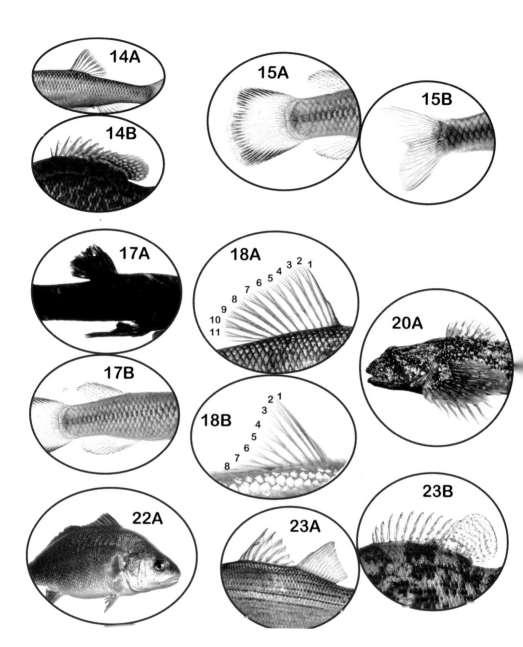

14A

14B

15A

15B

17A

17B

18A
1 2 3 4 5 6 7 8 9 10 11

18B
1 2 3 4 5 6 7 8

20A

22A

23A

23B

SPECIES DESCRIPTIONS AND RANGES

A thorough treatment of the 900-plus species would fill at least an entire book and include details for those with advanced ichthyological experience. Therefore, complete species accounts in the following pages include those that are commonly collected, locally or regionally abundant, endangered (globally or locally), ecologically important, and/ or sought after by anglers. Representative species of nearly all truly freshwater North American fish families are described.

Each account also includes geographic range maps that color states or provinces if the species is found within their freshwater environments. Two colors appear on the range maps: 1) green indicates the species is native, and 2) red denotes where the species is nonnative but viable populations have been established. Environmental degradation has caused dramatic declines of many freshwater fish populations. Many species ranges have substantially contracted, including some that were once abundant. Range maps shown in this chapter include watersheds where species currently or formerly existed; thus contemporary ranges may be significantly reduced. Data used to create the native ranges appearing on maps are derived from NatureServe.

Humans have intentionally or accidentally introduced many fishes across geographic boundaries, resulting in new populations far from where they evolved. Many introduced species cause ecological harm by competing with or consuming native species, altering lotic habitats, and/or interbreeding with native species. The range maps include watersheds colored red where the species has established nonnative populations, though these areas may change if the species range expands (or if it becomes eradicated). For more in-depth information on nonnative species in the United States, see the USGS Nonindigenous Aquatic Species database (https://nas.er.usgs.gov); data for introduced ranges shown on maps in the following pages come from this source.

PETROMYZONTIDAE (LAMPREYS)

Diversity and distribution: The family Petromyzontidae of North America include twenty-one species from five genera. Species are more concentrated in cooler regions and are found among all continental drainage basins.

Ecology and life history: The popular conception of lamprey involves a blood-sucking parasite that hitches a ride on other fishes using a grotesque circle of teeth. Although some freshwater lamprey species are parasitic, others are not. All lampreys start life in a larval stage called **ammocoete** for four to six years. Ammocoete-stage lamprey remain buried in substrate, filter-feeding on algae and microscopic animals. When a lamprey transitions into adulthood, its mouth grows, a circular pattern of teeth develops, the fleshy mouth covering disappears, and the eyes protrude. Parasitic species feed on other vertebrates after the transition.

Both parasitic and nonparasitic species occur within the same genus. Nonparasitic species (often termed brook lamprey) do not feed as adults and only live long enough to spawn, while parasitic species feed on the blood of other fishes and may live two to three years post-transformation. Parasitic species usually grow later than closely related, nonparasitic species.

Nearly all lampreys migrate to spawn. Some migrations are short, involving movements within a lotic system from a sandy to a more porous substrate where eggs are well oxygenated. Others migrate impressive distances upstream in lotic systems from lakes or the ocean. The Pacific Lamprey (*Entosphenus tridentatus*), for example, migrates from the Pacific Ocean as far as Idaho, several hundred miles up the Columbia River watershed.

Identifying species: Distinguishing lampreys can be very difficult, even for experts. The most useful and consistent strategy for identifying species is counting the number of vertical body muscle segments called **myomeres**, but this is impossible to do with live specimens in the field because they are small and impossible to tally on a moving organism. Therefore, amateur naturalists may be unable to be fully confident of the species identity. Nevertheless, collection location and/or the size often help identify among local species.

The following anatomical traits and geographic ranges may be applied as tools for identifying lamprey to genus:

Genus (# of North American species)	Geographic range	Anatomical features
Entosphenus (7)	Pacific-draining watersheds from California to Alaska	Caudal fin often slightly darker than body
Ichthyomyzon (6)	Eastern and central North America	Dorsal fin single, with potentially a shallow notch
Lampetra (4)	Throughout North America	Often with peppered pigmentation at base of caudal fin
Lethenteron (3)	Mississippi, Atlantic, and Arctic drainages	Dorsal fins deeply notched but connected
Petromyzon (1)	Native to Atlantic slope drainages and introduced to upper Great Lakes	Usually grows longer than 7 inches in parasitic adulthood

Genus *Entosphenus*

The seven North American species of lamprey in the genus *Entosphenus* can be difficult to distinguish. The most widespread and abundant species is the Pacific Lamprey (*Entosphenus tridentatus*), an anadromous, parasitic species with a range spanning Alaska to California. All other *Entosphenus* species have very limited ranges. For example, the nonparasitic Kern Brook Lamprey (*Entosphenus hubsii*) is found only within the Kern River drainage of eastern California. The smallest lamprey species in the world, the parasitic Miller Lake Lamprey (*Entosphenus minimus*), is restricted to Miller Lake, Oregon, and tributaries.

Entosphenus tridentatus—Pacific Lamprey

Figure 10.4. A Pacific Lamprey (*Entosphenus tridentatus*) adult. SEAN CONNOLLY/USFWS

Description: Pacific Lamprey are likely to be considerably larger than other *Entosphenus* and *Lampetra* species in western North America due to their anadromous life history strategy.

Size: Adults can grow up to 30 inches.

Habitat: Ammocoetes live in lotic systems of various sizes before migrating to the ocean as adults.

Diet: The Pacific Lamprey feeds on a diverse range of marine hosts, including salmon, sole, rockfish, and even whales.

Remarks: Pacific Lamprey range throughout the northern Pacific Rim, from the Japanese island of Hokkaido to California. Although not threatened with extinction, populations have been greatly reduced where humans have significantly degraded spawning habitat. Some Native American tribes in the Pacific Northwest consider the Pacific Lamprey an important food source.

Genus *Ichthyomyzon*

All six species within the genus *Ichthyomyzon* are found exclusively within North American freshwaters. Three species are parasitic—Silver Lamprey (*I. unicupsis*), Chestnut Lamprey (*I. castaneus*), and Ohio Lamprey (*I. bdellium*)—while the remaining three are not—Northern Brook Lamprey (*I. fossor*), Southern Brook Lamprey (*I. gagei*), and Mountain Brook Lamprey (*I. greeleyi*).

Two characteristics help identify species of *Ichthyomyzon* in the field. The first is their range, as all species are found exclusively within the Mississippi, Great Lakes, and Hudson River drainages. Second, all species of *Ichthyomyzon* have a <u>fully contiguous dorsal fin with only a small, shallow notch separating the fin into two sections</u> (Figure 10.5). All other freshwater North American lamprey genera possess caudal fins that are divided into two discontiguous sections.

Identifying *Ichthyomyzon* to species, however, is difficult. Ranges often offer the best clue, although many overlap. Parasitic adults tend to be larger than their nonparasitic relatives, but ammocoetes among species of both feeding types are very similar in appearance and size.

Ichthyomyzon fossor—Northern Brook Lamprey and *Ichthyomyzon gagei*—Southern Brook Lamprey

Figure 10.5. A Southern Brook Lamprey (*Ichthyomyzon gagei*) adult, with A) a shallow notch between dorsal fins highlighted. ZACH ALLEY

Description: The Northern and Southern Brook Lamprey are both small-bodied, nonparasitic lamprey with ranges in the Mississippi and Gulf of Mexico watersheds. Distinguishing between the Northern and Southern Brook Lamprey in the field where their ranges overlap is very difficult.

Size: No more than 7 inches.

Habitat: Found in shallow, small- to medium-sized lotic systems, including coldwater streams.

Diet: Both feed on detritus, single-celled algae, and microcrustaceans while buried in sediment.

Remarks: Both require pollutant-free water to survive, a trait that has led to population decline throughout their ranges. Several states list one or both species as threatened or endangered.

Genus *Lampetra*

Lampetra lamprey occur throughout the temperate Northern Hemisphere, from Turkey to western North America. Only one North American species, the Western River Lamprey (*Lampetra ayresii*) is parasitic. *Lampetra* species may often exhibit mottled patterns unusual for lamprey, but this trait is not consistent even within a species.

Lampetra species filter-feed on microscopic organisms during the ammocoete stage. The Western River Lamprey parasitizes smelt, herring, and salmon.

Lampetra aepyptera—Least Brook Lamprey

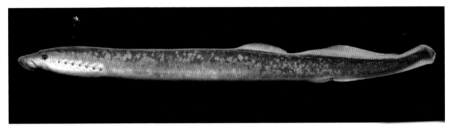

Figure 10.6. A Least Brook Lamprey (*Lampetra aepyptera*) adult. ZACH ALLEY

Description: A small-bodied, nonparasitic lamprey with a tan color during the ammocoete stage and gray to dark brown as adults.
Size: No more than 7 inches.
Habitat: Prefers slow-moving and warm lotic systems with silty or sandy substrate. Spawning occurs in pool-riffle transition zones.

Genus *Lethenteron*

Lamprey in the genus *Lethenteron* are found throughout the far Northern Hemisphere. The parasitic and anadromous Arctic Lamprey (*Lethenteron camtschaticum*) has the northernmost distribution of any lamprey species and ranges from Canada and Alaska to Siberia. Only one species, the nonparasitic American Brook Lamprey (*Lethenteron appendix*), occurs in the contiguous United States.

Lethenteron appendix—American Brook Lamprey

Figure 10.7. An American Brook Lamprey (*Lethenteron appendix*). KONRAD SCHMIDT

Description: A widely distributed, nonparasitic lamprey that is difficult to distinguish from *Lampetra* lamprey. Characteristics that verify American Brook Lamprey include teeth patterns and myomere counts that challenge even experienced ichthyologists.

Size: Typically about 6 to 7 inches, with large individuals more than 10 inches.

Habitat: Occupies small, cold streams to medium-sized, warm rivers but always with clear water.

Remarks: Older literature places American Brook Lamprey in the genus *Lampetra*. Genetic surveys, however, revealed that the species belongs in the genus *Lethenteron*.

Genus *Petromyzon*

The genus *Petromyzon* includes only one species globally, the parasitic Sea Lamprey (*Petromyzon marinus*). Sea Lamprey are anadromous and possess an impressively large native geographic range, from Florida to Newfoundland in North America to drainages of the Black and Mediterranean Seas of Europe.

Petromyzon marinus—Sea Lamprey

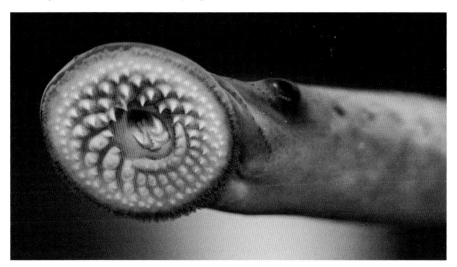

Figure 10.8.   A Sea Lamprey (*Petromyzon marinus*) adult mouth up close. T. LAWRENCE/GREAT LAKES FISHERY COMMISSION

Description: A parasitic species similar in appearance to other lamprey, but adult Sea Lamprey <u>attain a much larger size</u> than others with overlapping ranges.
Size: Larger individuals up to 3 feet.
Habitat: Ammocoetes are found in typical lamprey habitat with sandy or silty substrate for burrowing. Adults migrate to marine environments or lakes as parasites.
Diet: The Sea Lamprey feeds on a very large number of host fishes, including sturgeon, herring, large minnows, cod, and striped bass.
Remarks: Sea Lamprey were accidentally introduced to the Great Lakes above Niagara Falls during the twentieth century and have since caused substantial ecological damage to many lake fish populations, including those with commercial and recreational value. Fisheries biologists have initiated programs to reduce invasive Sea Lamprey populations by building small waterfall barriers (as lamprey cannot jump) and applying chemicals that disrupt larval development, called lampricides.

ACIPENSERIDAE (STURGEONS)

Diversity and distribution: The sturgeon family *Acipenseridae* includes twenty-five species found in the temperate Northern Hemisphere. Four sturgeon genera exist globally with two in North America: *Acipenser* (five species) and *Scaphirhynchus* (three species). Sturgeons can be found in freshwater, estuary, and coastal habitats, with many undergoing migrations that may exceed 700 miles from the ocean into rivers to spawn. Sturgeons are typically restricted to lakes and large rivers in freshwaters, as most require spacious habitat.

Ecology and life history: All sturgeons are predators that feed on invertebrates and small fish found on or near the benthic zone. Species in the genus *Scaphirhynchus*, especially *S. albus* (Pallid Sturgeon), become primarily piscivorous as adults after feeding on a mix of fish and invertebrates as juveniles. In contrast, the diets of sturgeon in the *Acipenser* consist more of invertebrates such as worms, insect larvae, and amphipods. Sturgeons cruise the bottom of their habitat to seek prey, a swimming style supported by the asymmetric caudal fin that extends longer at the top. Some anadromous species may feed very little while migrating into rivers.

Spawning occurs over riffle habitat, most often with strong, swift currents that ensure high dissolved oxygen concentrations for developing embryos. The spawning migration period may last up to two years and involve long resting periods in lotic habitat prior to reproduction. As a result, two to twelve years may pass between reproductive intervals.

Sturgeons rank among the longest-living fish on Earth. The record-holder for sturgeon age was a 154-year-old *Acipenser fulvescens* (Lake Sturgeon) caught in Lake Michigan.

Nearly all North American sturgeons have declined dramatically since European colonization. Dams block access to critical spawning habitat, and many species have limited tolerance to water pollution. Furthermore, sturgeon roe is highly prized as caviar and centuries of overfishing have greatly contributed to population declines. Many state and federal agencies support population restoration programs, but they will require decades to assess success due to the long lifespan and complex reproductive cycle of sturgeon.

Identifying species: Sturgeons are difficult to mistake for other fishes. The caudal fin is **heterocercal**, meaning it extends longer (often much longer) at the top relative to the bottom. Sturgeon lack true scales but possess five rows of bony plates called **scutes** that run along the body from front to back, a structural feature that limits predation. All species possess a snout that extends quite far beyond the downward-facing mouth, with four conspicuous barbels used for sensing prey positioned ahead of the mouth opening. Two nostrils positioned in front of the eyes on the snout are larger than the eyes in most species. The dorsal fin is positioned far back on the body, much closer to the caudal fin than the head.

Caudal fins allow for easy field identification between species of *Acipenser* and *Scaphirhynchus*. The latter possess a very long upper caudal tail filament called a **circus** that extends many times the length of the lower caudal tail extent. The large number of nerves on the circus likely means that the structure is used as a sensory organ. In contrast, the upper caudal tail lobe in *Acipenser* sturgeon is about twice the length of the lower lobe. Furthermore, the ranges of all North American species of *Scaphirhynchus* are restricted to the Mississippi River basin, while *Acipenser* species are found throughout the continent.

Genus *Acipenser*

The largest genus of sturgeon, *Acipenser* includes seventeen species worldwide and five in North America. Many species are anadromous and have transcontinental native ranges. *Acipenser* sturgeon consume a wide range of invertebrates from the benthic zone of lotic systems, including worms, crustaceans, insect larvae, and snails and the occasional benthic fish. Anadromous species in marine environments consume fish as large as salmon.

Acipenser oxyrinchus—Atlantic and Gulf Sturgeon

Figure 10.9. Gulf Sturgeon (*Acipenser oxyrinchus desotoi*), with A) a long, V-shaped snout and B) a lack of circus on the caudal fin. RYAN HAGERTY/USFWS

Description: Two subspecies of closely related *Acipenser oxyrinchus* exist in North America: the Gulf Sturgeon (*A. oxyrinchus desotoi*) and the Atlantic Sturgeon (*A. oxyrinchus oxyrinchus*). The snout in both subspecies is relatively long and sharply V-shaped. Color ranges from bluish black (typical in Atlantic Sturgeon of Canadian provinces) to olive brown farther south (Gulf Sturgeon) on the back with a pale white underside. Only one other species of *Acipenser* possesses an overlapping range with Gulf and Atlantic Sturgeon—the Shortnose Sturgeon (*A. brevirostrum*), which is smaller, rarer, and has a blunter snout with a larger mouth.

Size: Males typically grow to 6.5 feet while females are commonly beyond 8 feet.

Habitat: Atlantic and Gulf Sturgeon are both anadromous and adults feed primarily in marine or estuarine environments. Both subspecies use large lotic systems as spawning and nursery habitat.

Remarks: Atlantic Sturgeon once ranged from eastern North America to Europe. Severe overfishing and habitat degradation extirpated the species from Europe, although a small population has been established in the Baltic region.

Acipenser fulvescens—Lake Sturgeon

Figure 10.10. A juvenile Lake Sturgeon (*Acipenser fulvescens*). The brown and black mottling disappears with age. RYAN HAGERTY/USFWS

Description: Lake Sturgeon are torpedo shaped and possess a flattened, cone-shaped mouth. Color is typically <u>yellow brown to pale grayish green</u>. Range includes the mid/upper Mississippi and Great Lakes drainages.
Size: Commonly to 3 feet.
Habitat: Occupies a wide range of habitats, from shallow lakeshores to deep river runs. Feeding habitat consists of soft-bottom benthic zones.
Remarks: Most states list Lake Sturgeon as endangered due to overfishing, pollution, and especially dams that block migration. Populations that persisted through the twentieth century have mostly stabilized and, in some instances, recovered moderately.

Acipenser transmontanus—White Sturgeon

Figure 10.11. White Sturgeon (*Acipenser transmontanus*). OREGON DEPARTMENT OF FISH & WILDLIFE

Description: A large, anadromous fish with some landlocked populations ranging throughout the Pacific Coast drainages, including Alaska and British Columbia. <u>Barbels are positioned closer to the snout tip than the mouth</u>. Color is light gray above and white on belly. Only one other sturgeon possesses an overlapping native range with White Sturgeon: the Green Sturgeon (*A. medirostris*), which is dark green and exhibits a broad stripe on the belly that matches the color of the back.
Size: The largest freshwater fish in North America. Twelve-foot individuals are common, and the largest females may grow up to 20 feet. Record-holding individuals approach 1,800 pounds.
Habitat: Occupies large rivers for migration, spawning, and as nursery habitat. Adults feed in a variety of marine habitats, from estuaries to offshore.
Remarks: Some White Sturgeon populations are landlocked and migrate exclusively within freshwater habitats (including lakes).

Genus *Scaphirhynchus*

The genus *Scaphirhynchus* is endemic to the Mississippi and Gulf drainages of North America and consists of three species. All possess at least one long, flexible filament (circus) on the upper lobe of the caudal fin and a long, rounded, upward-pointed snout. One nearly extinct species, the Alabama Sturgeon (*Scaphirhynchus suttkusi*) is endemic to Mobile Bay drainages.

Scaphirhynchus sturgeon consume worms, crustaceans, and aquatic insects found in sand or gravel benthic habitat when young. Adults also consume benthic fish.

Scaphirhynchus albus—Pallid Sturgeon

Figure 10.12. Pallid Sturgeon (*Scaphirhynchus albus*). SAM STUKEL/USFWS

Description: Color on the Pallid Sturgeon is grayish white with a white belly. Barbels are positioned closer to the mouth than snout tip, with the middle two barbels set slightly closer to the snout. The belly lacks scutes.
Size: Frequently beyond 3 feet and 10 pounds.
Habitat: Large, turbid rivers; primarily the Misssissippi and Missouri River mainstems.
Remarks: Pallid Sturgeon are considered globally imperiled and are endangered in the United States. If a *Scaphirhynchus* sturgeon is caught in a river where Pallid and Shovelnose Sturgeon are both found, be sure that the specimen is a Shovelnose Sturgeon before keeping the fish.

Scaphirhynchus platorynchus—Shovelnose Sturgeon

Figure 10.13. Shovelnose Sturgeon (*Scaphirhynchus platorynchus*), with A) the circus highlighted, a caudal tail extension characteristic of the genus. SAM STUKEL/USFWS

Description: Color on the Shovelnose Sturgeon ranges from olive to yellow or reddish brown on the back and white on the belly. Barbels are evenly spaced between the snout tip and mouth and set in a single row. Abundant, thin scutes are found on the belly.

Size: Commonly to 2.5 feet (not including circus) and up to 5 pounds.

Habitat: Deep sections of large, turbid rivers with soft or gravel benthic zones.

Remarks: Shovelnose Sturgeon can be caught on a hook and line and are commercially harvested in some states.

AMIIDAE (BOWFIN)

Diversity and distribution: The family Amiidae consists of only one species, the Bowfin (*Amia calva*). The Bowfin is found exclusively in the Mississippi and Atlantic drainages of North America plus the Lake Champlain drainages of Vermont.

Evolutionary record: The Bowfin is a living fossil, the only remaining member of the family Amiidae that once included many freshwater and marine species found around the world. Fossil specimens suggest that this group has changed very little over about 100 million years, much older than nearly all other modern fishes.

Ecology and life history: The Bowfin possesses unique reproductive and parental care traits. Male Bowfin attract females by creating a large (2- to 4-foot), circular nest in shallow water. An elaborate courtship occurs in the nest region, during which the female places her snout in the mouth of the male for several minutes before dispersing eggs into the nest. The female permanently departs the nest post-spawning, but the male carefully protects the fertilized embryos and young fish. He watches over the tightly schooling brood by chasing away potential predators and conceals the young by kicking up sediment until the young grow to about 4 inches.

Like other species of primitive fishes, the Bowfin is capable of air breathing. Gulped air is directed to the swim bladder, which is surrounded by blood vessels capable of extracting oxygen.

Genus *Amia*

The Bowfin is a generalist predator that consumes a wide variety of invertebrate and vertebrate prey, especially minnows and crayfish. Feeding occurs almost exclusively during the night.

Amia calva—Bowfin

Figure 10.14. A Bowfin (*Amia calva*) adult. Identifying traits include A) a long dorsal fin and B) a large, dark spot at the base of the caudal fin. ZACH ALLEY

Description: Bowfin are stout and cylindrical with a very long dorsal fin that sometimes appears contiguous with the caudal fin. One odd anatomical feature of the Bowfin is a gular plate—a bony structure on the lower jaw. A large, dark spot at the upper base of the caudal fin that grows larger with age characterizes Bowfin from species with superficial resemblance.

Size: Can grow to more than 2 feet long, though most adults attain a length of about 20 inches.

Habitat: Most associated with lotic systems featuring slow-moving, deep water and abundant emergent vegetation. Especially fond of blackwater systems adjacent to swamps.

Remarks: Bowfin might be easily confused with the Northern Snakehead (*Channa argus*), an invasive species in the Potomac River watershed of Maryland and Virginia. Snakeheads have a much more mottled pattern resembling a python, lack a large, distinct black blotch centered at the base of the caudal fin, and grow much larger.

POLYODONTIDAE (PADDLEFISHES)

Diversity and distribution: Only two species of the family Polyodontidae exist globally, one in North America (*Polyodon spathula*) and another in China (*Psephurus gladius*). However, in 2019 scientists declared the latter species to be extinct, a tragic loss caused by dam-induced habitat fragmentation.

Genus *Polyodon*

The unmistakably long snout of the paddlefish serves at least two purposes: 1) as a sensory organ for detecting food and 2) as a hydrodynamic counterweight to their large gapes that would otherwise pull the fish down while swimming. When their mouth is open, the jaw may extend to twice the body height.

Adult American Paddlefish are planktivorous and feed by opening their large jaws to filter small organisms from the water column using their gill rakers. Very young American Paddlefish prey on crustaceans or insect larvae using teeth that vanish with age.

Polyodon spathula—American Paddlefish

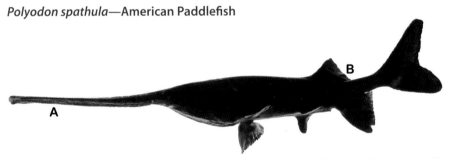

Figure 10.15. An American Paddlefish (*Polyodon spathula*) adult, characterized by A) a very large snout and B) dorsal fin set far back near the caudal fin. RYAN HAGERTY/USFWS

Description: American Paddlefish are hard to confuse with any other species due to their large snout and immense gape. The dorsal fin is set back very far, closer to the caudal fin than to the head. Most of the body is smooth and lacks scales. American Paddlefish are blue- or green-gray colored throughout their lives.

Size: Commonly grow to more than 3 feet long from snout tip to edge of caudal fin.

Habitat: Prefers large, slow-moving, and warm rivers with deep pools, although spawning occurs in reaches with clean gravel substrate.

Remarks: American Paddlefish populations are reduced throughout their native range due to habitat destruction and barriers to migration. Dams typically prevent individuals from reaching spawning beds. Additionally, American Paddlefish roe is prized as caviar and some populations have been overharvested beyond sustainable limits.

ANGUILLIDAE (EELS)

Diversity and distribution: Only one species of the eel family Anguillidae, the American Eel (*Anguilla rostrata*), is found in North America. Closely related species in the genus *Anguilla* can be found on all continents except Antarctica.

Ecology and life history: Freshwater eels in the *Anguilla* genus possess a truly remarkable life history. Nearly all *Anguilla* species are **catadromous**: They spend their adult life in freshwater ecosystems then migrate to the ocean to spawn and die soon after. The American Eel breeds in the Sargasso Sea, a zone in the Atlantic Ocean several hundred miles east of the Carolinas. Microscopic young eels are carried by the Gulf Stream throughout the Atlantic Ocean to nursery coastal and estuary habitats. Once large enough, young eels migrate upstream to spend adulthood in freshwater ecosystems. Individuals may remain as adults in lotic environments for several decades before migrating to spawn. Adult eels die shortly after spawning.

Genus *Anguilla*

Only one species of *Anguilla* exists in North America: the American Eel (*A. rostrata*). The American Eel is native to watersheds draining into Atlantic and Gulf coasts in mainland North America/Mesoamerica and Caribbean islands, from Trinidad to Greenland. Found as far upstream in the Mississippi River watershed as Minnesota and Ohio. The American Eel feeds on a large range of alive and recently dead organisms, mostly invertebrates and other fishes.

Anguilla rostrata—**American Eel**

Figure 10.16. An American Eel (*Anguilla rostrata*) adult. A) the dorsal, anal, and caudal fins are all contiguous in eels. SAM STUKEL/USFWS

Description: The American Eel has a <u>very elongate body</u> with <u>dorsal, anal, and caudal fins all contiguous</u>. Body color varies from <u>dull brown to greenish yellow</u> to silver when adults migrate toward the ocean to spawn. Possibly confused with lampreys, but the eel possesses paired pectoral fins and a jaw.

Size: Commonly to 20 inches long, but can grow to 60 inches and weigh up to 16 pounds.

Habitat: Occupies a very diverse range of habitats due to its migratory life history pattern. Juveniles are found in estuaries while adults occupy streams and ponds. In lotic systems, eels typically occupy pools and slow-moving waters. Eels are capable of crawling over land, allowing them to colonize waterbodies that other fishes cannot reach.

Remarks: American Eel are harvested by the thousands per pound from estuaries when very young, then transported to aquaculture farms to grow for the sushi market. The practice prevents the eels from completing their life cycle. Additionally, dams often prohibit young eels from migrating upstream.

LEPISOSTEIDAE (GARS)

Diversity and distribution: The Lepisosteidae is a small family, with seven species all restricted to the Western Hemisphere. Five species occur in eastern North America, one is endemic to Cuba, and another species is found in the American tropics. The only two genera in the family both occur in North America: *Lepisosteus* (four species) and *Atractosteus* (one species).

Ecology and life history: Gars primarily inhabit slow-moving waters, from lakes and swamps to backwaters of river channels. All species appear to tolerate brackish water and Alligator Gar (*Atractosteus spatula*) are capable of temporary forays into the open ocean. Some species partition habitat by age, with young gar found in protected habitat like oxbow lakes and adults in mainstream river channels. Gars do not school, but some species may aggregate during winter.

Gars are predators that patrol the water surface. To capture prey, gars will either stalk or remain very still until prey can be caught with a swift strike using their elongate, toothy jaws. Fish comprise the bulk of gar diets, although invertebrate prey are opportunistically consumed by many species. Feeding occurs primarily during the night.

All gar species are capable of breathing air to acquire oxygen, a strategy that helps them thrive in habitats where dissolved oxygen often falls to low concentrations due to warm temperatures and minimal surface turbulence. Air is gulped by mouth at the surface and forced into the swim bladder that also serves as a primitive lung.

Spawning takes place in quiet, slow-moving waters with abundant vegetation. Eggs are typically found attached to submerged vegetation or directly on substrate in the benthic zone. An impressive number of eggs may be deposited per spawn: A single Alligator Gar might deposit well over 100,000 eggs, while other species routinely release over 10,000 eggs per spawn. Gar eggs are toxic to many potential predators, including humans, though most fishes do not appear to be affected and will readily consume them. Young gar feed on invertebrates but transition to feeding on fish well before maturity.

Identifying species: Gars are unmistakable from other fishes thanks to their long, torpedo-shaped body; long snout with abundant sharp teeth; and diamond-shaped, interlocking, and tough scales. Gar species can be distinguished when viewed from above using coloration and snout shape. The Alligator Gar (genus *Atractosteus*) has a much shorter and blunt snout compared to those in *Lepisosteus*.

Genus *Atractosteus*

The sole species of *Atractosteus*, the Alligator Gar (*A. spatula*) is the largest North American freshwater fish that possesses an entirely freshwater life cycle, as White Sturgeon are anadromous and grow large by feeding in the ocean. The Alligator Gar will consume any fish that can be captured but also ducks, small mammals, and turtles.

Atractosteus spatula—**Alligator Gar**

Figure 10.17. The Alligator Gar (*Atractosteus spatula*), which A) has a shorter snout than any other gar.
LYNN CHAN

Description: The Alligator Gar has the <u>shortest snout but grows larger than any other gar</u>. Color can be shades of green, yellow, and brown.

Size: To 9 feet long and 300 pounds, though 5-foot-long individuals are more common.
Habitat: Slow-moving or still backwaters of large rivers, oxbow lakes, and bayous.
Remarks: The aquarium trade has potentially led to Alligator Gar introductions far beyond North America, including Iraq and Indonesia.

Genus *Lepisosteus*

The genus *Lepisosteus* includes four gar species. Both the Shortnose Gar (*L. platostomus*) and Spotted Gar (*L. oculatus*) have a snout length intermediate to the Alligator and Longnose Gars. The Spotted Gar has large spots all over the body, including on the fins and top of the head, while the Shortnose Gar lacks spots on the head and fins. The Florida Gar (*L. platyrhincus*) occurs only in Florida and Georgia and closely resembles Spotted Gar, but the spots in Florida Gar often form stripes. *Lepisosteus* gars feed on a broad array of fishes but also occasionally amphibians and small rodents.

Lepisosteus osseus—Longnose Gar

Figure 10.18. Longnose Gar (*Lepisosteus osseus*), with A) large spots on the dorsal, anal, and caudal fins but not the head or upper body. SAM STUKEL/USFWS

Description: Distinguishable from other gars by the very long, needle-like snout with a bulbous tip. The Longnose Gar often has large spots on the body, dorsal, caudal, and anal fins but never on the head and only very rarely on the pectoral fins.
Size: 2 to 4 feet long, including the snout.

ICTALURIDAE (CATFISHES)

Diversity and distribution: With forty-three species found north of Mexico, Ictaluridae is the fourth-largest freshwater fish family in North America. The most well-known catfishes are large-bodied species targeted by anglers. However, the twenty-nine small-bodied and often beautifully patterned catfishes in the genus *Noturus*, collectively known as madtoms, outnumber large species. All Ictaluridae possess native ranges east of the Rocky Mountains, although many have been introduced farther west. Lotic species include four genera: *Noturus*, *Ameiurus* (seven species), *Ictalurus* (three species), and *Pylodictis* (one species). The family also includes three species of catfishes that exclusively inhabit subterranean water.

Ecology and life history: Nearly all catfish species are restricted to warmwater environments. They are most often associated with benthic habitats ranging from lake bottoms to large river riffles. Catfish diets vary among species though they are largely omnivorous, with vegetation and seeds forming part of the diet in larger species. Many *Noturus* madtom catfish are exclusively predators. Feeding occurs mostly at dawn, dusk, and overnight. Catfish sensory capabilities are highly acute thanks to their conspicuous barbels, allowing them to detect food from significant distances and/or buried in substrate.

Some catfishes are tolerant to adverse environmental stressors. Large-bodied species in the genera *Ictalurus* and *Ameiurus* can live through periods with water temperatures above 80°F and dissolved oxygen levels as low as 1 to 2 mg/L, conditions that are lethal to most fishes.

Catfish reproductive behavior is relatively complex. One or both parents excavate a round cavity nest for the eggs. Parents care for embryos by fanning the water, which removes fine sediment and provides oxygen. The parents may carefully reposition the embryos by moving them with their mouth. Once hatched, males guard the young for several days until they are mature enough to feed.

Humans value many large-bodied catfish species for recreational and commercial purposes. Catfishes make an ideal aquaculture species due to their tolerance of low oxygen concentrations and ability to grow on a vegetarian diet.

Identifying species: Catfishes possess several traits that readily distinguish them from other fish families. All species have eight conspicuous barbels: two on top of the head near the nostrils, two on the mouth corners, and four on the chin. Catfishes lack scales and instead have thick, smooth skin. Large-bodied species feature a wholly separate adipose fin, and *Noturus* species possess an adipose fin contiguous with the caudal fin. Barbels are venomous in some species and can inflict significant pain.

Catfishes possess sharp, barbed spines on the edges of their pectoral and dorsal fins that become locked into place when they feel threatened. The spines can break off in the skin if mishandled. Some possess glands that deliver venom to the spines; thus catfishes must be handled with caution.

Field identification of four genera of catfishes is relatively easy using the traits listed in the table below.

Genus (# of North American species north of Mexico)	Range of adult sizes (inches)	Anatomical features
Ameiurus (7)	10–25	Caudal fin either moderately forked to less than half the length of entire caudal fin or rounded
Ictalurus (3)	40–70	Caudal fin deeply forked to more than half the length of total caudal fin
Noturus (29)	1.5–10	Adipose fin contiguous with caudal fin; caudal fin usually rounded; small-bodied as adults
Pylodictis (1)	Up to 68	Lower jaw protrudes beyond upper jaw; caudal fin only slightly notched

Genus *Ameiurus*

The bullhead catfishes (genus *Ameiurus*) are omnivores that occur in a range of lotic habitats, from medium-sized streams to large rivers. Males invest more parental care to their offspring than those in any other catfish genus and will protect the schooling ball of young until individuals grow to 2 inches. *Ameiurus* catfishes are larger than *Noturus* species but smaller than the other two North American genera, though some may grow beyond 24–30 inches.

Ameiurus catfishes can be identified to species using chin barbel colors, dorsal fin coloration, and caudal fin shape, although some species pairs (such as *A. melas* and *A. nebulosus*) are very difficult to distinguish. One major identifying feature is the presence or absence of a dark blotch at the base of the caudal fin. The table below lists the anatomical, color, and range traits to distinguish species (those not covered in further detail are noted with an asterisk).

Smaller *Ameiurus* species feed mostly on small invertebrates such as amphipods, aquatic insects, and the occasional fish egg or small fish. Larger species eat more fish, while vegetation and detritus represent secondary food.

Scientific name	Common name	Tail shape	Chin barbel color	Dorsal fin blotch	Range
A. brunneus*	Snail Bullhead	Rounded or very slightly notched	Dark	Present	Alabama to North Carolina, including Florida
A. catus	White Bullhead	Moderately forked	White	Absent	Native to Atlantic slope drainages
A. melas and A. nebulosus*	Black and Brown Bullhead	Rounded or very slightly notched	Dark brown to black	Absent	Most eastern United States
A. natalis	Yellow Bullhead	Rounded or very slightly notched	White or yellow	Absent	Most eastern/ midwestern United States
A. platychephalus*	Flat Bullhead	Rounded or very slightly notched	White	Present	Georgia to Virginia
A. serracanthus*	Spotted Bullhead	Rounded or very slightly notched	Dark	Present	Florida, Georgia, and Alabama

* NOT COVERED IN DETAIL FURTHER.

Ameiurus catus—White Bullhead

Figure 10.19. White Bullhead (*Ameiurus catus*), with A) white chin barbels and B) deeply forked caudal fin highlighted. ROBERT AGUILAR/SMITHSONIAN ENVIRONMENTAL RESEARCH CENTER

Description: The White Bullhead is colored brown gray to blue on the back, bright white or very pale yellow on the lower third of the body including the belly. Chin barbels are usually white. The caudal fork is deeper in the White Bullhead than any other *Ameiurus* species.
Size: Typically to 12 inches long, but can attain 36 inches.
Habitat: Mud-bottomed, large lotic systems, lakes, and reservoirs.

Ameiurus melas—Black Bullhead

Figure 10.20. Black Bullhead (*Ameiurus melas*), a catfish characterized by A) black chin barbels. JULIA WOOD

Description: The Black Bullhead is colored dark brown to black on the back, yellow to white on the belly. Dark brown or black chin barbels, especially dark away from the base. Very difficult to distinguish from Brown Bullhead (*A. nebulosus*) unless gill rakers can be counted (Black Bullhead 13 to 15, Brown Bullhead 17 to 19). Both species have broadly overlapping ranges.
Size: Typically to 8 to 10 inches long, but can grow to 14 inches.
Habitat: Slow backwaters of lotic systems and ponds. Capable of tolerating very warm and low oxygen conditions.

Ameiurus natalis—Yellow Bullhead

Figure 10.21. Yellow Bullhead (*Ameiurus natalis*), with A) yellow chin barbels. ROBERT AGUILAR/SMITHSONIAN ENVIRONMENTAL RESEARCH CENTER

Description: The Yellow Bullhead is olive brown on the back, and usually yellow on the belly and chin barbels.
Size: Typically 8 to 10 inches long.
Habitat: Inhabits a wide range of lotic conditions, including warmwater streams with moderate rapids. Very tolerant of acidic conditions and thrives in blackwater.

Genus *Ictalurus*

Three species comprise the genus *Ictalurus*: the Blue Catfish (*I. furcatus*), the Headwater Catfish (*I. lupus*), and the Channel Catfish (*I. punctatus*). They are most easily distinguished from other catfishes by their deeply forked caudal tail and large size. The Channel Catfish is most common with the broadest distribution, followed by the Blue Catfish. These two species are difficult to distinguish in the field. *Ictalurus* biodiversity is greater in southern North America, with five species endemic to Mexico. The Headwater Catfish is the rarest American *Ictalurus* species and is found only within the Rio Grande drainage in Texas, New Mexico, and Mexico.

All three species primarily consume animal prey as adults, mostly fish. Some Blue Catfish may consume large quantities of mussels and clams.

Ictalurus furcatus—Blue Catfish

Figure 10.22. Blue Catfish (*Ictalurus furcatus*), with A) straight-edged anal fin. SAM STUKEL/USFWS

Description: Color on a Blue Catfish is most often blue or gray on the back and lighter on the belly. The most reliable means of distinguishing Blue from Channel Catfish is the shape of the anal fin edge, which is straight in Blue Catfish.

Size: The largest member of the Ictaluridae family, the Blue Catfish can grow to more than 6 feet long and weigh over 300 pounds. Individuals exceeding 100 pounds and 4 feet are not uncommon.
Habitat: Deep, fast-moving waters in large rivers and estuaries.

Ictalurus punctatus—Channel Catfish

Figure 10.23. Channel Catfish (*Ictalurus punctatus*), distinguished from *Ictalurus furcatus* by A) a rounded anal fin edge. SAM STUKEL/USFWS

Description: The Channel Catfish has a gray, blue, dark olive, or black back and gray or silver belly with gray fins. The edge of the anal fin is distinctly more rounded than in Blue Catfish.

Size: Commonly grow to 2 feet long, with largest individuals up to 4 feet.

Habitat: Occupies a wide range of lotic conditions, from clear to turbid waters and large- to medium-sized rivers. Also found in ponds, reservoirs, and estuaries. Intolerant of high acidity.

Genus *Noturus*

With twenty-nine species, madtom catfishes in the genus *Noturus* comprise the bulk of species biodiversity in the Ictaluridae family. All species are small-bodied and only rarely grow beyond 8 inches long. The easiest means of distinguishing madtom catfishes from the juveniles of other genera is the adipose fin, which in *Noturus* is narrowly connected to the caudal fin. All madtoms are similarly colored various shades of brown, gray, and yellow green. Many species exhibit impressive mottle or banded patterns.

Although a small number of species are broadly distributed, most native geographic ranges are very restricted, and several species are endemic to a single state or river drainage. Such narrow geographic ranges elevate extinction risk. At least one species, the Scioto Madtom (*N. trautmani*), is likely extinct.

Anglers are unlikely to encounter madtom catfishes due to their small size. However, those interested in observing madtoms can capture them unharmed by baiting minnow traps with meat. The reward is a chance to observe some of the most beautifully patterned catfishes, though specimens should be handled with care as some deliver venom via their pectoral and dorsal spines.

Only seven widely distributed madtoms are covered here. Check with state fish agencies for further information on rarer species, some of which may closely resemble those described below. Madtoms are especially diverse in lotic systems of the southern Appalachian and Ozark Mountains. Many are endangered, often in part due to limited distributions. Others have established populations well outside their native ranges thanks to movement by anglers as bait or the aquarium trade.

All madtoms feed mainly on aquatic insects, primarily stonefly and mayfly nymphs plus caddisfly larvae and aquatic worms. Larger species occasionally feed on small crayfish or fish.

Noturus eleutherus—Mountain Madtom

Figure 10.24. Mountain Madtom (*Noturus eleutherus*), characterized by A) a broad white band on the caudal fin edge. NCFISHES.COM

Description: Mountain Madtom are <u>mottled with dark spots</u> throughout the fins and body, with a <u>pale, wide band at the fringe of the entire caudal fin</u>. Colored various shades of pale brown with darker mottling.
Size: Up to 5 inches long.
Habitat: Medium to large lotic systems with fast-flowing, clear water. Usually associated with sand or gravel substrate and submerged vegetation.

Noturus exilis—Slender Madtom

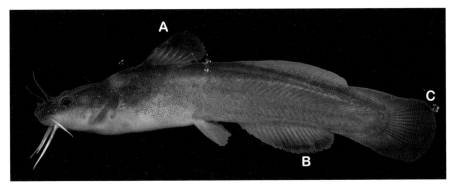

Figure 10.25. Slender Madtom (*Noturus exilis*), identified by dark, broad bands on the A) dorsal, B) anal, and C) caudal fins. JULIA WOOD

Description: The Slender Madtom is colored pale brown to yellow except for <u>dark, broad bands on the dorsal, anal, and caudal fins</u>. <u>Light yellow blotches also occur behind the head and at the base of the dorsal fin</u>.
Size: Usually 4 to 6 inches long.
Habitat: Riffles of lotic systems with large rocks to hide under during daylight hours.

Noturus flavus—Stonecat

Figure 10.26. Stonecat (*Noturus flavus*), with dark-colored A) dorsal and B) adipose fin bases highlighted. SAM STUKEL/USFWS

Description: Stonecats are olive yellow except for the top of the body, especially the head, which fades to a darker shade of brown. The <u>bases of the dorsal and adipose fins are also dark colored</u>.
Size: 3 to 5 inches long.
Habitat: Shallow riffles of medium-sized lotic systems, occasionally headwater streams or large rivers.

Noturus gyrinus—Tadpole Madtom

Figure 10.27. The Tadpole Madtom (*Noturus gyrinus*) has A) a distinct dark band running the body length. NCFISHES.COM

Description: <u>A dark, narrow but conspicuous band</u> runs the length of the body of the Tadpole Madtom; otherwise, colored golden brown with <u>no mottling</u>.
Size: Up to 5 inches long.
Habitat: Inhabits slower-moving lotic systems with finer substrate compared to most other madtom species and especially favors blackwater streams adjacent to swamps.
Remarks: The Tadpole Madtom possesses perhaps the most venomous spines among the catfishes and therefore delivers a very painful sting.

Noturus insignis—Margined Madtom

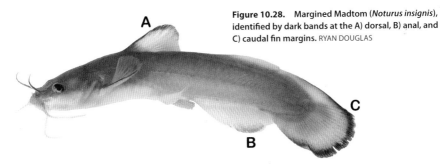

Figure 10.28. Margined Madtom (*Noturus insignis*), identified by dark bands at the A) dorsal, B) anal, and C) caudal fin margins. RYAN DOUGLAS

Description: Margined Madtoms are most easily distinguished by <u>dark, thick bands at the fringes of the caudal, dorsal, and anal fins</u>. Most are colored olive brown to pale yellow with no spots or mottling. Although similar in appearance to the Slender Madtom, the Margined Madtom lacks large, yellow blotches on the head and dorsal fin, plus the two species' ranges do not overlap.
Size: Usually 4 to 6 inches long.
Habitat: Headwater streams to medium-sized lotic systems with clear, fast-moving water.

Noturus miurus—Brindled Madtom

Figure 10.29. Brindled Madtom (*Noturus miurus*), with A) four distinctive dark saddles on the back and B) a dark band at the caudal fin base. ZACH ALLEY

Description: The Brindled Madtom is pale brown to yellow with a mottled pattern throughout the body. The species has <u>four broad, dark saddles</u> on the back, from just behind the head to the adipose fin, plus a <u>dark band at the caudal fin base</u>.
Size: 2 to 5 inches long, though usually to 4 inches.
Habitat: Warmwater lotic systems and lakes of all sizes, from headwater streams to large rivers.

Noturus nocturnus—Freckled Madtom

Figure 10.30. Freckled Madtom (*Noturus nocturnus*), with A) fine dots on the body and head. JULIA WOOD

Description: The Freckled Madtom is colored pale yellow to dark olive with fine, darker-colored spots throughout the body and head. The species is very difficult to distinguish from Black Madtom (*Noturus funebris*).

Size: Up to nearly 6 inches long, but usually 4 to 5 inches.

Habitat: Often associated with large woody debris and root snags in medium to large, pristine lotic systems.

Genus *Pylodictis*

The genus *Pylodictis* includes only one species in the world, the Flathead Catfish (*P. olivaris*), which is endemic to North America. The Flathead Catfish is an ambush predator that opportunistically feeds primarily on other fishes but also on insect larvae and crayfish as juveniles.

Pylodictis olivaris—Flathead Catfish

Figure 10.31. Flathead Catfish (*Pylodictis olivaris*), identified by A) a protruding lower jaw and B) a pale blotch on the upper caudal fin edge. SAM STUKEL/USFWS

Description: The Flathead Catfish is distinguished from other catfishes by the protruding lower jaw and toothy plate on the upper jaw. Young possess a large, pale blotch on the upper edge of the caudal fin. Colored dark brown to black on the back with mottled patterns, with a yellow belly.

Size: The Flathead Catfish is the second-largest Ictaluridae species behind Blue Catfish, growing up to 5 feet long and over 100 pounds.
Habitat: Large warmwater rivers, lakes, and reservoirs.

PERCOPSIDAE (TROUT-PERCHES)

Diversity and distribution: The only two species in the Percopsidae family, the Trout-Perch (*Percopsis omiscomaycus*) and the Sand Roller (*P. transmontana*), are neither trout nor perch but rather are small-bodied fishes not closely related to either of the more familiar families. With the two North American species representing the only members in the family, Percopsidae is indigenous to the continent.

Ecology and life history: Habitat ranges from small streams to rivers and lakes. In lotic habitats, *Percopsis* is most associated with sandy-bottomed pools. Trout-Perch are locally abundant in the Great Lakes.

Trout-perches spawn by aggregating in large groups over sandy substrate and broadcasting eggs and milt into the benthic zone. No parental care is offered to the young. Males tend to die earlier, resulting in sex ratios skewed toward females among adults.

Identifying species: Trout-perches are most easily distinguished from other fishes by their small but conspicuous adipose fin, which very few other fish families possess. The two *Percopsis* species are similar in appearance but cannot be confused in the field because their ranges do not overlap. The Trout-Perch ranges from Vermont and Quebec north to the lower Yukon River, while the Sand Roller is endemic to the Columbia River basin.

Genus *Percopsis*

Both *Percopsis* species are lightly colored, with a body and fins that appear translucent. Dark but faded green blotches run along the length of the body. Each has an adipose fin. Trout-perches feed at night on small invertebrates, especially larval insects and crustaceans. Small fishes are occasionally consumed by large adults.

Percopsis omiscomaycus—Trout-Perch

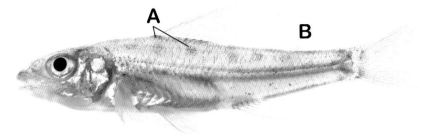

Figure 10.32a. Trout-Perch (*Percopsis omiscomaycus*), with A) adipose fin and B) characteristic dark blotches highlighted. The Sand Roller (*Percopsis transmontana*) shares both features with the Trout-Perch. SAM STUKEL/USFWS

Description: The Trout-Perch is the more slender and smaller of the two *Percopsis* species.
Size: Adults usually range 1.5 to 2 inches.
Habitat: Prefers to migrate into lakes to feed and spawns in lotic systems but will remain in large pools of lotic systems as well.

Percopsis transmontana—Sand Roller

Figure 10.32b. Sand Roller (*Percopsis transmontana*). BRIAN SIDLAUSKAS

Description: Sand Rollers are larger and have a deeper body than the Trout-Perch.
Size: Up to 4 inches long, but more commonly 2.5 to 3 inches.
Habitat: Medium to large lotic systems, especially those with abundant submerged vegetation.

CLUPEIDAE (HERRINGS)

Diversity and distribution: The herring family Clupeidae consists of 174 species world-wide found in marine, estuarine, and freshwater environments. Herring biodiversity is concentrated in the tropics. In the United States and Canada, 8 species from 2 genera are commonly found in freshwater as residents or anadromous migrants entering freshwater to spawn, all with native ranges in the Mississippi River and Atlantic coast watersheds. A few have established populations west of the Rockies following introductions by humans. Along the Pacific Coast, 2 marine species occasionally enter freshwater but are not covered further here.

Ecology and life history: Most herrings filter-feed on plankton by cruising the water and ensnaring prey using gill rakers, primarily at night to avoid predators. Specialized chambers in the mouth collect microscopic food particles until enough accumulate for swallowing. This feeding strategy means that they are mostly restricted to lotic systems large enough to support plankton prey.

Herrings are schooling fish and aggregate in large numbers as a strategy for protection from predators. Most represent a crucial link between small plankton and larger-bodied fish predators in lotic food webs.

Several North American species are anadromous and occur only in lotic systems when they are young and during spawning as adults. Dams completely block access to spawning habitat, resulting in substantial declines of many populations. Recent dam removal projects aimed at restoring fish populations have proven very successful, with sizable herring spawning runs returning faster than biologists anticipated.

Identifying species: Herrings can be distinguished from other families by body shape, as they are very flattened side to side, especially their belly, which tapers into a keel. Many species possess bony scutes on the belly with sharp angles such that they resemble a saw. All North American freshwater herrings are silvery and shiny, with some exhibiting green or blue tints on the back. Several possess a dark spot on the body just behind the gill opening.

The two freshwater North American genera can be identified from each other using the dorsal fin. Herrings in the genus *Dorosoma* (two species) possess a long, threadlike ray at the base of the dorsal fin that extends about halfway to the caudal fin. Genus *Alosa* herrings (six species) lack such a conspicuous ray.

Genus *Alosa*

Herrings in the genus *Alosa* are commonly referred to as river herrings. Most North American *Alosa* species are anadromous and grow large in marine or estuarine environments before returning to rivers for spawning. Several are commercially harvested and/or recreationally targeted, especially the American Shad (*Alosa sapidissima*).

Alosa species feed on plankton while in rivers, switching to shrimp and small fishes in marine environments. Most also feed on fish eggs and insect larvae in the water column.

Alosa pseudoharengus—Alewife

Figure 10.33. Alewife (*Alosa pseudoharengus*). ROBERT AGUILAR/SMITHSONIAN ENVIRONMENTAL RESEARCH CENTER

Description: Alewife appear similar to other herring species, especially Blueback Herring (*A. aestivalis*), but Alewife possess conspicuously <u>larger eyes</u>, which are typically <u>wider than the snout length</u>.
Size: Up to 11 inches long, but usually 8 to 9 inches.
Habitat: Both anadromous and landlocked native Alewife populations exist. Alewife make daily vertical migrations in marine and lake environments, spending daylight hours up to 300 feet below the surface. Lotic environments are occupied mostly for spawning and rearing, especially in large- to medium-sized rivers.
Remarks: The Alewife was most likely introduced into the upper Great Lakes during the middle of the twentieth century, and populations rapidly expanded, so much so that they fundamentally changed the Great Lakes' ecosystems by changing the composition of plankton communities. Large Alewife die-offs in the Great Lakes polluted beaches and contaminated cities like Chicago with an unpleasant smell. State fish agencies introduced Pacific salmon to the Great Lakes as a means of controlling Alewife populations.

Alosa sapidissima—American Shad

Figure 10.34. American Shad (*Alosa sapidissima*), characterized by A) a row of dark spots behind the gill. RENÉ REYES/US DEPARTMENT OF RECLAMATION

Description: American Shad <u>grow larger than any other herring species</u>. Adults often have one or (rarely) two <u>rows of dark spots</u> that start behind the gill opening. Most resemble Hickory Shad (*A. mediocris*), but the lower jaw of American Shad projects much less.

Size: Males frequently grow to 20 inches long, females to 24 inches. Record-holding specimens are 30 inches and up to 12 pounds.

Habitat: American Shad migrate along the Atlantic coast, traveling north in summer and south in winter. Adults spawn in the rivers where they were born then return to the ocean. Natural barriers, such as the Great Falls of the Potomac River, historically limited the farthest upstream American Shad could travel, but dams limit upstream migration today.

Remarks: American Shad is a historically important fish in the United States, as Native Americans and European colonists relied heavily on it for food. Anglers enthusiastically target American Shad during their spawning runs, as they fight terrifically when hooked.

Genus *Dorosoma*

The genus *Dorosoma* consists of five species found exclusively in the Western Hemisphere, with two species (*D. cepedianum*—Gizzard Shad and *D. petenense*—Threadfin Shad) found north of the Mexican border. Although they resemble other herrings, both *Dorosoma* species possess a <u>long, threadlike dorsal fin ray</u>. *Dorosoma* herring feed on small-bodied invertebrates, fish larvae, and algae suspended in the water.

Dorosoma cepedianum—Gizzard Shad

Figure 10.35. A Gizzard Shad (*Dorosoma cepedianum*) juvenile, with A) a dark spot that will fade with age. ROBERT AGUILAR/SMITHSONIAN ENVIRONMENTAL RESEARCH CENTER

Description: A large, black spot behind the gills of Gizzard Shad juveniles disappears with age.
Size: Adults commonly range 7 to 14 inches long.
Habitat: The Gizzard Shad is a freshwater species that only occasionally enters marine waters. Favored lotic habitats include the pools and runs of medium to large rivers.

Dorosoma petenense—Threadfin Shad

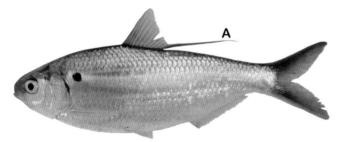

Figure 10.36. Threadfin Shad (*Dorosoma petenense*), with A) a long, threadlike dorsal fin ray characteristic of the genus. RENÉ REYES/US DEPARTMENT OF RECLAMATION

Description: Threadfin Shad are the smaller of the two North American *Dorosoma* species but otherwise very closely resemble Gizzard Shad.
Size: Adults typically grow to 3 to 7 inches long.
Habitat: Mostly freshwater environments, especially medium- to large-sized rivers. Also found in reservoirs.

ESOCIDAE (PIKES)

Diversity and distribution: The Esocidae is a relatively small fish family, with eleven species found worldwide exclusively in the Northern Hemisphere and seven species native to North America. Ichthyologists include three genera in the Esocidae: *Esox* (pikes), *Novumbra* (western mudminnows), and *Dallia* (blackfishes). All *Dallia* species possess native ranges in the far north, from Alaska to Siberia, and only one species, the Alaska Blackfish (*D. pectoralis*), is found in North America.

Ecology and life history: Ecological traits in the Ecosidae vary among genera, but some are common among all species. Pikes possess a sedentary lifestyle and spend most of their time lying in wait amid submerged vegetation waiting for prey to swim by. All species are mostly predators (*Esox* species exclusively so) and feed mainly during the day. Reproductive behavior and strategy varies among Ecosidae genera.

Identifying species: All fishes in Ecosidae possess dorsal fins set very far back on their body above the anal fin. Those in the genus *Esox* have a snout that resembles a duck's bill. Although *Novumbra* and *Dallia* species do not exhibit traits that readily identify them from other species, their restricted native ranges allow for deductive identification. The Alaska Blackfish (*Dallia pectoralis*) is endemic to western Alaska and eastern Siberia, while the Olympic Mudminnow (*Novumbra hubbsi*) is endemic to western Washington State.

Genus *Esox*

With four species, true pikes in the genus *Esox* comprise the bulk of Ecosidae biodiversity and include the largest species, the Muskellunge (*E. masquinongy*). All *Esox* prefer slow-moving to still water with abundant submerged plants. The familiar Muskellunge and Northern Pike (*E. lucius*) favor lakes but also hunt in large rivers.

All *Esox* species broadcast spawn in shallow waters and do not hold territories. Parents do not care for the young. *Esox* pikes are predators of fishes and large-bodied invertebrates, especially crayfishes.

Esox americanus—Redfin Pickerel

Figure 10.37. Redfin Pickerel (*Esox americanus*), distinguished from Chain Pickerel by A) a dark band under the eye tilted backward. ZACH ALLEY

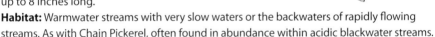

Description: The smallest *Esox* species, the Redfin Pickerel has a similar appearance to Chain Pickerel but can be distinguished by a <u>dark bar under the eye that is tilted backward</u>.
Size: This smallest North American *Esox* species grows up to 8 inches long.
Habitat: Warmwater streams with very slow waters or the backwaters of rapidly flowing streams. As with Chain Pickerel, often found in abundance within acidic blackwater streams.

Esox lucius—Northern Pike

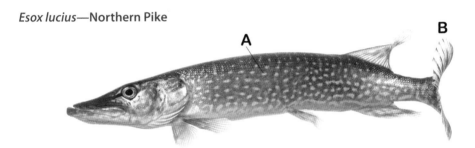

Figure 10.38. Northern Pike (*Esox lucius*), distinguished from Muskellunge by having A) light, oval spots and B) more rounded caudal fin tips. SAM STUKEL/USFWS

Description: The Northern Pike is a large *Esox* species with a <u>dark body and pale, oval spots</u> that run length-wise. <u>Caudal fin tips are relatively rounded</u> compared to the Muskellunge.
Size: Up to 4 feet long.
Habitat: Primarily a resident of lakes, but also occupies large, sluggish rivers with abundant vegetation.
Remarks: The Northern Pike attracts anglers but causes significant ecological harm when introduced outside its native range to create fisheries. As a top predator, Northern Pike often reduce prey populations so much that the food eaten by prey fishes becomes more abundant, an ecological phenomenon known as a trophic cascade.

Esox masquinongy—Muskellunge

Figure 10.39. Muskellunge (*Esox masquinongy*), characterized by A) dark vertical bars and B) large fin spots.
SAM STUKEL/USFWS

Description: The Muskellunge is the largest *Esox* species. Complex patterning covers the body, including dark vertical bars on the body and large spots on the fins. The Muskellunge possesses more sharply pointed caudal fin tips than the Northern Pike.
Size: Commonly 2 to 4 feet long, but can grow to nearly 6 feet.
Habitat: Sluggish or still water with abundant vegetation when young transitioning to open water in adulthood.
Remarks: The Muskellunge is targeted by anglers because of its large size, impressive fight, and culinary quality. Many state agencies stock Muskellunge to support recreational fisheries.

Esox niger—Chain Pickerel

Figure 10.40. Chain Pickerel (*Esox niger*), with A) a dark, vertical bar underneath the eye. NCFISHES.COM

Description: A relatively small *Esox* species, the Chain Pickerel has a dark, vertical bar set just below the eye and pale fins.
Size: Up to 20 inches long.
Habitat: More associated with lotic systems than the larger *Esox* species, especially slow-moving small- to medium-sized streams. Often abundant in acidic blackwater streams.

Genus *Novumbra*

The genus *Novumbra* includes only one species: the Olympic Mudminnow (*N. hubbsi*).

Novumbra hubbsi—Olympic Mudminnow

Figure 10.41. Olympic Mudminnow (*Novumbra hubbsi*). ROGER TABOR/USFWS

Description: The Olympic Mudminnow resembles the Eastern (*Umbra pygmaeus*) and Central (*U. limi*) Mudminnows, but genetics suggest that the Olympic Mudminnow is closely related to *Esox* pikes. Endemic to western Washington State, the Olympic Mudminnow is brightly colored, beautifully patterned, and small. Males possess <u>a dark body with bright, narrow, vertical bands</u>.
Size: No more than 2 to 3 inches long.
Habitat: Sluggish waters with abundant vegetation, including wetlands and ponds. Usually the only fish species present in habitats where it is found.

UMBRIDAE (MUDMINNOWS)

Diversity and distribution: The entire mudminnow family consists of one genus (*Umbra*) with three species, one endemic to Europe and two to North America. The North American species are the Eastern Mudminnow (*Umbra pygmaea*) and the Central Mudminnow (*U. limi*). Native mudminnow ranges span the eastern and central thirds of the continent, from Florida to Canada in the Mississippi, Atlantic, and Hudson Bay drainages.

Evolutionary record: Mudminnow are most closely related to pikes. The two lineages diverged about 60 million years ago, which coincides with the earliest mudminnow fossils.

Ecology and life history: Unlike their pike cousins, mudminnows feed at night and hide within submerged vegetation during the day. Both species tolerate very low oxygen conditions and can breathe air by drawing oxygen from their swim bladders.

Male mudminnows are territorial and court females over several days. After accepting a male, the female will excavate a shallow nest in the benthic zone substrate, which is followed by the release of embryos and milt by the pair. The female will then become aggressive toward males and guard her nest, occasionally fanning the embryos to deliver oxygen.

Identifying species: The position of the dorsal fin, far back above the anal and pelvic fins near the caudal fin, separates mudminnows from other fishes. Although fishes in Ecosidae (pikes) also possess this trait, mudminnows are much smaller and lack the duckbill-like snout that characterizes pikes.

Genus *Umbra*

The two North American *Umbra* species look alike but possess disjunct ranges, with the Eastern Mudminnow found only in Atlantic slope drainages from southern New York to Florida and the Central Mudminnow distributed mainly in the Great Lakes, Mississippi River, and Hudson Bay drainages. Both species possess a stout body, rounded fins that lack spines, and a very dark blotch at the caudal fin base. Females grow larger than males. The Eastern Mudminnow usually has a snout shorter than its eye diameter.

Both mudminnow species are predators, most often of invertebrates such as insect larvae, crustaceans, and terrestrial insects that fall into the water. Female Central Mudminnow may also consume small fish.

Umbra limi—Central Mudminnow

Figure 10.42.
Central Mudminnow
(*Umbra limi*), with
A) a dark blotch
characteristic of the
genus. ZACH ALLEY

Description: The Central Mudminnow possesses a snout that is typically equal to or slightly longer than its eye diameter and usually possesses vertical bars or blotches on the body.

Size: Somewhat larger than the Eastern Mudminnow, typically 3 to 6 inches long and up to 7 inches.

Habitat: Slow water with abundant vegetation, often in headwater streams.

Umbra pygmaea—Eastern Mudminnow

Figure 10.43.
Eastern
Mudminnow
(*Umbra pygmaea*).
NCFISHES.COM

Description: The smaller of the two *Umbra* species, the Eastern Mudminnow has a snout that is typically shorter than its eye diameter, and the body patternation consists of horizontal stripes.

Size: Usually range 2 to 4 inches long.

Habitat: Slow-moving waters of any type. A high tolerance to low dissolved oxygen means that Eastern Mudminnow are sometimes the only fish species present in a very small water body.

SALMONIDAE (TROUT AND SALMON)

Diversity and distribution: Native trout and salmon are found throughout temperate, subarctic, and Arctic North America, Asia, and Europe. All species require cold water, and many are anadromous or potamodromous.

The United States and Canada harbor thirty-eight native species of Salmonidae. More than half are whitefish (genera *Coregonus* and *Prosopium*), of which most occur exclusively in lakes and therefore are not covered further here.

Ecology and life history: Despite being predators, multiple organisms feed on Salmonidae species to the extent that they are considered keystone organisms in many ecosystems. Bald eagles, otters, kingfishers, and ospreys all feed on trout and salmon in lotic and lentic environments. Salmon fall prey to sea lions and killer whales, while in the open ocean. The large runs of salmon that return to lotic systems to spawn offer a feast to numerous aquatic and terrestrial species, so much so that they can serve as the primary source of nitrogen in their natal watershed ecosystems (see page 42).

Most species of trout and salmon spawn by digging round nests called **redds** in riffles with gravel and pebble substrates. Eggs are deposited by the female in the redds and the male releases milt to fertilize them. Redds are intentionally dug in riffle habitat to ensure adequate oxygen delivery to the fertilized embryos. Parents abandon the redds shortly after fertilization. After hatching, Salmonidae fry rely on a nutritious yolk sac for sustenance until eventually weaning to feed on small invertebrates.

The long-standing trout and salmon angling tradition nurtured a body of terminology for the life history of the species. Individuals are called **alevin** during the earliest life history stage, when the yolk sac is still attached to the fish. Once the yolk sac has disappeared and individuals start feeding on their own, they are called **parr.** Most species possess distinct colors or patterns during the parr stage, including dark vertical bands called **parr marks.** Older juvenile fish that begin their migration toward the ocean (if that is part of their life history) are called **smolt.** During this stage, trout and salmon largely lose their colors and adopt a more silvery sheen.

Anglers target trout and salmon more than any other fish in the colder climates where they thrive. The passion of the fly-fishing community does convey a strong imperative for conservation. However, the desire to catch both familiar and exotic species led to widespread intentional introductions of trout to waters beyond their native ranges. As a result, many rare trout species or subspecies are critically threatened and, in some cases, have gone extinct. Numerous anadromous salmon populations are also threatened by overfishing, water extraction, and especially dams. As cold-loving fishes, trout and salmon are also acutely sensitive to climate change.

Identifying species: Fishes in the Salmonidae are among the very few that possess adipose fins. They differ from the other two adipose-possessing families (trout-perches and catfishes) by their beautiful patterning, large size, and lack of barbels.

The Salmonidae in North America includes seven genera. One genus, *Coregonus* (commonly called whitefish or ciscos) consists of about fourteen species that are almost entirely restricted to lakes. The genus *Stenodus* includes one species, the Sheefish (*S. leucichthys*), found only in large, Arctic rivers. The other five genera can be easily distinguished in the field using the traits listed below.

Genus (# of North American species north of Mexico)	Color and pattern	Anatomical features
Oncorhynchus (10)	Light-colored body with darker spots, usually with hints of many colors in pattern	Fine scales, more flattened body shape
Prosopium (6, but only 2 in lotic systems)	Light colored with almost no conspicuous colors or patterns	Large scales, cylindrical body shape
Salvelinus (5)	Dark-colored body with light spots, often with bright colors and complex patterns	Fine scales, more flattened body shape
Salmo (2, but 1 nonnative)	Light-colored body with dark, often large and red or black spots	Fine scales, more flattened body shape
Thymallus (1)	Blue or silver body sometimes with dark spots and a bluish-purple sheen	Very large and conspicuous dorsal fin, large scales set in neat lateral rows

Genus *Oncorhynchus*

Trout and salmon in the genus *Oncorhynchus* rank among the most recognizable fishes in the world, largely thanks to the Rainbow Trout (*O. mykiss*), which has been introduced to streams in every continent except Antarctica. *Oncorhynchus* salmon species also comprise the last intact wild salmon runs in the world, although many populations south of Alaska are at risk of extinction.

Of the ten *Oncorhynchus* species, six are anadromous and spawn only once in their lifetime before dying shortly after. Rainbow Trout (*O. mykiss*) that migrate to the ocean, known as **steelhead**, can survive to spawn more than once. Anadromous Salmonidae species return to the streams where they were born to spawn by using an acute sense of smell. Specific combinations of trace chemicals in the rivers provide the salmon guidance on where to swim to find their birth stream.

Oncorhynchus trout diets vary by life stage. In lotic systems, *Oncorhynchus* trout and young salmon feed on aquatic and terrestrial insects, crustaceans, and the occasional fish. Anadromous salmon in marine environments feed on shrimp, crab, squid, tunicates, and fish.

Oncorhynchus clarkia—Cutthroat Trout

Figure 10.44. Coastal Cutthroat Trout (*Oncorhynchus clarkii clarkii*). Each subspecies exhibits unique colors and patterns but all have A) a red slash below the mouth. ROGER TABOR/USFWS

Description: The Cutthroat Trout includes eleven surviving subspecies with very different appearances. However, all possess a <u>prominent bright red stripe on the jaw</u>.
Size: Typically 10 to 20 inches long, but up to 40 inches in large rivers, lakes, and among sea-run individuals.
Habitat: Very diverse among subspecies, but all spawn in small- to medium-sized lotic systems. Adults forage in streams, lakes, or (in one subspecies) estuaries and along coasts.
Remarks: The Cutthroat Trout is a species complex, with subspecies exhibiting very distinct patterns. During the last ice age, Cutthroat Trout occupied freshwater habitats of western North America that looked very different from today, with large, cold lakes present in many modern-day deserts and ice sheets capping mountain ranges. As the climate shifted, Cutthroat Trout populations became isolated and evolved into up to thirteen distinctly patterned subspecies. Two subspecies, the Yellowfin and Alvord Cutthroat Trout, went extinct during the twentieth century due to environmental degradation. The remaining eleven subspecies range from Alaska to New Mexico, some with broad ranges and others restricted to a single, small watershed. Each possesses a unique pattern and combination of colors.

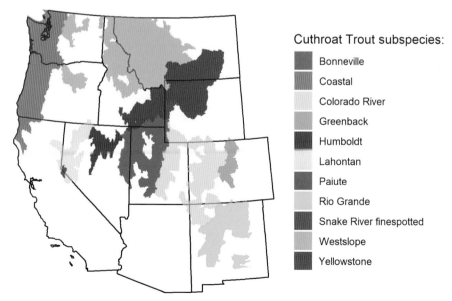

Cuthroat Trout subspecies:
- Bonneville
- Coastal
- Colorado River
- Greenback
- Humboldt
- Lahontan
- Paiute
- Rio Grande
- Snake River finespotted
- Westslope
- Yellowstone

Figure 10.45. Range maps of the surviving eleven Cutthroat Trout subspecies.

Cutthroat Trout are very closely related to Rainbow Trout, and intermixing produces fertile offspring. Consequently, many Cutthroat Trout subspecies are severely threatened by Rainbow Trout introductions. For example, only one population of Greenback Cutthroat Trout (*Oncorhynchus clarkii stomias*) without Rainbow Trout genes persists in a small Colorado stream.

The Cutthroat Trout is named after the iconic American explorer William Clark, who first scientifically described the species.

Oncorhynchus gorbuscha—Pink Salmon

Figure 10.46. Spawning male (two above) and female (below) Pink Salmon (*Oncorhynchus gorbuscha*), distinguished by A) a large hump in front of the dorsal fin in males and B) a cream-colored belly. ROGER TABOR/USFWS

Description: Pink Salmon parr are silvery with no parr marks and a dark green back. Spawning adults are green gray on the back and cream colored below during the spawn, with large oval spots on the caudal fin. Spawning males develop a large hump in front of the dorsal fin.

Size: Pink Salmon are the smallest anadromous *Oncorhynchus* species and typically grow to 18 to 24 inches long and 3 to 5 pounds.

Habitat: Young Pink Salmon quickly leave their natal streams for the ocean, where they usually remain near coasts.

Remarks: Pink Salmon complete their life cycle in only two years, the shortest lifespan of any anadromous Pacific salmon.

Oncorhynchus keta—Chum Salmon

Figure 10.47. A spawning Chum Salmon (*Oncorhynchus keta*), distinguished by A) maroon vertical bars. Roger Tabor/ USFWS

Description: Chum Salmon parr possess faint but conspicuous parr marks that are primarily on the upper half of the body. Spawning adults are light olive green with dull and <u>maroon vertical bands</u>. Males possess conspicuous, sharp teeth during the spawn.

Size: Usually 24 to 30 inches long and 10 to 12 pounds, but up to 3.5 feet and 15 pounds; the second-largest Pacific salmon species after Chinook.

Habitat: Most Chum Salmon spawn and rear in lower sections or mouths of rivers, though some will migrate more than 1,000 miles inland.

Oncorhynchus kisutch—Coho Salmon

Figure 10.48. A Coho Salmon (*Oncorhynchus kisutch*) spawning adult, distinguished from Sockeye Salmon by A) a green back. ROGER TABOR/USFWS

Description: Coho Salmon parr can be easily distinguished from other salmon by a <u>white band followed by a black band on the anal and dorsal fins</u>. They also have a reddish caudal fin. Spawning adult males possess a very pronounced hook on the upper jaw. Both sexes turn <u>bluish green on the back and red on the body</u> (a duller red than Sockeye Salmon).

Size: Typically 2 to 2.5 feet long and 8 to 12 pounds.

Habitat: Young Coho Salmon prefer slow-moving water like the margins of pools in rivers, ponds, or lakes.

Oncorhynchus mykiss—Rainbow Trout

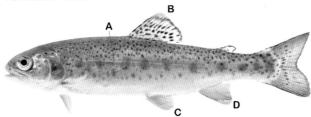

Figure 10.49. Rainbow Trout (*Oncorhynchus mykiss*), distinguished by A) a broad, pink stripe and white margins on the B) dorsal, C) pelvic, and D) anal fins. SAM STUKEL/ USFWS

Description: Rainbow Trout parr can be distinguished by <u>well-developed parr marks and mottling</u>, <u>white tips on the dorsal, anal, and pelvic fins</u>, and a <u>dark edge around the adipose fin</u>. As adults, Rainbow Trout have <u>many spots</u> and a <u>faint, broad, pink stripe along the body</u>. Steelhead are silvery but retain typical rainbow trout traits.

Size: Typically 10 to 20 inches long, but steelhead can grow to 40 inches and weigh more than 40 pounds.

Habitat: Rainbow Trout occupy a very diverse range of freshwater and marine habitats, from alpine lakes to the open ocean. The species requires cold, clean water to spawn.

Remarks: Rainbow Trout may be the most abundant freshwater fish in the world thanks to widespread stocking to support recreational fisheries. Some introduced populations cause substantial ecological damage when they outcompete native fishes for resources or hybridize with closely related species, including Cutthroat, Apache, and Golden Trout.

Oncorhynchus nerka—Sockeye Salmon

Figure 10.50. Spawning male Sockeye Salmon (*Oncorhynchus nerka*), the species that turns vibrant red during migration. ROGER TABOR/USFWS

Description: Sockeye Salmon parr have relatively short parr marks located primarily on the upper half of the body and a green back. As spawning adults, however, Sockeye Salmon possess a strikingly <u>vibrant shade of red on the body</u>, a <u>green head</u>, <u>arched back</u>, and well-developed kype. Some populations are naturally landlocked and migrate to lakes.

Size: 1.5 to 2.5 feet long and up to 15 pounds.

Habitat: Cold, clear streams as juveniles; the open ocean (or lakes in landlocked populations) as adults until spawning.

Oncorhynchus tshawytscha—Chinook Salmon

Figure 10.51. A Chinook Salmon (*Oncorhynchus tshawytscha*) spawning adult. RENÉ REYES/US DEPARTMENT OF RECLAMATION

Description: The Chinook is the largest species of salmon in the world. Parr can be distinguished from other salmon by dark edges on the adipose fin and first ray of the dorsal fin. Spawning adults are silver at first but turn brown to light red as their flesh deteriorates during migration. Adults also possess conspicuously black-colored gums on the lower jaw.

Size: Typically 3 feet long and 30 pounds, but up to 58 inches and 120-plus pounds.

Habitat: Coldwater streams as juveniles. Adults migrate long distances to feed in the ocean.

Remarks: Chinook Salmon are the most commercially valued wild salmon. Although humans have driven populations in the south of their range to extinction, healthy populations persist in Alaska and support a valuable fishery.

Genus *Prosopium*

Fishes in the genus *Prosopium*, commonly referred to as whitefishes, primarily inhabit lakes and are rarely encountered in lotic habitat. Three *Prosopium* species are found exclusively in Bear Lake on the Idaho-Utah border. However, one species, the Mountain Whitefish (*P. williamsoni*) can be found in streams and rivers throughout western North America. Whitefish feed on aquatic insects, fish eggs, and small fishes in the water column.

Prosopium williamsoni—Mountain Whitefish

Figure 10.52. Mountain Whitefish (*Prosopium williamsoni*). GLACIER NPS

Description: The Mountain Whitefish superficially resembles large-bodied minnows due to its cylindrical shape, large scales, and lack of colors or patterns that appear in trout species. However, like other Salmonidae, it has an adipose fin. Fins are often tinted orange red.
Size: Typically 7 to 10 inches long, but can grow to 25 inches.
Habitat: Clear, cold streams and lakes.

Genus *Salvelinus*

Fishes in the genus *Salvelinus* are collectively referred to as charr. All species have a <u>dark body with light spots and mottled patterns</u>. Males develop streaks of vibrant orange or red on the fins and belly when spawning. The widely distributed Lake Trout (*S. namaycush*) completes its entire life cycle in lakes. All other *Salvelinus* species primarily inhabit lotic systems. The Arctic Charr (*S. alpinus*) and Dolly Varden (*S. malma*) are mostly found north of the Canadian border.

Charr primarily feed on aquatic insects and crustaceans in smaller streams, while larger adults consume fish. Bull Trout are known to eat American Dipper (*Cinclus mexicanus*), a diving songbird.

Salvelinus confluentus—Bull Trout

Figure 10.53. Bull Trout (*Salvelinus confluentus*), distinguished from Brook Trout by A) fewer spots on fins and B) dull pink spots. JARED BERNARD

Description: Bull Trout appearances vary significantly among populations and by size. Most individuals are dull gray to greenish gray to silver with large white or yellow spots peppered throughout the body. Some spots are dull pink. Bull Trout fins have far fewer spots than Brook Trout fins.

Size: Usually 8 to 16 inches long, but can grow to more than 3 feet and more than 20 pounds.

Habitat: Lotic systems with cold water and large, deep pools. Bull Trout also occupy cold lakes. In coastal watersheds, some Bull Trout will migrate to estuaries in search of food.

Remarks: Many Bull Trout populations are critically threatened by pollution, climate change, and Brook Trout introductions. Offspring between Bull and Brook Trout are viable and quickly replace pure Bull Trout.

Salvelinus fontinalis—Brook Trout

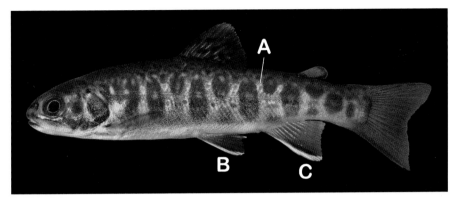

Figure 10.54. Brook Trout (*Salvelinus fontinalis*), easily identified by A) bright red-orange spots and a white stripe on the B) pelvic and C) anal fins. JULIA WOOD

Description: The Brook Trout body is mottled dark yellow, green, and gray on the back fading to a dull white below with <u>bright orange-red spots</u> on the sides. The <u>first rays of the pectoral, pelvic, and anal fins have bright white stripes but are otherwise tinted red</u>. During the autumn spawn, males turn bright red on the belly.

Size: Typically 5 to 12 inches long, with larger habitats supporting larger individuals. The largest grow up to 28 inches and over 14 pounds.

Habitat: Restricted to cold, clear headwater streams in the southern end of its range, extending to larger rivers, lakes, and ponds in the north. Some populations are anadromous to lakes or estuaries.

Remarks: The Brook Trout is the only native Salmonidae in eastern North America south of New England. Environmental degradation has reduced many populations in their native range. Anglers keen to catch familiar fish introduced Brook Trout throughout the West, where they now compete with native trout and hybridize with Bull Trout.

Genus *Salmo*

Two species of *Salmo* are found in North America: the native Atlantic Salmon (*S. salar*) and the nonnative Brown Trout (*S. trutta*). Both species exhibit wildly variable appearances and life history strategies in their native ranges, with some populations adopting an anadromous migration strategy and others remaining in freshwater habitats their entire lives.

Salmo trout and salmon feed on aquatic insects and small fish in freshwater; shrimp and fishes such as capelin and herring in the ocean. Larger resident freshwater individuals often transition to a diet of fish as well.

Salmo salar—Atlantic Salmon

Figure 10.55. Atlantic Salmon (*Salmo salar*) parr rearing in a stream before migrating to the ocean.
HARALD OLSEN/NTNU

Description: Atlantic Salmon are bronze to dull green with dark black and occasionally maroon blotches on the back. Appearances vary with life history: Landlocked individuals never attain the silvery sheen that develops in anadromous individuals.

Size: Anadromous individuals typically grow to 28 to 36 inches long and 10 to 20 pounds, with a maximum of 30 pounds. Landlocked individuals are much smaller.

Habitat: Streams, lakes, and rivers with cold water. Anadromous individuals can migrate well over 100 miles in the open ocean.

Remarks: The Atlantic Salmon ranges from Connecticut to Labrador in North America, Iceland and Greenland in the North Atlantic, and Russia to Portugal in Europe. Some populations never migrate to the ocean and instead remain in freshwater environments their entire lives.

Although the Atlantic Salmon is globally the most abundant salmon thanks to aquaculture, wild populations have severely declined due to overfishing, dams, pollution, and predation by introduced species. Now listed as endangered in the United States, major dam removal projects in Maine aim to restore Atlantic Salmon.

Salmo trutta—Brown Trout

Figure 10.56. Brown Trout (*Salmo trutta*), identified by A) black and red spots, B) red or orange spots on the adipose fin, and C) a caudal fin lacking spots. NCFISHES.COM

Description: Most Brown Trout in North America are yellow to orange with black and red spots on the body. The adipose fin has red or orange spots, while the caudal fin almost always lacks spots.

Size: In lotic systems 10 to 24 inches long.
Habitat: Lotic systems and lakes with cold, clear water. Some individuals in coastal watersheds will travel to estuaries.
Remarks: The Brown Trout was imported from Europe during the late nineteenth century by immigrant anglers wanting to catch familiar species. Since introduction, the Brown Trout has established viable populations throughout North America and outcompetes native trout.

Genus *Thymallus*

The genus *Thymallus* includes over a dozen species mainly found in Siberia and far eastern Asia. Only one species occurs in North America: the Arctic Grayling (*T. arcticus*). Arctic Grayling feed on aquatic and terrestrial insects, salmon eggs, and small fish.

Thymallus arcticus—Arctic Grayling

Figure 10.57. Arctic Grayling (*Thymallus arcticus*), easily identified by A) a sail-like dorsal fin, B) black spots behind the head, and C) large, iridescent scales. RYAN HAGERTY/USFWS

Description: The most striking feature of the Arctic Grayling is its <u>prominent, sail-like dorsal fin with brightly colored spots and a red, orange, or white fringe</u>. The <u>scales are large and iridescent</u>. Most individuals have large, black spots behind the head.

Size: Most Arctic Grayling in the southern extent of their range grow 10 to 14 inches long. The largest individuals exceed 24 inches and 5 pounds.

Habitat: Clear, cold, and clean lotic systems and lakes.

APHREDODERIDAE (PIRATE PERCH)

Diversity and distribution: Only one species of fish in the family Aphredoderidae exists in the world—the Pirate Perch (*Aphredoderus sayanus*). The Pirate Perch is endemic to North America.

Evolutionary record: The Pirate Perch is most closely related to cavefishes (Amblyopsidae) and trout-perches (Percopsidae). Fossils dating to about 45 to 55 million years ago suggest that the family once had a much wider distribution.

Ecology and life history: The Pirate Perch is a mostly nocturnal invertebrate predator that thrives in swamp-like habitat, such as cypress bottomlands.

During the winter to spring spawning season, adults create tunnel-like structures in submerged vegetation or root masses that direct flow over embryos to provide oxygen. Adults do not offer parental care.

Identifying species: The most unusual trait of the Pirate Perch is the location of the anus, which is found right behind the head between the gill openings in adults. The Pirate Perch superficially resembles livebearers (Poeciliidae).

Genus *Aphredoderus*

The Pirate Perch feeds on aquatic insects, small fish, and soft-bodied crustaceans by sucking prey from muddy or sandy substrate.

Aphredoderus sayanus—Pirate Perch

Figure 10.58. Pirate Perch (*Aphredoderus sayanus*), characterized by A) dark bands below the eye, B) black specks on the belly, and C) a dark band on the caudal fin base. ALAN CRESSLER

Description: The Pirate Perch is colored olive gray to deep purple on the back and side, lighter on the belly but with dark specks, and dark vertical bands below the eyes and at the caudal fin base. The body is stout with the caudal fin starting at the top.

Size: Usually 2.5 to 4.5 inches long, rarely to 5.5 inches.

Habitat: Primarily lakes and swamps but also pools and backwaters of small streams, especially in submerged plants.

GASTEROSTEIDAE (STICKLEBACKS)

Diversity and distribution: The stickleback family Gasterosteidae includes about seven species worldwide, all found in the Northern Hemisphere in both freshwater and marine environments. Although the family includes relatively few species, they are very widely distributed and often found in high abundance. Three species of sticklebacks, each in their own genus, commonly occur in North American freshwaters. All are found in higher latitudes and cool to cold water. An additional species, the Fourspine Stickleback (*Apeltes quadracus*) is primarily found in marine environments but occasionally enters freshwater.

Ecology and life history: Each stickleback species occurs in a very wide range of habitats, from the open ocean to freshwater. Thanks to their ability to tolerate diverse conditions, two North American stickleback species (the Threespine Stickleback—*Gasterosteus aculeatus* and Ninespine Stickleback—*Pungitius pungitius*) have native geographic ranges that span the Northern Hemisphere, from Asia to Europe. Some populations are anadromous.

All sticklebacks are predators of small-bodied invertebrates and larval fish. Most prefer to feed within submerged vegetation or the benthic zone, only rarely in open water.

Male sticklebacks construct spherical nests by secreting an adhesive from their kidney to bind plant fragments together. The nest design can be elaborate, with separate entrance and exit portals. Females enter the nest to deposit eggs, after which males fertilize, aerate, and guard them against predators. Males become extremely territorial when guarding their nests and protect the young until they are large enough to forage on their own.

Sticklebacks are important prey for many predators, including other fishes and birds. They therefore represent important links in the food webs of many ecosystems.

Identifying species: Sticklebacks are easily distinguished from other fishes by large, conspicuous spines projecting from their back in front of the dorsal fin and belly, disproportionately large eyes, a small body (less than 4 inches), and lack of scales.

The three common lotic species of sticklebacks are easily distinguished from one another using dorsal spine count. Brook Stickleback (*Culaea inconstans*) typically have *four regularly spaced spines*, Ninespine Stickleback have eight to twelve *dorsal spines* (usually nine or ten), and Threespine Stickleback typically have *three dorsal spines*. Males become brightly colored when spawning.

Genus *Culaea*

The genus *Culaea* includes just one species: the Brook Stickleback (*C. inconstans*). The Brook Stickleback feeds on small invertebrate prey, fish eggs, and small larval fish.

Culaea inconstans—Brook Stickleback

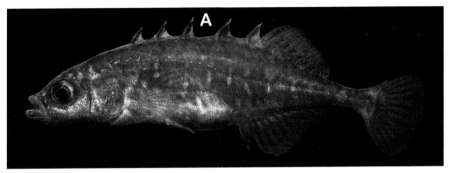

Figure 10.59. Brook Stickleback (*Culaea inconstans*), identified by A) four (sometimes five or six) dorsal spines.
ZACH ALLEY

Description: The Brook Stickleback is olive green colored with light speckling. They typically have <u>four evenly spaced dorsal spines</u>, but some individuals may have five or six.
Size: Usually 1.5 to 2.5 inches long.
Habitat: Cold, clear waters in ponds, lakes, and the pools of lotic systems with abundant submerged vegetation.
Remarks: Except during the breeding season, Brook Stickleback form schools and will even share large food items by passing prey from mouth to mouth.

Genus *Gasterosteus*

Six species of sticklebacks that range widely throughout the Northern Hemisphere in marine and freshwaters are included in the genus *Gasterosteus*, but only the Threespine Stickleback (*Gasterosteus aculeatus*) is commonly found in lotic systems. The Threespine Stickleback feeds on worms, small crustaceans, aquatic and terrestrial insects, and small fishes.

Gasterosteus aculeatus—Threespine Stickleback

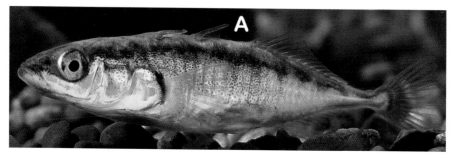

Figure 10.60. Threespine Stickleback (*Gasterosteus aculeatus*), with A) three dorsal spines highlighted. KONRAD SCHMIDT

Description: The Threespine Stickleback varies in appearance among habitats, with open water–dwelling species exhibiting a more torpedo-shaped body than benthic dwellers. They possess <u>three dorsal spines</u>.
Size: Typically 1 to 3.5 inches long.
Habitat: A very wide range of marine and freshwater habitats, from small ephemeral streams to the open ocean. Most frequently encountered in lotic environments near coasts or lakes.

Genus *Pungitius*

Nine species that range widely throughout the Northern Hemisphere comprise the genus *Pungitius*, including the Ninespine Stickleback (*P. pungitius*) that frequents lotic systems. The Ninespine Stickleback consumes any small invertebrate that can be captured, from aquatic insects to zooplankton.

Pungitius pungitius—Ninespine Stickleback

Figure 10.61. Ninespine Stickleback, identified by A) eight to ten dorsal spines. KONRAD SCHMIDT

Description: The Ninespine Stickleback is easily recognized from other stickleback species by the <u>large number (usually nine) of dorsal spines</u>, spines on the belly, and a slender body. The body color is olive green to black.
Size: Usually 1 to 2 inches long, but up to 3.5 inches.
Habitat: Lakes, rivers, and estuaries. Most associated with submerged vegetation in all habitats.

POECILIIDAE (LIVEBEARERS)

Diversity and distribution: The livebearer family Poeciliidae consists of about 300 species distributed throughout eastern North America, South America, and Africa. As is usually the case in plant and animal groups, livebearer species diversity increases with proximity to the equator. In North America, 16 species from 4 genera have ranges in waters that extend above the Mexican border, but even among these species only a handful are found north of Florida or south Texas. No species are native to Canada, and Mexican waters support a far greater proportion of Poeciliidae biodiversity.

Ecology and life history: The livebearer family gets its common name from a unique reproductive strategy. Eggs are fertilized internally, and females give birth to as many as one hundred young that are immediately ready to swim about three weeks later.

The livebearer diet is usually omnivorous and consists of small aquatic insect larvae, terrestrial insects, fish larvae, small tadpoles, algae, and detritus. The typical proportion of animal versus vegetable matter in diets varies among species. Those that consume animal prey possess sharper teeth, while more vegetarian species have flat teeth for grinding. Nearly all livebearer species remain at or near the water surface while foraging.

Several livebearer species are very familiar to non-naturalists as popular aquarium species, including swordtails (genus *Xiphophorus*), mollies, and guppies (both genus *Poecilia*). Livebearer species for the aquarium trade have been selectively bred for bright colors, showy patterns, and/or flaring fins. However, the males of some wild, native species do exhibit a similar aesthetic appeal.

Most livebearer species prefer still water and are only found in ponds, lakes, wetlands, and springs. Many other species possess very restrictive native ranges and are found only in a few watersheds of the Rio Grande drainage. The exceptions to these rules, those that do routinely occupy lotic waters north of the borderlands, are covered below.

Identifying species: Livebearers tend to have a small and stubby body (less than 3 inches long), large scales, an extended anal fin in males, a rounded caudal fin, and an upturned mouth. Livebearers very closely resemble killifish (family Fundulidae) and the two families can be easily confused in the field. In common North American lotic Poeciliidae, except fishes in the genus *Poecilia*, the first ray of the dorsal fin is clearly set behind the first ray of the anal fin (this trait does not necessarily apply south of the United States).

The table of genus attributes below applies *only* to North American Poeciliidae species north of Mexico found in lotic waters and is not meant to serve as a means of comprehensively distinguishing among genera beyond the United States.

Genus (# of North American species north of Mexico)	Traits or range of common lotic species
Gambusia (about 14 plus 2 extinct species)	Gray body; females often exhibit a dark spot above base of anal fin and are much stouter; New Mexico to Delaware and north to Illinois; one species introduced broadly beyond native range
Heterandria (1)	Very small fish (less than 1.5 inches) with a broad, dark band running the length of the body; southeastern United States from Louisiana to North Carolina
Poecilia (2)	Males have a large, conspicuous dorsal fin with a speckled pattern; dorsal fin set in front of anal fin; southeastern United States from Texas to North Carolina
Poeciliopsis (1)	Females colored pale olive and smaller males dark gray, otherwise a drably colored fish; Arizona and far western New Mexico

Genus *Gambusia*

Gambusia fishes include the most widely distributed Poeciliidae species. Most possess very narrow ranges in south Texas and New Mexico, with some confined to single springs. However, the Eastern and Western Mosquitofish (*G. holbrooki* and *G. affinis*, respectively) are widely distributed and often abundant in lotic systems.

Both species were introduced throughout the world to control mosquitoes, although the strategy proved not very effective. They tolerate a wide range of conditions, including waters with warm temperatures, pollution, or low dissolved oxygen. Mosquitofish introductions often negatively impact native amphibians and fishes, as both species are aggressive and voracious predators.

Mosquitofish are omnivorous and feed on emerging aquatic insects or terrestrial insects that fall onto the water surface, eggs and larvae of other fishes, and algae.

Gambusia affinis—Western Mosquitofish

Figure 10.62. A male Western Mosquitofish (*Gambusia affinis*), with A) spots on the caudal fin. NCFISHES.COM

Description: Western Mosquitofish (*Gambusia affinis*) have a dull gray body and a <u>caudal fin peppered with spots</u>. Females are larger and have a dark spot above the anal fin.
Size: Typically 1 to 3 inches long; females grow much larger than males.
Habitat: Standing water of all types, from ponds and lakes to lotic system pools; tolerates brackish water.

Gambusia holbrooki—Eastern Mosquitofish

Figure 10.63. A female Eastern Mosquitofish (*Gambusia holbrooki*), characterized by A) a dark spot above the belly. ROBERT AGUILAR/SMITHSONIAN ENVIRONMENTAL RESEARCH CENTER

Description: Very similar to Western Mosquitofish. Gray body with darker olive to brown on the back. Female Eastern Mosquitofish possess a large, dark spot on the belly.
Size: Typically 1.5 to 3 inches long; females grow much larger than males.
Habitat: Occupies a wide range of habitats, from still to moving waters and freshwater to saltwater, usually within submerged vegetation.

Genus *Heterandria*

Only three species worldwide comprise the genus *Heterandria*: two endemic to Mexico and *H. formosa*, the Least Killifish. The latter is not a killifish but rather a livebearer. The Least Killifish feeds on small invertebrates, zooplankton, and snails but also algae secondarily.

Heterandria formosa—Least Killifish

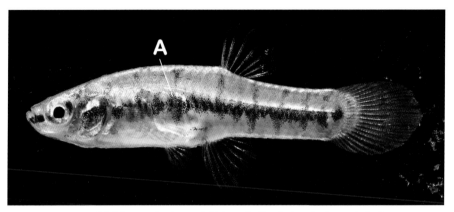

Figure 10.64. Least Killifish (*Heterandria formosa*), distinguished by A) a broad stripe on the body. NCFISHES.COM

Description: The Least Killifish is a tiny livebearer, the smallest vertebrate in North America, with a <u>broad stripe running through the body</u> and a dark spot on the dorsal fin.

Size: Rarely grows beyond 1 inch long.
Habitat: Standing or slow-moving water including ponds, lakes, ditches, and lotic system pools with submerged vegetation; tolerates brackish water.

Genus *Poecilia*

Fishes in the genus *Poecilia* are familiar to aquarium hobbyists as the ubiquitous molly. Two species are native north of the Mexican border: the Amazon Molly (*P. formosa*), found only in far southern Texas, and the Sailfin Molly (*P. latipinna*), which ranges from Texas to North Carolina coastal watersheds.

Poecilia livebearers feed on algae and parts of submerged plants, also small insect larvae including mosquitoes.

Poecilia latipinna—Sailfin Molly

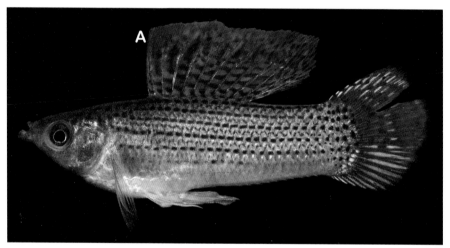

Figure 10.65. The Sailfin Molly (*Poecilia latipinna*), easily identified by A) a large, patterned dorsal fin in males. ZACH ALLEY

Description: The Sailfin Molly gets its name from the large, showy dorsal fin of the male that is about as tall as the body is deep. The dorsal fin is also covered in spots with a row of long, dark spots. The body is bluish gray with rows of dark spots.

Size: Unlike many other livebearers, Sailfin Molly males and females are about the same size, though females are usually slightly larger, about 0.6 to 2 inches long.

Habitat: Slow-moving or standing water, including lowland lotic systems; can survive in estuaries.

Remarks: The Sailfin Molly is a popular aquarium fish. Selective breeding has created varieties with extra-showy colors and dorsal fin patterns.

FUNDULIDAE (KILLIFISH)

Diversity and distribution: The family Fundulidae, fishes commonly called killifish or topminnows, includes about forty species, with the center of biodiversity located in the southeastern United States. About thirty-seven species occur in the United States, nine in Mexico, and three in Canada. Some are broadly distributed across eastern and central North America while others are found only within a single, small watershed.

Four killifish genera are commonly encountered in North America north of Mexico. The genus *Fundulus* dominates the family with thirty-four species. The genus *Adinia* includes one species, the Diamond Killifish (*A. xenica*), found only in salt marshes. The genera *Leptolucania* and *Lucania* are composed of one and three species, respectively. One species of *Fundulus* is considered extinct and up to seven species are threatened.

Ecology and life history: The common name topminnow comes from the tendency of killifish to remain near the water surface while feeding. Killifish are predators of invertebrates living near or traversing the water surface, including aquatic and terrestrial insects, zooplankton, and fish eggs. Numerous species consume large numbers of mosquito larvae. Some killifish species symbiotically clean parasites off other fish of the same or different species, including minnows.

Several killifish species are tolerant to high salinity and low dissolved oxygen, conditions that would prove fatal to many fishes. Dissolved oxygen concentrations tend to be higher near the interface between water and air: typical killifish habitat. Some killifish are found exclusively in very saline environments such as salt marshes or estuaries.

Killifish reproduce by attaching large, adhesive eggs to vegetation or benthic substrate. Males are territorial and will chase off competitors during courtship, which usually involves pairs swimming together over several days and depositing eggs one at a time followed by fertilization. Young receive no parental care after hatching. The males of most species are more brightly colored but grow to about the same size as females.

Identifying species: Killifish are characterized by their small body size, <u>rounded tail</u>, large scales, <u>anal and dorsal fins set far back on the body</u>, <u>upturned mouth</u>, and bright colors. Distinguishing killifish from livebearers (family Poeciliidae) can be difficult in the field if unfamiliar with the local species. However, killifish males do not have extended anal fins, are usually more brightly colored than northern livebearers, and are about the same size as females. In the most diverse and widespread genus, *Fundulus*, the first ray of the anal fin is usually set behind, equal to, or very slightly ahead of the first ray of the dorsal fin, whereas in most North American livebearers north of Mexico (except for the Sailfin Molly), the anal fin is set well ahead of the dorsal fin. Most killifish (especially males) are also more brightly colored and patterned than common livebearer species.

Genus (# of North American species north of Mexico)	Traits or range of common lotic species
Adinia (1)	Very stout body with abundant vertical stripes; almost exclusively found in marine and estuarine environments
Fundulus (about 34)	Dorsal fin set ahead of, above, or very slightly behind the anal fin; as a genus, distributed throughout eastern and central North America
Leptolucania (1)	Large, conspicuous, dark spot at the base of the caudal fin surrounded by a yellow halo; slow-moving lotic systems of Florida, Georgia, and Alabama
Lucania (3)	Dorsal fin clearly set ahead of the anal fin; coastal watersheds of the Southeast

Genus *Fundulus*

The genus *Fundulus* comprises most of the biodiversity within the Fundulidae family. Many species have very restricted ranges, with some found only within a single medium-sized watershed. *Fundulus* species outlined below are those with the widest ranges and/or most abundant in lotic systems. Some *Fundulus* species form schools while others usually remain solitary.

Killifish in the genus *Fundulus* are omnivorous, with aquatic insect larvae and small algae cells from the water column comprising most of their diet. Some species seem to specialize on mayfly nymphs or snails.

Fundulus catenatus—Northern Studfish

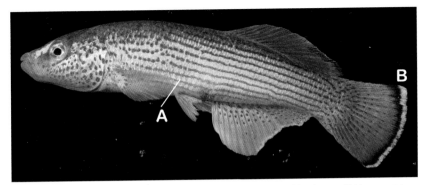

Figure 10.66. A male Northern Studfish (*Fundulus catenatus*), identified by A) rows of iridescent stripes and B) a black and orange or yellow stripe at the caudal fin edge. ZACH ALLEY

Description: The male Northern Studfish exhibits horizontal rows of small, iridescent blue dots or stripes that run from the cheek to the caudal fin and (when breeding) an <u>orange or yellow and black stripe at the caudal fin edge</u>. Both sexes are <u>iridescent pale blue</u> with orange to cream fins and have a <u>gold stripe on the back</u> in front of the dorsal fin.

Size: A larger killifish that grows up to 6 inches long.

Habitat: Lotic systems with clear water and sandy to rocky substrate.

Fundulus chrysotus—Golden Topminnow

Figure 10.67. A male Golden Topminnow (*Fundulus chrysotus*), identified by A) large, orange spots when spawning. SMITHSONIAN ENVIRONMENTAL RESEARCH CENTER

Description: The Golden Topminnow gets its name from its <u>gold to pearly color</u>. Both sexes lack a dark spot below the eye. Males have orange spots (especially toward the caudal fin) and may exhibit a bluish sheen.

Size: Usually about 2.5 to 3 inches long.

Habitat: Very slow-moving, shallow lotic systems with abundant submerged vegetation. Also wetlands and oxbow lakes.

Fundulus diaphanus—Banded Killifish

Figure 10.68. A Banded Killifish (*Fundulus diaphanus*), which gets its name from A) prominent vertical bands.
NCFISHES.COM

Description: The Banded Killifish exhibits <u>many conspicuous vertical bands from the gill to the caudal fin base</u>. The body is olive to gold with darker stripes and often a spot at the base of the caudal fin.
Size: Up to 5 inches long.
Habitat: Lakes, ponds, and slow-moving streams with sandy or muddy substrate.

Fundulus dispar—Starhead Topminnow

Figure 10.69. A male Starhead Topminnow (*Fundulus dispar*), a species characterized by A) a dark blotch below the eye and males with B) vertical stripes and horizontal rows of spots. KONRAD SCHMIDT

Description: The Starhead Topminnow has a very <u>conspicuous gold spot on the head</u> and usually a <u>dark blotch below the eye</u>. The body is colored yellow to pale blue green. Males have thin, dark, vertical bars and horizontally positioned red spots.
Size: Usually up to 2 inches long.
Habitat: Wetlands, lakes, and quiet backwater pools of lotic systems.

Fundulus lineolatus—Lined Topminnow

Figure 10.70. A male Lined Topminnow (*Fundulus lineolatus*), identified by A) twelve to fifteen dark vertical bars. NCFISHES.COM

Description: Males have twelve to fifteen large, conspicuous, vertical bars while females display about <u>six dark horizontal bars that run from the gill to the caudal fin base</u>. Both sexes have dark coloration below the eye and an <u>iridescent spot on the head</u>.
Size: Typically 3 to 3.5 inches long.
Habitat: Wetlands, ponds, and slow-moving lotic systems with clear water and abundant vegetation.

Fundulus notatus—Blackstripe Topminnow

Figure 10.71. A Blackstripe Topminnow (*Fundulus notatus*), which always has A) a dark band running the body length. ZACH ALLEY

Description: Both sexes possess a <u>broad, dark band that runs from the caudal fin base through the eye to the snout</u> and small spots on the caudal, anal, and dorsal fin. Color is olive above the line and white below. <u>Lacks conspicuous dark spots above the lateral band</u>.
Size: Up to about 2.5 inches long.
Habitat: Most often found in lotic systems of all sizes with turbid waters.

Fundulus olivaceus—Blackspotted Topminnow

Figure 10.72. A Blackspotted Topminnow (*Fundulus olivaceus*), distinguished by A) a dark lateral band and B) dark spots above the band. ZACH ALLEY

Description: The Blackspotted Topminnow has a <u>dark, broad lateral band runs from the caudal fin base to the snout</u>. Both sexes are flecked with <u>numerous small, dark spots above the band</u> and on the caudal and dorsal fins. Males also exhibit spots below the dark band.
Size: A large killifish that grows to 4 inches long.
Habitat: The Blackspotted Topminnow prefers faster-moving water (compared to other topminnows) and lives in lotic systems with sandy substrate and clear water.

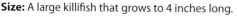

Fundulus sciadicus—Plains Topminnow

Figure 10.73. A male Plains Topminnow (*Fundulus sciadicus*), identified by A) red-tinted fin edges.
SAM STUKEL/USFWS

Description: The Plains Topminnow is colored light olive and <u>lacks vertical black bars</u> or a <u>spot below the eye</u>. Males develop <u>red tints on fin edges</u>.
Size: 1.5 to 2.5 inches long.
Habitat: Occupies a variety of lotic habitats, from clear to turbid water. Prefers habitats with abundant submerged vegetation.

Genus *Leptolucania*

The genus *Leptolucania* consists of one species, the Pygmy Killifish (*L. ommata*), which is endemic to the southeastern United States. The Pygmy Killifish diet consists of small-bodied invertebrates primarily and algae secondarily.

Leptolucania ommata—Pygmy Killifish

Figure 10.74. A Pygmy Killifish (*Leptolucania ommata*), identified by A) a dark spot at the caudal fin base.
ZACH ALLEY

Description: Both sexes possess a dark spot at the base of the caudal fin surrounded by a yellow halo. Males are colored gold orange while females are more darkly colored with a very broad horizontal band on the body.
Size: Rarely grows more than 1 inch long.
Habitat: Slow-moving lotic systems adjacent to swamps.

Genus *Lucania*

Three species comprise the genus *Lucania*, all endemic to North America. The Cuatrocienegas Killifish (*L. interioris*) is endemic to wetlands in the deserts of northern Mexico, while the Bluefin Killifish (*L. goodei*) is mainly found in Florida. The Rainwater Killifish (*L. parva*) is widely distributed in eastern and southern North America. *Lucania* killifish diets consist of small-bodied invertebrates, including mosquito larvae.

Lucania parva—Rainwater Killifish

Figure 10.75. A female Rainwater Killifish (*Lucania parva*), which has A) a dorsal fin clearly set ahead of the anal fin. ROBERT AGUILAR/SMITHSONIAN ENVIRONMENTAL RESEARCH CENTER

Description: The Rainwater Killifish has a <u>dorsal fin clearly positioned ahead of the anal fin</u> and is colored yellow to light brown. Males exhibit a <u>very dark, large spot at the base of the caudal fin</u>, an <u>orange spot at the end of the dorsal fin</u>, and an <u>orange-tinted anal fin with a thin black edge</u>.

Size: Rarely grows more than 2.5 inches long.

Habitat: Lotic systems of variable size but always with abundant submerged vegetation. Very tolerant of saltwater.

CATOSTOMIDAE (SUCKERS)

Diversity and distribution: The Catostomidae family includes seventy-four species, with only one found outside North America. Although the Mississippi drainage harbors the greatest concentration of sucker biodiversity, native sucker species occur throughout the continent, including rare desert suckers. Suckers inhabit lotic systems of all sizes, from headwater streams to large rivers.

The sucker family includes ten genera. Most diverse is the *Catostomus* genus, fishes commonly referred to as suckers, with twenty-six species. The genus *Moxostoma* (commonly called redhorse) includes twenty-two large-bodied species. The other eight genera consist of one to five species.

Ecology and life history: Although the Catostomidae includes species with a diverse range of body sizes and habitats, nearly all have a mouth aimed downward for sucking up detritus, plant matter, and small prey. Most are omnivorous, and many feed on decomposing organic matter. The most consumed food item often reflects what is locally abundant. Some suckers specialize on prey such as snails and fish eggs. Invertebrates comprise at least 50 percent of dietary intake for most sucker species. Nearly all suckers form schools to forage but especially when threatened by predators or migrating.

Large-bodied species migrate over 100 miles within lotic systems to spawn, often to channel reaches where they were born. Spawning takes place in riffles with current capable of delivering adequate oxygen to fertilized eggs. Suckers do not care for young, and fishes within only one genus, *Moxostoma* (redhorses) excavate nests in substrate. All others broadcast spawn into coarse substrate or nest mounds built by other species.

Like fishes in the family Cyprinidae, the males of many sucker species develop **tubercles**—hard, sharp, but stout projections on the head and below the mouth made of keratin, the same organic molecule that makes hair in mammals. Tubercles are used to defend spawning territory and attract females.

Environmental tolerance varies significantly among suckers, with some being very sensitive to pollution while others can thrive in highly degraded urban waters. All suckers strictly inhabit freshwater and do not enter estuaries or coastal waters. The habitat preferences of several species shift with age or vary within geographic ranges. A minority of species reside in lakes and rarely enter lotic systems.

Identifying species: Few traits reliably distinguish suckers as a family, though nearly all possess a mouth aimed downward for sucking up prey. Typical colors range from brown to dull gray, and bright colors rarely appear except in the males of a few species when spawning. Some suckers grow beyond 4 feet and weigh over 70 pounds.

Suckers most closely resemble minnows (family Cyprinidae), and several large-bodied species could be confused with carp. However, suckers lack the conspicuous mouth barbels easily observed on carp.

Due to the large family size, traits to reliably distinguish genera in the field are not always available. Therefore, range maps can offer a useful means of field identification. In addition, three sucker genera possess dorsal fins that grow much longer in the first few rays then narrow toward the caudal fin, creating a hooklike shape that ichthyologists call **falcate**.

Genus (# of North American species)	Traits or range of common lotic species (*genera not covered further)	Falcate dorsal fins
Carpiodes (3)	Medium-sized suckers native to eastern and central US and Great Lakes basins.	Yes
Catostomus (26)	Small- to medium-sized suckers with traits significantly varying among species. Distributed throughout all major US basins and southern Canada.	No
Chamistes* (4)	The four surviving species are restricted to very isolated basins or single lakes in the western United States. The Snake River Sucker, C. murieri, went extinct in the twentieth century.	No
Cycleptus (2)	Large suckers of the Mississippi and Rio Grande basins.	Yes
Deltistes* (1)	Sole species is the Lost River Sucker, D. luxatus, which only occurs in the Klamath River drainage of California and Oregon.	
Erimyzon (3)	Small suckers often with a broad, dark lateral band on the body. Central and eastern United States to Canada.	No
Hypentelium (3)	Small- to medium-sized suckers with indented forehead and dark saddles on the back. Eastern to central United States and Great Lakes.	No
Ictiobus (5)	The largest members of the sucker family. Mississippi and Great Lakes drainages.	Yes
Minytrema (1)	Sole species is the Spotted Sucker (M. melanops), a large-bodied, gold-colored sucker with conspicuous dark spots on most scales. Central and southeastern United States to Ontario.	No
Moxostoma (22)	Very large suckers with fins often red pigmented. Throughout Mississippi, Great Lakes, and Atlantic coast basins, but biodiversity is concentrated in eastern United States.	Some species moderately so, others not
Thoburnia (3)	Smaller-bodied suckers with conspicuous colors and patterns: either orange pigmentation, fine lateral body stripes, or dark mottling. Restricted to Virginia, West Virginia, North Carolina, Kentucky, and Tennessee.	No
Xyrauchen (1)	Sole species is the Razorback Sucker (X. texanus), a sucker with a large, conspicuous keel on the head and back. Restricted to the Colorado River basin.	Slightly

Genus *Carpiodes*

Suckers in the genus *Carpiodes* superficially resemble carp and are commonly referred to as carpsuckers. They are medium bodied with big scales and a dull gray to gold color, and inhabit the same large rivers where carp have successfully invaded. Unlike carp, however, on *Carpiodes* the first five to seven rays of the dorsal fin extend much farther than the rest of the fin to create a hooklike shape.

Carpsuckers feed by ingesting detritus in river benthic zones and digesting whatever plant or animal matter is consumed, including small invertebrates, clams and mussels, snails, and vegetation.

Carpiodes carpio—River Carpsucker

Figure 10.76. A River Carpsucker (*Carpiodes carpio*). KONRAD SCHMIDT

Description: The River Carpsucker is brown to olive on the back, somewhat lighter on the belly. Fins are opaque and dark yellow in older individuals.
Size: Typically 12 to 20 inches long.
Habitat: Large, deep rivers with sandy or silty substrate.

Carpiodes cyprinus—Quillback

Figure 10.77. A Quillback (*Carpiodes cyprinus*). SAM STUKEL/USFWS

Description: A silvery sucker that is compressed side to side.
Size: Usually to 24 inches long, rarely to 28 inches.
Habitat: Unlike others in the genus, the Quillback prefers medium to large rivers with clear water.

Carpiodes velifer—Highfin Carpsucker

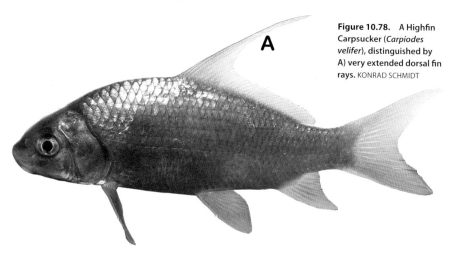

Figure 10.78. A Highfin Carpsucker (*Carpiodes velifer*), distinguished by A) very extended dorsal fin rays. KONRAD SCHMIDT

Description: The Highfin Carpsucker has a <u>very long dorsal fin extension in the first several rays</u>. Color is shiny silver to gold, often with red-tinted fins.
Size: Usually 12 to 15 inches long, but can grow to 20 inches.
Habitat: Lotic systems with deep, protected pools but with swift currents nearby. Turbid or clear water.

Genus *Catostomus*

The genus *Catostomus* is the most diverse and widespread among the suckers. *Catostomus* body shapes tend to be more elongate than suckers of other genera, and their scales are relatively small. Many species have extremely narrow natural distributions, especially in western species that may occupy only a few small watersheds.

Catostomus suckers feed on zooplankton when young then transition to midges, fish eggs, the occasional small fish, amphipods, and vegetation in the benthic zone as adults. Some species, such as the Bluehead Sucker (*C. discolobus*), specialize on vegetation.

Catostomus catostomus—Longnose Sucker

Figure 10.79. Schooling Longnose Sucker (*Catostomus catostomus*), identified by A) a dark lateral band in males and B) a very white belly. PAUL VECSEI

Description: A sucker with a <u>red to olive back and silver to white belly</u>. Spawning males develop a pronounced dark lateral band.
Size: Usually 8 to 10 inches long, but can grow to 24 inches.
Habitat: Deep water of rivers and lakes, especially in colder water (32–60°F).
Remarks: The Longnose Sucker sometimes hybridizes with the White Sucker (*C. commersonii*), which is very similar in appearance.

Catostomus commersonii—White Sucker

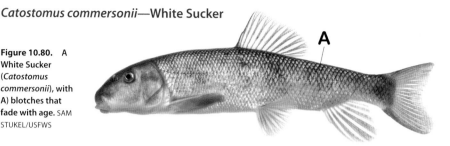

Figure 10.80. A White Sucker (*Catostomus commersonii*), with A) blotches that fade with age. SAM STUKEL/USFWS

Description: Brown to pale green on the back, gold to orange on the side, and a pale cream to white belly. Young White Suckers have large, fading blotches on the side. The body is long and round in cross section.
Size: Usually to 10 inches long, but up to 25 inches.
Habitat: Occupies a diverse range of habitats, but usually headwater to medium-sized lotic systems with clear water.
Remarks: The White Sucker is the most common and abundant of all suckers and can tolerate very polluted conditions. White Suckers hybridize with other *Catostomus* species in western ecosystems where it has been introduced.

Catostomus macrocheilus—Largescale Sucker

Figure 10.81. A school of Largescale Suckers (*Catostomus macrocheilus*), identified by A) abrupt color transition. GLACIER NPS

Description: Very dark on the back and abruptly transitioning to white on the belly with a dark lateral band extending from the mouth to the caudal fin. The dorsal fin is somewhat concave. The Largescale Sucker may be similar in appearance to the Bridgelip Sucker, but its scales are relatively larger.
Size: 14 to 18 inches long, occasionally to 24 inches.
Habitat: Medium- to large-sized lotic systems but also in lakes to depths exceeding 75 feet.

Catostomus platyrhynchus—Mountain Sucker

Figure 10.82. A Mountain Sucker (*Catostomus platyrhynchus*). TOM TAYLOR

Description: Color of a Mountain Sucker is dusky gray or green on the back with a cream to white belly. During the spawning season, males develop tubercles and both sexes may exhibit a bright orange band.

Size: A small *Catostomus* species, rarely grows larger than 10 inches long.

Habitat: Can thrive in a diverse range of ecosystems, from headwater streams to large rivers, lakes, and reservoirs.

Genus *Cycleptus*

The two species of *Cycleptus* are large suckers with <u>falcate dorsal fins</u> that inhabit large rivers. The Southeastern Blue Sucker, *C. meridionalis*, is restricted to swift-flowing rivers of Louisiana, Mississippi, and Alabama, while the Blue Sucker (*C. elongatus*) is widespread. *Cycleptus* suckers feed on benthic invertebrates, vegetation, and algae.

Cycleptus elongatus—Blue Sucker

Figure 10.83. A Blue Sucker (*Cycleptus elongatus*), identified by drab blue colors and A) a falcate dorsal fin.
RYAN HAGERTY/USFWS

Description: A slender, compressed sucker colored olive to blue black on the back with a bluish-white belly and a falcate dorsal fin. Fins are bluish and turn darker during the spawning season.

Size: Up to 32 inches long.
Habitat: Large rivers with gravel substrates and strong, swift flow.
Remarks: The Blue Sucker was once very abundant throughout its range but has declined significantly, mostly because of dams and locks that restrict migration.

Genus *Erimyzon*

The genus *Erimyzon* consists of three small-bodied sucker species of the eastern and central United States. One species, the Lake Chubsucker (*E. succetta*) is found mainly in lakes, ponds, and wetlands. The Sharpfin Sucker (*E. tenuis*) range is limited to large rivers of the Mobile and Pensacola Bays of Mississippi and Alabama. *Erimyzon* suckers feed on about equal parts vegetation/detritus and small invertebrates.

Erimyzon oblongus—Creek Chubsucker

Figure 10.84.   An adult Creek Chubsucker (*Erimyzon oblongus*). NCFISHES.COM

Description: A stout, medium-sized sucker. Young Creek Chubsuckers exhibit a dark horizontal band, while larger individuals show blotches or saddles. Color is olive to gold on the back and pale yellow to white on the belly, often with <u>red-tinted fins</u>. The <u>scales are often dark at the edges</u>.

Size: Up to 16 inches long, but usually 8 to 10 inches.
Habitat: Small- to medium-sized lotic systems with abundant submerged vegetation.

Genus *Ictiobus*

The *Ictiobus* suckers are commonly called buffalo and represent the largest species in the family. Buffalo possess <u>large scales</u> and <u>falcate fins</u>, though the longest rays do not extend as far as those in *Carpiodes*. All buffalo species inhabit large rivers. Distinguishing among species of buffalo can be difficult in the field.

Buffalo occupy the same ecological niche as introduced carp, which can outcompete them for limited resources. They consume a wide variety of organisms of the benthic zone and water column, from insect larvae and zooplankton to detritus and algae.

Ictiobus bubalus—Smallmouth Buffalo

Figure 10.85. A Smallmouth Buffalo (*Ictiobus bubalus*). SAM STUKEL/USFWS

Description: The Smallmouth Buffalo has a stout body with a brown to green tint on the back, lighter on the belly. Fins grow dark during the spawning season and males develop tubercles. The <u>mouth is relatively small and set below the eye</u>.
Size: Typically to 30 inches long. A record weight in Texas recorded 97 pounds.
Habitat: Large rivers with silt substrate and abundant submerged vegetation.

Ictiobus cyprinellus—Bigmouth Buffalo

Figure 10.86. An adult Bigmouth Buffalo (*Ictiobus cyprinellus*), a sucker with a rare A) forward-facing mouth. KONRAD SCHMIDT

Description: The Bigmouth Buffalo is one of the few sucker species with a <u>mouth facing forward</u> rather than downward. Color is dull gray to olive, lighter on the belly.

Size: Up to 48 inches long and over 75 pounds.

Habitat: Large lotic systems with slow-moving water and muddy substrate.

Remarks: With some individuals exceeding 110 years old, the Bigmouth Buffalo is one of the longest-living fishes in the world. It is also one of the few suckers prized for food, with small commercial fisheries targeting the species.

Ictiobus niger—Black Buffalo

Figure 10.87. A Black Buffalo (*Ictiobus niger*), a sucker with A) thicker lips than most others in the family. KONRAD SCHMIDT

Description: Colored black on the back and dark green to gold on the side, fading to smoky white on the belly. Black Buffalo possess <u>thicker lips</u> and a more stream-lined body than other *Ictiobus* species.

Size: Typically 20 to 24 inches long, but up to 48 inches.

Habitat: Large, deep lotic systems and lakes.

Genus *Hypentelium*

The genus *Hypentelium* (commonly called hog suckers) includes three small-bodied species. They can usually be distinguished from other suckers by their <u>indented head, which is concave between the eyes and gives the head a boxy appearance</u>. All *Hypentelium* species also have dark mottling and/or saddles throughout the body.

The Alabama Hog Sucker (*H. etowanum*) range spans Georgia to eastern Mississippi, while the Roanoke Hogsucker (*H. roanokense*) is found only within the Dan and Roanoke River drainages of Virginia and North Carolina. The Northern Hogsucker (*H. nigricans*) distribution is widespread.

Hogsuckers forage in the benthic zone by overturning rocks and disturbing sediment to feed on invertebrates, algae, and detritus. Other fish species may position themselves downstream of foraging hogsuckers to feed on items swept into the current.

Hypentelium nigricans—Northern Hogsucker

Figure 10.88. A Northern Hogsucker (*Hypentelium nigricans*), identified by A) a concave, angular head and B) dark saddles on the back. NCFISHES.COM

Description: A slender sucker with about four dark saddles on the back, otherwise colored gold to olive on the back and pale on the belly.
Size: Usually 6 to 12 inches long.
Habitat: Cold to cool lotic systems with clear water, from headwater streams to medium-sized rivers.

Genus *Minytrema*

The genus *Minytrema* consists of just one species—the Spotted Sucker. An omnivorous species, the Spotted Sucker feeds on both plant and animal matter in the benthic zone.

Minytrema melanops—Spotted Sucker

Figure 10.89. A Spotted Sucker (*Minytrema melanops*), identified by A) ubiquitous dark spots on most scales.
ZACH ALLEY

Description: The Spotted Sucker can be easily field identified by the <u>dark spots on most scales</u>. Body color is gold to brown colored to white on the belly. Males display two dark lateral bands with pink pigmentation in between when spawning.
Size: Usually 6 to 12 inches long.
Habitat: Deep pools of small- to medium-sized, warm-water lotic systems with sandy or gravel substrate.

Genus *Moxostoma*

Fishes in the genus *Moxostoma*, the second most diverse sucker genus, are commonly referred to as redhorse. Redhorses are medium- to large-bodied suckers of medium to large rivers that get their common name from their usually red-tinted fins. Some redhorses are endangered due to intense habitat modification of large rivers and/or extremely limited distributions. One extinct species, the Harelip Sucker (*M. lacerum*), was last observed in 1893.

All redhorses have a gold to silver body, large scales, reddish fins, a forked caudal fin, and a pale belly. Distinguishing among species usually requires inspection of the mouthparts. Another useful anatomical feature is the shape of the dorsal fin, which is concave in some species.

Redhorses feed on a diverse diet of primarily animal prey such as snails, insect larvae, amphipods, clams, and mussels. Most species also secondarily consume detritus and algae. The River Redhorse (*M. carinatum*) specializes on mollusks.

Moxostoma anisurum—Silver Redhorse

Figure 10.90. A Silver Redhorse (*Moxostoma anisurum*), which A) does not have a falcate dorsal fin.
KONRAD SCHMIDT

Description: The Silver Redhorse has a V-shaped lower lip with a smooth upper lip. The dorsal fin edge is not concave.
Size: Usually to 12 inches long, but up to 26 inches.
Habitat: Deep pools with slow-moving water in lotic systems, also associated with undercut banks and large woody debris. Also inhabits lakes.

Moxostoma breviceps—Smallmouth Redhorse

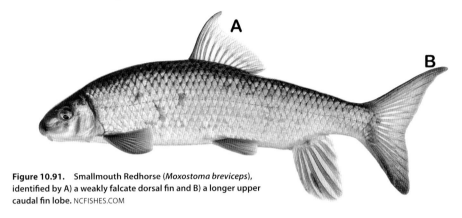

Figure 10.91. Smallmouth Redhorse (*Moxostoma breviceps*), identified by A) a weakly falcate dorsal fin and B) a longer upper caudal fin lobe. NCFISHES.COM

Description: The Smallmouth Redhorse gets its name from its small mouth and short head. It has a slightly to moderately falcate dorsal fin, and the upper lobe of the caudal fin is typically longer than the lower lobe. The lower lip of the mouth is very bumpy.
Size: Up to 24 inches long, but usually shorter.
Habitat: Lotic systems with fast-moving water and gravel to boulder substrate.

Moxostoma carinatum—River Redhorse

Figure 10.92. A River Redhorse (*Moxostoma carinatum*), which has A) a relatively thicker lower lip and B) a slightly longer upper caudal fin lobe. NCFISHES.COM

Description: One of the largest redhorse species, the River Redhorse has a longer upper caudal lobe relative to the lower lobe and a lower lip that is much thicker than the upper lip. Dark spots also commonly appear on larger scales.
Size: Usually 10 to 20 inches long, but up to 30 inches and over 10 pounds.
Habitat: Lotic systems with rocky substrate, clear water, and swift currents.

Moxostoma erythrurum—Golden Redhorse

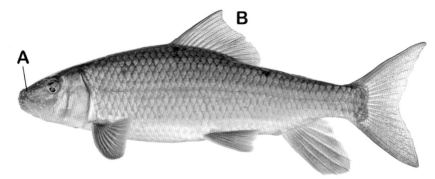

Figure 10.93. A male Golden Redhorse (*Moxostoma erythrurum*), characterized by A) tubercles and B) a slightly falcate dorsal fin. NCFISHES.COM

Description: A gold-colored redhorse with a stout, U-shaped lower lip and a <u>slightly falcate dorsal fin</u>. Males develop <u>conspicuous tubercles</u> during the spawning season.
Size: Usually 12 to 20 inches long.
Habitat: Pools of small- to medium-sized lotic systems with silty or sandy substrate.

Moxostoma macrolepidotum—Shorthead Redhorse

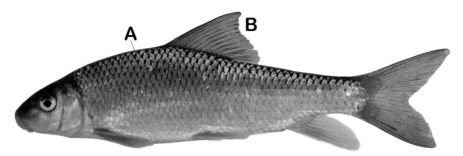

Figure 10.94. Shorthead Redhorse (*Moxostoma macrolepidotum*), identified by A) dark scale bases and B) a slightly falcate dorsal fin. ROBERT AGUILAR/SMITHSONIAN ENVIRONMENTAL RESEARCH CENTER

Description: A redhorse with a short, stout head, <u>slightly falcate dorsal fin</u>, and brassy colored body. <u>Scale bases are darkly colored</u>.
Size: Usually 10 to 18 inches long.
Habitat: Lotic systems with sand or gravel substrate and swift currents, usually with clear water.

Moxostoma valenciennesi—Greater Redhorse

Figure 10.95. A Greater Redhorse (*Moxostoma valenciennesi*), identified by A) a non-falcate dorsal fin and B) dark scale margins. KONRAD SCHMIDT

Description: A redhorse with a large head, non-falcate dorsal fin, and dark pigmentation on scale margins.
Size: Up to 25 inches long.
Habitat: Fast-moving medium- to large-sized lotic systems plus lakes with rocky substrate.
Remarks: The ecological attributes of the Greater Redhorse are not well known, but the species may be in severe decline throughout its range. Further surveys are needed to determine if populations are stable.

Genus *Thoburnia*

The three species in the genus *Thoburnia* are restricted to the central Appalachian foothills. The Rustyside Sucker (*T. hamiltoni*) occurs only in the Dan and Roanoke Rivers of Virginia and North Carolina, and the blackfin sucker (*T. atripinnis*) exclusively occupies the Dan River headwaters in Kentucky. One species, the Torrent Sucker (*T. rhothoeca*), is relatively widely distributed. *Thoburnia* suckers are omnivorous species that primarily consume fly larvae and algae.

Thoburnia rhothoeca—Torrent Sucker

Figure 10.96. A Torrent Sucker (*Thoburnia rhothoeca*), identified by A) a broad orange lateral stripe and B) dark saddles on the back. LOUGHRAN CABE

Description: A small-bodied sucker with black mottling or saddles and often a prominent orange stripe on the body sides.
Size: No more than 7 inches long.
Habitat: Lotic systems with clear water, high gradients, and gravel substrate, including mountain streams.

Genus *Xyrauchen*

The genus *Xyrauchen* includes only one species, the unmistakable Razorback Sucker (*X. texanus*) that is endemic to the Colorado River basin of the southwestern United States. Razorback Suckers consume plankton when young, while adults primarily feed on mayfly, caddisfly, and fly larvae.

Xyrauchen texanus—Razorback Sucker

Figure 10.97. A Razorback Sucker (*Xyrauchen texanus*), easily identified by A) a large keel on the back.
SAM STUKEL/USFWS

Description: A large sucker with a pronounced keel that runs from the back of the head to the terminus of the dorsal fin. Colored gray green on the back and yellow on the belly.

Size: Over 3 feet long and up to 12 pounds.

Habitat: Historically occupied backwaters of large rivers, sand flats, and floodplains, but these habitats are largely absent in the modern Southwest. The largest remaining populations in some regions are in reservoirs.

Remarks: The Razorback Sucker is critically imperiled because the Colorado River has been so heavily modified by dams, irrigation, an altered sediment regime, and introduced species. Populations are supported by hatchery operations.

CYPRINIDAE (MINNOWS AND CARPS)

Diversity and distribution: The family Cyprinidae dominates freshwater fish biodiversity in North America but also to varying degrees in Europe, Asia, and Africa. Approximately 3,000 species comprise the family, which accounts for about a quarter of freshwater fishes and nearly 10 percent of all fishes. An unknown number of species remain undescribed or undiscovered by science, especially in tropical waters. Species diversity tends to increase toward the equator, but North American Cyprinidae diversity is nevertheless vast. About 260 native Cyprinidae species occur north of the Mexican border.

Very recent studies of Cyprinidae genetics suggest that the family should really be considered multiple families. Resolving such matters in evolutionary science requires time and many genetic comparisons, work that is currently ongoing. Therefore, this book will treat Cyprinidae fishes using the classic approach: as one large family. Readers should be aware that this framework may be adjusted by scientists soon, although if that occurs the genus and species names (plus common names) will largely endure.

Cyprinidae fishes inhabit the entire spectrum of freshwater habitats, from frigid Arctic streams to tropical lakes. Some are very highly localized, such as the Desert Dace (*Eremichthys acros*), which is exclusively found within marshes fed by hot springs in northwestern Nevada. Entire genera, including *Dionda* and *Lepidomeda*, are limited to a very few watersheds in the desert Southwest. Others, like the Creek Chub (*Semotilus atromaculatus*), seem to occupy all waterbodies and rank among the most abundant fish in the continent.

Ecology and life history: Generalizing anything about fishes in the Cyprinidae is very difficult because they occupy so many ecological niches. The popular conception of a minnow is a small, silvery fish that does little other than fall prey to larger fish. However, within the Cyprinidae are pikeminnow (*Ptychocheilus* spp.), voracious predators that grow to 6 feet and nearly 100 pounds. The familiar but invasive carp species, which grow to well over 30 pounds on an omnivorous diet, are also in the Cyprinidae.

A few traits and behaviors can be generalized, however. Cyprinidae fishes are almost entirely freshwater, with only a small minority able to reside in brackish water. All species lack true teeth and instead break apart food using modified bony structures in their throat called **pharyngeal** teeth. Cyprinidae fishes also do not have stomachs and absorb nutrition from ingested prey via long intestines. Intricate nerve connections between the swim bladder and inner ear give Cyprinidae fishes excellent hearing ability.

Reproductive strategies vary considerably among species, ranging from broadcast spawning to nest building and guarding. The males of many species develop tubercles while spawning. Some species (especially those in *Nocomis*) construct large mounds of rock and gravel in riffles or runs for their fertilized eggs, as these structures ensure offspring receive plenty of oxygen. Many other species deposit their own eggs in these structures; thus the mounds become nurseries for the whole fish community.

Identifying species: A few anatomical traits are consistent among the Cyprinidae. All species lack 1) teeth on the jaw, 2) scales on the head, 3) an adipose fin, and 4) a second dorsal fin. The caudal fin is almost always forked. Cyprinidae fishes most resemble some species of suckers (Catostomidae), but a minnow mouth is typically oriented forward or upward rather than downward (although some minnows do have a downward-facing mouth). The

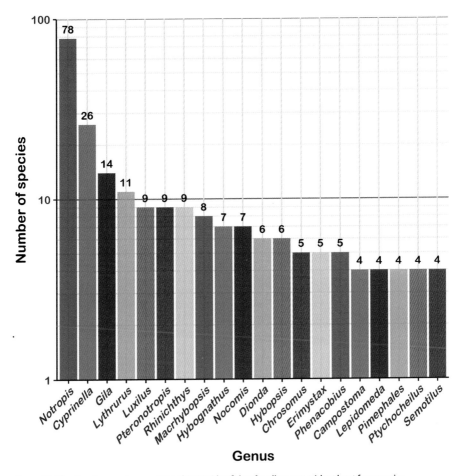

Figure 10.98. Species counts per genus of Cyprinidae fishes for all genera with at least four species.

Cyprinidae that most resemble suckers are the carps, which typically have large barbels that are absent in suckers. The best way to tell a minnow from a sucker is by counting dorsal fin rays: Suckers have ten or more, while minnows have nine or fewer.

Identifying Cyprinidae fishes to genus or species can prove challenging even for experienced ichthyologists. Species found north of the Mexican border in North America fall into forty-nine genera. As is the case for most diverse plant and animal groups, the family includes a minority of genera with many species and many genera with few species (Figure 10.98).

Comprehensive coverage of North American Cyprinidae could fill an entire book; thus the genera and species accounts below include common widespread, ecologically important, and/or unique species.

Genus *Campostoma*

Minnows in the genus *Campostoma* are called stonerollers because of their tendency to build nests out of substrate. The most distinguishing trait of the genus is a hard ridge on the lower jaw used to scrape algae. A stoneroller mouth lacks barbels and is positioned at the bottom of the head, and the body is stout, giving them the appearance of a sucker. Males develop abundant tubercles on the head and along the back when spawning. All four species are native to east of the continental divide, and two have very limited ranges.

Stonerollers feed on algae primarily and detritus secondarily. Introducing stonerollers results in significant algae control. They have especially long intestines to help digest vegetative matter.

Campostoma anomalum—Central Stoneroller

Figure 10.99. A male Central Stoneroller (*Campostoma anomalum*) during the spawning season, as indicated by tubercles and A) stripes on the dorsal fin. ZACH ALLEY

Description: The Central Stoneroller is brassy-colored with <u>small, randomly scattered dark spots</u>. Males develop broad stripes on the dorsal and anal fins.
Size: 2.5 to 6 inches long.
Habitat: Small- to medium-sized lotic systems with cool, clear water, high gradients, and hard substrate.

Genus *Chrosomus*

Minnows in the genus *Chrosomus* are known as redbelly dace thanks to the bright red color that develops on the lower half of their body when spawning. Redbelly Dace lack barbels. All five species are native to east of the continental divide, and three have very restricted native ranges. Redbelly dace are omnivorous, primarily consuming vegetative matter but also small invertebrates.

Chrosomus eos—Northern Redbelly Dace

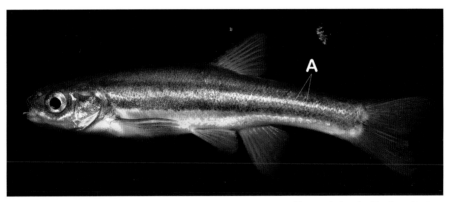

Figure 10.100. A Northern Redbelly Dace (*Chrosomus eos*), characterized by A) a dark and yellow lateral stripe.
ZACH ALLEY

Description: The Northern Redbelly Dace has <u>two broad bands, one yellow and the other black, that run the length of the body and end with a caudal tail spot</u>. In summer, males develop yellow-tinted fins.
Size: Usually to 3 inches long.
Habitat: Most often in blackwater lotic systems, ponds, and wetlands, sometimes in headwater streams.

Chrosomus erythrogaster—Southern Redbelly Dace

Figure 10.101. A Southern Redbelly Dace (*Chrosomus erythrogaster*) during the spawning season. ZACH ALLEY

Description: The Southern Redbelly Dace exhibits the same color pattern as the Northern Redbelly Dace (*C. eos*) but also often has a line of dark spots running along the back.
Size: Up to 2.75 inches long.
Habitat: Headwater lotic systems with clear water.

Genus *Clinostomus*

The two species of beautifully colored *Clinostomus* minnows known as redside dace are broadly distributed throughout the eastern United States. Redside dace lack barbels and have an upturned mouth for feeding in the water column and on insects on the surface. Males develop abundant tubercles during the spawning season. Redside dace chiefly consume aquatic and terrestrial insects, secondarily feeding on algae.

Clinostomus elongatus—Redside Dace

Figure 10.102. A Redside Dace (*Clinostomus elongatus*), identified by A) an upturned mouth and B) a dark band that runs through the eye and body underneath C) a yellow band. During the spawning season, D) a dark red band appears as well. KONRAD SCHMIDT

Description: The Redside Dace has a dark, well-developed lateral band that runs through the eye and is interrupted by a thicker but shorter bright red band during the spawning season. Outside of the spawning season, both sexes have light pink coloration on the lower half of the body. On either side of the two lateral bands is yellow pigmentation, while the back is olive colored.
Size: Usually to 3 inches long.
Habitat: Small lotic systems with cool, clear water and gravel substrate.

Clinostomus funduloides—Rosyside Dace

Figure 10.103. A spawning male Rosyside Dace (*Clinostomus funduloides*). NCFISHES.COM

Description: The Rosyside Dace is <u>very similar in appearance to the Redside Dace</u>. Colors in both species are brighter during spawning and in males.
Size: Usually to 3 inches long.
Habitat: Usually headwater lotic systems with gravel riffles.

Genus *Cyprinella*

Fishes of the second-largest Cyprinidae genus in North America, *Cyprinella*, are commonly known as satinfin shiners. Satinfin shiners are <u>small-bodied (less than 5 inches)</u>, and most species <u>lack barbels</u>. The genus is characterized by <u>colorful pigments in the dorsal fin</u> membranes and <u>large scales with a distinct diamond pattern and dark pigments at the edges</u>. Most *Cyprinella* species possess limited ranges in one to three states of the southeastern United States west to Texas. Widespread species are covered here.

Satinfin shiners are omnivorous and consume a diet of aquatic insects, algae, and even seeds that fall into water. Most species form schools

Cyprinella analostana—Satinfin Shiner

Figure 10.104. A male Satinfin Shiner (*Cyprinella analostana*), identified by A) milky-white fringes on the fins when spawning. NCFISHES.COM

Description: The Spotfin Shiner is colored metallic silver to blue. Spawning males exhibit a milky-white hue on fin margins. Spotfin Shiners can be easily confused with Steelcolor Shiners (*C. whipplei*), and distinguishing the two species outside of the spawning season requires counting fin rays.
Size: 1.5 to 2.75 inches long.
Habitat: Medium- to large-sized lotic systems with warm water.

Cyprinella lutrensis—Red Shiner

Figure 10.105. A male Red Shiner (*Cyprinella lutrensis*), which has red fins except for the dorsal fin.
SAM STUKEL/USFWS

Description: The Red Shiner gets its name from a bright red hue on all fins of the male *except* the dorsal fin. Some individuals may show red behind the gill and on the head as well. Scales have a blue sheen and the belly is white.
Size: 2 to 3.5 inches long.
Habitat: Low-gradient lotic systems with abundant pools. Also found in lakes and reservoirs.

Cyprinella spiloptera—Spotfin Shiner

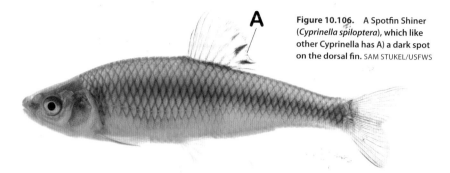

Figure 10.106. A Spotfin Shiner (*Cyprinella spiloptera*), which like other Cyprinella has A) a dark spot on the dorsal fin. SAM STUKEL/USFWS

Description: The Spotfin Shiner lacks conspicuous pigmentation, even in spawning males. Membranes in the latter half of the dorsal fin exhibit dark-colored spots, but this is also true of other *Cyprinella* species with overlapping ranges.
Size: Up to 4.75 inches long.
Habitat: Medium- to large-sized lotic systems with clear water.

Cyprinella venusta—Blacktail Shiner

Figure 10.107. A male Blacktail Shiner (*Cyprinella venusta*), identified by A) a large, black spot on the caudal fin base. JULIA WOOD

Description: The Blacktail Shiner can be easily identified using the large, black spot on the caudal fin base. Spawning males develop yellow-tinted fins.
Size: Up to 6 inches long.
Habitat: Lotic systems of all sizes, both in pools and riffles.

Cyprinella whipplei—Steelcolor Shiner

Figure 10.108.   A male Steelcolor Shiner (*Cyprinella whipplei*), identified by A) a large, rounded dorsal fin.
ZACH ALLEY

Description: Steelcolor Shiner males have <u>large, rounded dorsal fins</u>. Color is metallic silver to blue, with spawning males developing a light purple tinge and a red snout. Fins in both sexes are light yellow.
Size: Up to 5 inches long.
Habitat: Medium-sized lotic systems with warm water and mud to sand substrate.

Genus *Cyprinus*

One species of large-bodied minnows in the genus *Cyprinus*, native to Europe and central Asia, is invasive and widespread in North America: the Common Carp (*C. carpio*). The Common Carp grows very large feeding on invertebrates by sucking up sediment and filtering out prey, leaving behind trails of small holes but often damaging or removing submerged vegetation in the process. Common Carp are widely grown for human consumption in aquaculture operations worldwide.

Cyprinus carpio—Common Carp

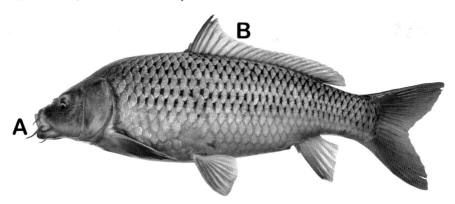

Figure 10.109. A Common Carp (*Cyprinus carpio*), identified by A) conspicuous barbels and B) a falcate dorsal fin. NCFISHES.COM

Description: The Common Carp has a stout body with large scales, a long falcate dorsal fin, conspicuous barbels, and large scales. Color ranges from brassy to steel blue or dark olive. Resembles some suckers but is distinguished by the barbels.
Size: Commonly 1 to 2 feet long and up to 40 pounds.
Habitat: Thrives in a wide range of conditions but usually aquatic ecosystems with soft substrate and slow-moving to still water.

Genus *Hybognathus*

Hybognathus species are collectively known as silvery minnows and are small- and elongate-bodied, very shimmering fishes with blunt snouts and no barbels. Males form tubercles throughout the body when spawning. Distinguishing some species, such as between the Plains Minnow (*H. placitus*) and the Western Silvery Minnow (*H. argyritis*), is extremely difficult and requires head dissections. All consume algae, detritus, and plant material.

Hybognathus hankinsoni—Brassy Minnow

Figure 10.110. A Brassy Minnow (*Hybognathus hankinsoni*), a green-gold shimmering minnow with A) a well-defined lateral dark band. KONRAD SCHMIDT

Description: The Brassy Minnow is colored shimmering gold, often tinted green. The lateral band is well developed and ranges from dark gray to dull purple.
Size: Up to 3.5 inches long.
Habitat: Small, clear headwater lotic systems.

Hybognathus nuchalis—Mississippi Silvery Minnow

Figure 10.111. A Misssissippi Silvery Minnow (*Hybognathus nuchalis*). JULIA WOOD

Description: The Mississippi Silvery Minnow is iridescent silver to gold, sometimes tinted green.
Size: Up to 7 inches long.
Habitat: Medium- to large-sized lowland lotic systems.

Genus *Hybopsis*

Minnows in the genus *Hybopsis* are called bigeye chubs thanks to dis-proportionally large eyes. Bigeye Chubs have barbels, though they may be difficult to see in the field. All species are native to the southeast-ern United States, with one species found far north in the Mississippi River. Bigeye chubs are small-bodied predators of small insect larvae and amphipods.

Hybopsis amblops—Bigeye Chub

Figure 10.112. A Bigeye Chub (*Hybopsis amblops*), which like others in the genus has A) very large eyes.
NCFISHES.COM

Description: The Bigeye Chub has large, upturned eyes, a small mouth, blunt snout, and a well-defined dark lateral band. The dorsal fins are slightly falcate.
Size: Up to 3 inches long.
Habitat: Small- to medium-sized lotic systems with clear water and abundant submerged vegetation.

Genus *Hypophthalmichthys*

Two invasive, ecologically destructive carp native to Asia in the genus *Hypophthalmichthys* are now common in North American rivers. *Hypo-phthalmichthys* carps were originally brought to the United States to control algae blooms but escaped cultivation and established popula-tions in rivers that continue to expand. Field identification is very easy. Both species grow large and have eyes positioned on the lower half of the head as adults. Unlike Common Carp (*Cyprinus carpio*), barbels are absent. *Hypophthalmichthys* carps filter-feed on plankton using gill rakers. In North American rivers, *Hypophthalmichthys* carps outcom-pete native species for food and habitat. Both species are cultivated in aquaculture for human consumption, mostly in Asia. The two invasive North American species are closely related and hybridize.

Hypophthalmichthys molitrix—Silver Carp

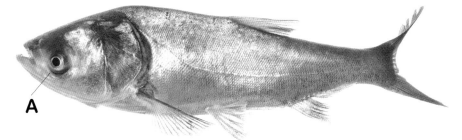

Figure 10.113. A Silver Carp (*Hypophthalmichthys molitrix*), in a genus identified by A) eyes positioned in the lower half of the head during adulthood. SAM STUKEL/USFWS

Description: The Silver Carp has a stout body with a large, conical head and is colored silver to dull dark gray, sometimes with yellow-tinted fins. Large eyes are positioned at the bottom of the head, at or below the mouth.

Size: Up to 3 inches long and over 60 pounds, though usually smaller.

Habitat: Large, slow-moving lotic systems, lakes, and reservoirs with warm water.

Remarks: The Silver Carp is now infamous for leaping into the air to escape danger, sometimes injuring boaters.

Hypophthalmichthys nobilis—Bighead Carp

Figure 10.114. A Bighead Carp (*Hypophthalmichthys nobilis*). RYAN HAGERTY/USFWS

Description: Very similar in appearance to Silver Carp (*H. molitrix*), but Bighead Carp tend to have large, faded blotches throughout the body in adulthood.

Size: Up to 4 inches long and approaching 100 pounds.

Habitat: Large lotic systems, usually in cool to cold water.

Genus *Luxilus*

Minnows in the genus *Luxilus* were once included in *Notropis* but were separated following genetic studies. Although some species look like shiners, they tend to grow a larger and deeper body. *Luxilus* minnows are commonly called highscale shiners because of their <u>tall scales</u>. All species lack barbels and are native to east of the continental divide. The two species with broad distributions are covered below.

All *Luxilus* species feed on aquatic and terrestrial insects. Several are known to leap from the water to pursue flying prey.

Luxilus chrysocephalus—Striped Shiner

Figure 10.115. A spawning male Striped Shiner (*Luxilus chrysocephalus*), identified by A) dark crescents on the scales. ZACH ALLEY

Description: The Striped Shiner has an olive-colored back and silver sides, often with <u>dark crescents on the scales</u>.
Size: Typically 2.5 to 4 inches long.
Habitat: Lotic systems of all sizes and temperatures, also lakes.

Luxilus cornutus—Common Shiner

Figure 10.116. A male Common Shiner (*Luxilus cornutus*), distinguished by A) a dark band on the back.
ZACH ALLEY

Description: The Common Shiner has a dark stripe running on the back. Otherwise, the body is olive to silver with small, dark spots. Spawning males grow tubercles.
Size: Usually to 4 inches long, but up to 6 inches, larger than most others in the genus.
Habitat: Small- to medium-sized lotic systems with cool, clear water and no submerged vegetation.

Genus *Lythrurus*

Like the genus *Luxilis*, *Lythrurus* minnow species were once considered in genus *Notropis*, and most species resemble minnows in that genus. However, genetic studies revealed that *Lythrurus* minnows, commonly called smallscale shiners, warrant a separate genus. Most of the eleven smallscale shiners possess native ranges limited to a few southeastern states. All except one is native only to the southern Mississippi River and Atlantic slope basins, while the Redfin Shiner (*L. umbratilis*) is also native to the southern Great Lakes basin.

Smallscale shiners feed on an omnivorous diet of aquatic and terrestrial insect larvae, vegetative matter, and detritus. All species form schools.

Lythrurus fasciolaris—Scarlet Shiner

Figure 10.117. A male Scarlet Shiner (*Lythrurus fasciolaris*). Both sexes have A) faint vertical bars and B) red-tinted fins. ZACH ALLEY

Description: Both sexes have <u>red-tinted fins</u> and <u>faint vertical bars</u> throughout the body, though such traits are more easily seen in males, especially when spawning. Color is otherwise silvery blue with a lighter belly.
Size: Usually to 3.5 inches long.
Habitat: Headwater to medium-sized lotic systems with clear water and limited silt.

Lythrurus umbratilis—Redfin Shiner

Figure 10.118. A male Redfin Shiner (*Lythrurus umbratilis*). Both sexes have A) a dark spot at the caudal fin base. ZACH ALLEY

Description: The Redfin Shiner has a deeper, more compressed body than other shiners. Spawning males have <u>bright red fins, a silver body, and abundant tubercles</u>. Both sexes have a dark spot at the caudal fin base.
Size: Usually to 3.5 inches long.
Habitat: Pools in lotic systems of all sizes.

Genus *Macrhybopsis*

Macrhybopsis minnows, commonly called blacktail chubs, include twelve species of medium-sized minnows with <u>prominent barbels</u> and a <u>mouth aimed downward</u>. Many species have large, slightly <u>darkened speckles and/or fine, black spots</u>. Males do not develop tubercles on the head.

Blacktail Chubs are omnivores and primarily feed on insect larvae, amphipods, and algae.

Macrhybopsis hyostoma—Shoal Chub

Figure 10.119.   A Shoal Chub (*Macrhybopsis hyostoma*). Macrhybopsis minnows have A) a downward-facing mouth, B) prominent barbels, and C) abundant, dark spots. ZACH ALLEY

Description: The Shoal Chub has a bright silver sheen, tiny black spots, and often a broad lateral band.
Size: Up to 3 inches long.
Habitat: Runs of large rivers with clean water and gravel substrate.

Macrhybopsis storeriana—Silver Chub

Figure 10.120.   A Silver Chub (*Macrhybopsis storeriana*). KONRAD SCHMIDT

Description: The Silver Chub has a greenish back, very faint lateral band, and white belly.
Size: Up to 9 inches long.
Habitat: Large lotic systems with turbid water.

Genus *Nocomis*

Fishes in the genus *Nocomis* are medium-bodied minnows collectively called chubs. *Nocomis* minnows are enormously ecologically important, as they build large mound nests out of coarse sediment in riffles. Water flowing through the nests is oxygen-rich, so many other fishes use the nests as well and are therefore dependent on *Nocomis* chubs for their own reproduction.

Three species of *Nocomis* chubs are widely distributed while four have narrow ranges in the southeastern United States. All are endemic to the Mississippi and Atlantic slope watersheds. All species have a torpedo-shaped, stout body with large scales that are absent on the head and small barbels. Males develop abundant tubercles and a hump on the head when spawning. Minnows with similar appearances have spots on the dorsal fin, but *Nocomis* species lack such coloration.

Nocomis chubs feed on a broad range of plant and animal matter, including aquatic insects, snails, crayfish, and vegetation.

Nocomis biguttatus—Hornyhead Chub

Figure 10.121.   A male Hornyhead Chub (*Nocomis biguttatus*), identified by A) abundant tubercles, B) a red spot behind the eye, and C) a broad, dark stripe. KONRAD SCHMIDT

Description: The Hornyhead Chub has a broad, dark, lateral stripe. Above the stripe scales are colored olive brown, scales below are cream colored. Spawning males have abundant tubercles. A large, bright spot appears behind the eye, colored red in males and brassy in females.

Size: Typically 6 to 9 inches long.

Habitat: Lotic systems with warm water and abundant submerged vegetation.

Nocomis leptocephalus—Bluehead Chub

Figure 10.122. A male Bluehead Chub (*Nocomis leptocephalus*), identified by A) a steel-blue head and B) a fading orange band behind the gills. NCFISHES.COM

Description: The Bluehead Chub has an olive-covered back, a faded orange band on the side, and a cream-colored belly. Fins are often tinted orange to reddish. Males develop a steel-blue head when spawning and have fewer tubercles than other *Nocomis* species.
Size: Usually 2.75 to 6 inches long.
Habitat: The Bluehead Chub resides in lotic systems further upstream than other *Nocomis* species, typically headwater streams with cold to cool and clear water.

Nocomis micropogon—River Chub

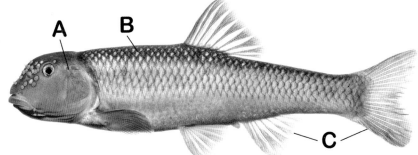

Figure 10.123. A male River Chub (*Nocomis micropogon*), characterized by A) a blue-purple head, B) a green back, and C) orange-yellow-tinted fins. NCFISHES.COM

Description: The River Chub has a green-colored back, bluish-purple head, and fins tinged orange to yellow. Spawning males have abundant tubercles.
Size: Typically 3.5 to 7 inches long.
Habitat: Medium-sized lotic systems with warm, clear water, swift currents, and abundant riffles.

Genus *Notemigonus*

Only one species is included in the genus *Notemigonus*: the Golden Shiner (*N. chrysoleucas*). The Golden Shiner is a well-known species thanks to its broad use as a bait fish. Golden Shiners school and usually feed in the water column on small aquatic insect larvae and terrestrial insects.

Notemigonus crysoleucas—Golden Shiner

Figure 10.124. A Golden Shiner (*Notemigonus crysoleucas*), identified by A) a slightly concave head and B) a falcate anal fin. NCFISHES.COM

Description: The Golden Shiner is brassy colored with slightly darker, greenish back scales. Both sexes have a falcate anal fin, and large individuals may have a slightly concave head. Barbels are absent.
Size: Typically 3 to 5 inches long.
Habitat: Medium- to large-sized, warmwater lotic systems, including blackwater.

Genus *Notropis*

With about seventy-eight species, *Notropis* is the second-largest freshwater fish genus in North America after the *Etheostoma* darters. *Notropis* species fit the archetype minnow: small and usually silvery fish that lack barbels and tend to school. However, some *Notropis* species exhibit vivid, beautiful colors when spawning. All species are native to east of the continental divide, and many have very limited ranges. Most are called shiners.

Identifying *Notropis* to species can be very difficult in species-rich areas, especially in the southeastern United States. All *Notropis* species lack barbels, <u>grow to no more than 5 inches</u>, have <u>forked caudal fins</u>, and often exhibit a <u>broad, dark lateral stripe along the body</u>. In many cases, field identification may come down to range and habitat, as characteristics distinguishing species involves counting fin rays or pharyngeal teeth.

Notropis minnows are omnivorous but prefer animal prey, which consists of very small invertebrates, terrestrial insects, and fish larvae typically taken from the water column.

Notropis atherinoides—Emerald Shiner

Figure 10.125. An Emerald Shiner (*Notropis atherinoides*). SAM STUKEL/USFWS

Description: The Emerald Shiner has a bright silver-green sheen with a faint, dark lateral band. Spawning individuals show no special colors. Forms very large schools.
Size: Usually to about 4 inches long.
Habitat: Large lotic systems and lakes, typically in the water column.

Notropis blennius—River Shiner

Figure 10.126. A River Shiner (*Notropis blennius*). KONRAD SCHMIDT

Description: The River Shiner is colored pale olive on the back and silver white on the body, with a faint lateral band separating the colors.
Size: Up to 5 inches long.
Habitat: Large lotic systems, often in turbid water.

Notropis buccatus—Silverjaw Minnow

Figure 10.127. A Silverjaw Minnow (*Notropis buccatus*), distinguished by A) large, square chambers below the eye. BRIAN ZIMMERMAN

Description: The Silverjaw Minnow is most easily distinguished by <u>large, square chambers below the eye</u>. A dark, broad stripe often occurs along the body, and scales are tinted darker above than below.
Size: Up to 3 inches long.
Habitat: Small but lowland lotic systems with warm water. Unlike many others in the genus, the Silverjaw Minnow occupies the bottom of the water column.

Notropis buchanani—Ghost Shiner

Figure 10.128. A Ghost Shiner (Notropis buchanani). ZACH ALLEY

Description: The Ghost Shiner is colored very pale silver to white and has a stouter body and more rounded snout than other *Notropis*.
Size: Up to 2.5 inches long.
Habitat: Medium- to large-sized lotic systems with slow current, typically in water less than 3 feet deep.

Notropis dorsalis—Bigmouth Shiner

Figure 10.129. A Bigmouth Shiner (*Notropis dorsalis*). ZACH ALLEY

Description: The Bigmouth Shiner has a flattened head and a relatively narrow lateral band that runs from the gill to the caudal fin.
Size: Up to 3 inches long.
Habitat: Small- to medium-sized, swiftly flowing, and shallow lotic systems.

Notropis heterodon—Blackchin Shiner

Figure 10.130. A Blackchin Shiner (*Notropis heterodon*), identified by A) a prominent lateral band that runs through the eye. KONRAD SCHMIDT

Description: The Blackchin Shiner can be distinguished from other *Notropis* by a well-defined black lateral band that runs from the snout to the caudal fin through the eye. Above the band the scales are colored yellow to olive and pale cream below.
Size: Up to 3.5 inches long.
Habitat: Cool to cold lotic systems with slow-moving flow and clean, clear water.

Notropis heterolepis—Blacknose Shiner

Figure 10.131. A Blacknose Shiner (*Notropis heterolepis*), defined by A) a well-defined lateral band with a gold stripe above. KONRAD SCHMIDT

Description: As with *N. heterodon*, the Blacknose Shiner has a <u>well-defined lateral band</u> that runs from the snout to the caudal fin through the eye, with a <u>gold stripe above</u>.
Size: Typically 2 to 3 inches long.
Habitat: Lotic systems with clear, cold waters, sandy substrate, and abundant vegetation.

Notropis hudsonius—Spottail Shiner

Figure 10.132. A Spottail Shiner (*Notropis hudsonius*), identified by A) a distinct, black spot on the caudal fin base. KONRAD SCHMIDT

Description: The Spottail Shiner has a well-defined dark spot on the caudal fin base. Scales on the upper half of the body are pale green and white on the lower half.
Size: Usually 4 to 5 inches long, occasionally to 6 inches.
Habitat: Lotic systems of all sizes and conditions. Spawns in gravel riffles.

Notropis percobromus—Carmine Shiner

Figure 10.133. A Carmine Shiner (*Notropis percobromus*), easily identified by A) an upturned mouth and B) bright red pigmentation. KONRAD SCHMIDT

Description: The Carmine Shiner has an <u>upturned mouth</u> and <u>bright red behind the gill, on the snout, and on the dorsal fin base</u>.
Size: Usually 2 to 3 inches long.
Habitat: Lotic systems with clear water and fast flows.
Remarks: Carmine and Rosyface Shiners (*N. rubellus*) were once considered the same species and look very similar.

Notropis rubellus—Rosyface Shiner

Figure 10.134. A Rosyface Shiner (*Notropis rubellus*), which develops A) a bright red face and pectoral fin base when spawning. ZACH ALLEY

Description: The Rosyface Shiner develops a <u>bright red face and fin base</u> that fades outside of the spawning season. Both sexes have a faint to well-defined lateral band with bluish-green scales above and silver to white scales below. Slenderer than others in the genus.
Size: Usually 2 to 3 inches long.
Habitat: Medium- to large-sized lotic systems with clear water and rocky substrate.

Notropis stramineus—Sand Shiner

Figure 10.135. A Sand Shiner (*Notropis stramineus*), identified by A) a downturned mouth. ZACH ALLEY

Description: The Sand Shiner has a <u>downturned mouth</u> and a lateral band that fades toward the head. Scales above the band are olive colored.
Size: No more than 3.5 inches long.
Habitat: Lotic systems with sand substrate, warm water, and slow flows.

Notropis volucellus—Mimic Shiner

Figure 10.136. A Mimic Shiner (*Notropis volucellus*). NCFISHES.COM

Description: The Mimic Shiner has a short, rounded snout and a lateral band that is well defined more toward the caudal fin.
Size: Up to 2.5 inches long.
Habitat: Pools of medium- to large-sized lotic systems with clear water and slow current.

Genus *Phenacobius*

Phenacobius minnows are commonly called suckermouth minnows because of their rounded, sucker-like mouth. Only one species possesses a large native range, and all are native to drainages east of the continental divide. Suckermouth minnows feed on very small invertebrates, especially fly larvae, in the benthic zone and water column.

Phenacobius mirabilis—Suckermouth Minnow

Figure 10.137. A Suckermouth Minnow (*Phenacobius mirabilis*), identified by A) a downward-facing, sucker-like mouth and B) a large, dark spot on the caudal fin base. KONRAD SCHMIDT

Description: The Suckermouth Minnow has a well-defined lateral band that ends in a very dark spot and a downward-facing mouth. Central Stoneroller (*Campostoma anomalum*) looks much like the Suckermouth Minnow but lacks a fleshy, sucker-like mouth.
Size: 2 to 5 inches long.
Habitat: Lotic systems with turbid water and abundant riffles.

Genus *Pimephales*

Pimephales minnows, commonly called bluntnose minnows, can be distinguished by their small, tightly clustered scales at the base of the dorsal fin and short, blunt snouts. Barbels are absent. Males form tubercles when spawning. Of the four species, three are very widely distributed and introduced beyond their native ranges thanks to their use as bait. Bluntnose minnows are omnivores, with detritus, insects, and vegetation comprising their diets.

Pimephales notatus—Bluntnose Minnow

Figure 10.138. A female Bluntnose Minnow (*Pimephales notatus*), characterized by A) a narrow dark band that ends in a caudal fin base spot. ZACH ALLEY

Description: The Bluntnose Minnow has a streamlined body and a relatively narrow, dark lateral band that ends with a dark spot at the base of the caudal fin.
Size: 1.5 to 2.5 inches long.
Habitat: A very wide range of conditions in lotic systems of all sizes.

Pimephales promelas—Fathead Minnow

Figure 10.139. A male Fathead Minnow (*Pimephales promelas*), identified by A) a faint, dusky lateral band.
KONRAD SCHMIDT

Description: The Fathead Minnow has a <u>dusky lateral band</u> and is colored olive to tan above and below. Males have particularly blunt snouts.
Size: Up to 2.5 inches long.
Habitat: Pools of small- to medium-sized, warmwater streams; also lakes and ponds.

Pimephales vigilax—Bullhead Minnow

Figure 10.140. A Bullhead Minnow (*Pimephales vigilax*), identified by dark spots on the A) dorsal fin and B) caudal fin base. ZACH ALLEY

Description: The Bullhead Minnow has a <u>faint to prominent spot on the dorsal fin and a spot near the caudal fin base</u>.
Size: Up to 3 inches long.
Habitat: Usually medium- to large-sized lotic systems.

Genus *Platygobio*

The sole species of *Platygobio*, the Flathead Chub (*P. gracilis*) is a large-bodied minnow native to the plains of the midwestern United States north to the Yukon River. The Flathead Chub is an invertebrate predator of anything it can capture in the water column, primarily aquatic and terrestrial insects.

Platygobio gracilis—Flathead Chub

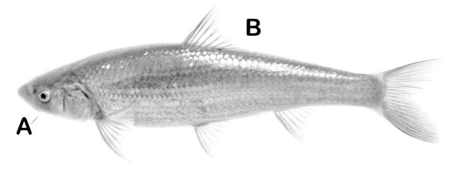

Figure 10.141. A Flathead Chub (*Platygobio gracilis*), distinguished by A) prominent barbels and B) a falcate dorsal fin. SAM STUKEL/USFWS

Description: The Flathead Chub has a large, somewhat upturned mouth on the bottom of the head, prominent barbels, and a falcate dorsal fin.
Size: Up to 12 inches long.
Habitat: Lotic systems of all sizes, but usually with sandy substrate.

Genus *Ptychocheilus*

Minnows in the genus *Ptychocheilus* are the largest native Cyprinidae species in North America, known as pikeminnow. All are torpedo-shaped, voracious predators with a <u>large, flattened head</u>, deeply forked caudal fin, and a <u>mouth lacking barbels that extends to below the eye</u>. The four *Ptychocheilus* species are native to western North America, with one species each in the Colorado, Columbia, Sacramento/San Joaquin, and coastal Oregon basins.

Pikeminnow adopt a fish diet in adulthood, which unjustly vilifies them because they consume trout and salmon. However, they are native and help ensure trout and salmon populations consist of individuals capable of escaping predators.

Ptychocheilus grandis—Sacramento Pikeminnow

Figure 10.142. A spawning Sacramento Pikeminnow (*Ptychocheilus grandis*). The genus is distinguished by A) a large, flat head and B) a mouth that extends below the eye. RENÉ REYES/US DEPARTMENT OF RECLAMATION

Description: The Sacramento Pikeminnow is typically silvery to dull green. Young have a lateral band, and spawning adults develop rose-tinted fins.
Size: Commonly 2 to 3 feet long, up to 3.75 feet.
Habitat: Large lotic systems with clear water and rocky or sandy substrate.

Genus *Rhinichthys*

The eight *Rhinichthys* minnow species, commonly called dace, represent some of the most widespread and abundant freshwater fishes in North America. All have very fine scales and a mouth that aims downward. Each species also possesses very small barbels that are hard to see without magnification. The four species not profiled here have very limited native ranges in the western United States.

Rhinichthys minnows are omnivorous and primarily feed on insect larvae and algae.

Rhinichthys atratulus—Eastern Blacknose Dace

Figure 10.143. An Eastern Blacknose Dace (*Rhinichthys atratulus*), which has A) a well-defined lateral band that runs through the eye. NCFISHES.COM

Description: The Eastern Blacknose Dace has a broad, black band that runs from the mouth to the caudal fin. Fine scales above are colored gold above the stripe and cream below. Spawning males turn bright orange.
Size: Up to 4.5 inches long, but usually about 2.5 inches.
Habitat: Headwater to medium-sized lotic systems. Often occupies the smallest lotic habitats among minnows within their range.
Remarks: Both Eastern and Western Blacknose Dace are very tolerant of pollution and can be abundant in degraded waters.

Rhinichthys cataractae—Longnose Dace

Figure 10.144.
A Longnose Dace
(*Rhinichthys cataractae*), identified by rose-colored fins and A) a long snout.
ZACH ALLEY

Description: The Longnose Dace has a snout that extends far beyond the mouth and an elongate body. Dark mottling appears throughout the body, and the fins are tinted red.
Size: 2 to 9 inches long.
Habitat: Lotic systems with swift current and cold water, often in riffles.
Remarks: The Longnose Dace possesses the widest native distribution of any Cyprinidae species, with populations found in the Arctic. Unlike most other minnows, the Longnose Dace forages primarily at night.

Rhinichthys obtusus—Western Blacknose Dace

Figure 10.145. A Western Blacknose Dace (*Rhinichthys obtusus*), which has A) a less well-defined lateral band than Eastern Blacknose Dace and B) mottled spots. ZACH ALLEY

Description: Western Blacknose Dace have a lateral stripe like Eastern Blacknose Dace but with less definition. The body is mottled with dark brown spots. Spawning males turn bright orange.
Size: Typically 2 to 4 inches long.
Habitat: Primarily headwater streams, from cool to cold water.
Remarks: Western and Eastern Blacknose Dace were considered one species until recent genetic studies showed they were distinct. Both species have similar habitat preferences.

Rhinichthys osculus—Speckled Dace

Figure 10.146. A Speckled Dace (*Rhinichthys osculus*). ROGER TABOR/USFWS

Description: The Speckled Dace is colored tan with abundant dark brown spots of various sizes throughout the body. Fins turn red in both sexes during the spawning season.
Size: Up to 4.5 inches long.
Habitat: Able to occupy diverse conditions and a wide range of water temperatures, from small springs to large rivers but usually in clear water.

Genus *Semotilus*

Although the genus *Semotilus* includes only four species of medium- to large-sized minnows, the Creek Chub (*S. atromaculatus*) represents one of the most widespread and abundant species in the family. Like fishes in the genera *Nocomis* and *Gila*, those in *Semotilus* are commonly called chubs. All species have small barbels and a dark spot at the dorsal fin base. Males form tubercles when spawning.

Semotilus chubs are omnivorous but strongly favor invertebrate prey, mostly aquatic insects and (when large enough) other fish.

Semotilus atromaculatus—Creek Chub

Figure 10.147. A male Creek Chub (*Semotilus atromaculatus*), which has A) a dark spot on the dorsal fin base. ZACH ALLEY

Description: The Creek Chub exhibits colors ranging from olive brown on the back to a purplish sheen. Spots often appear at the base of the dorsal and caudal fins, but the former fades with age. Males develop tubercles.
Size: Up to 4.5 inches long.
Habitat: Typically headwater streams, although not those with steep gradients.
Remarks: The Creek Chub tolerates very degraded conditions and can thrive in urban waters.

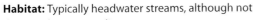
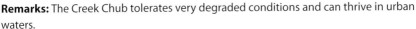

Semotilus corporalis—Fallfish

Figure 10.148. A Fallfish (*Semotilus corporalis*), identified by A) black scale edges in adulthood. ZACH ALLEY

Description: The Fallfish is shiny silver or brass colored with scales showing black edges in adulthood.
Size: The largest minnow species east of the Mississippi River. Usually 6 to 12 inches long, but up to 17 inches.
Habitat: Medium- to large-sized lotic systems with warm to cool and clear water; almost always in pools.

Fishes **249**

ATHERINOPSIDAE (SILVERSIDES)

Diversity and distribution: The silverside family Atherinopsidae includes over one hundred species, about half of which inhabit exclusively marine waters. Approximately forty-seven species migrate to or fully reside in North American freshwater ecosystems, but diversity is centered in the tropics, with only four encountered in lotic systems north of Mexico. All four northern North American freshwater silversides possess native ranges in the Mississippi and Atlantic coast drainages, although the Inland Silverside (*Menidia beryllina*) has established populations in California.

Silversides feed on plankton, larval fish, and small invertebrates from the water column, which restricts their habitat to waterbodies large enough to support such prey. Consequently, they are primarily found in larger rivers when in freshwater. All species form schools.

Ecology and life history: Silversides are small-bodied fishes with short lifespans ranging from seventeen months to a maximum of four years. They occupy low positions on aquatic food pyramids and represent important prey species for larger fish-eating predators in all environments where they are found. Silverside diets vary with age, with larval fish often consumed while young and zooplankton as adults, though this varies among species.

To spawn, silversides aggregate in the hundreds to thousands in shallow habitat with abundant submerged vegetation. Males chase females until they release eggs in batches, which are subsequently fertilized. The chase can lead to females jumping out of the water and ending up on land. Eggs affix to plant matter or substrate, and no parental care is provided to the offspring.

Identifying species: Silversides are very narrow-bodied, pale fish with a silver sheen and upturned mouth. The anal and pelvic fins are often as large as or larger than the dorsal fins and their caudal fin is moderately forked. Very few other freshwater fishes could be mistaken for silversides. A few minnow (Cyprinidae) species superficially resemble silversides, but minnows have one dorsal fin while silversides have two.

As most of the North American silverside diversity is concentrated south of the Mexican border, only four fishes in two genera occur in lotic waters of the United States. The two genera have very similar appearances but can be distinguished by patterns on the back: Those in *Menidia* display large diamond-shaped crosshatch patterns while fishes in *Labidesthes* lack such a pattern.

Genus *Labidesthes*

The genus *Labidesthes* is composed of only two fishes, one found in the American tropics and *L. sicculus*, the Brook Silverside, which is distributed throughout the central United States and southern Canada. Unlike most other silversides, fishes in this genus exclusively inhabit freshwater. The Brook Silverside feeds on meiofauna and very small insects.

Labidesthes sicculus—Brook Silverside

Figure 10.149. A Brook Silverside (*Labidesthes sicculus*), identified by A) a red snout and B) a dark, narrow band. ZACH ALLEY

Description: The Brook Silverside has a pale olive-green body. A dark, narrow band runs from the gill to the caudal fin base. Adults may have red-colored fins and snout.
Size: Usually 3 to 4 inches long.
Habitat: Warm, clear lotic systems with slow to still currents; also lakes and reservoirs.
Remarks: Recent genetic studies advocate for a separate southern species along the coast from Texas to Florida north to Arkansas, the Southern Brook Silverside (*L. vanhyningi*), which exhibits a yellow hue.

Genus *Menidia*

Two of the four *Menidia* species occur in the United States. The Inland Silverside (*M. beryllina*) inhabits streams, estuaries, and the coast from Texas to Massachusetts. The very rare Waccamaw Silverside (*M. extensa*) is found only in Lake Waccamaw in coastal North Carolina. *Menidia* silversides primarily consume zooplankton but also aquatic and terrestrial insects.

Menidia beryllina—Inland Silverside

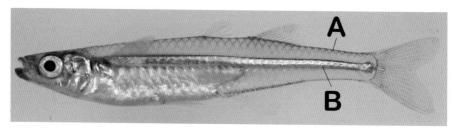

Figure 10.150. An Inland Silverside (*Menidia beryllina*), characterized by A) diamond-shaped patterns on the back and B) a narrow lateral band. ROBERT AGUILAR/SMITHSONIAN ENVIRONMENTAL RESEARCH CENTER

Description: The Inland Silverside has a pale yellow to olive-green body with diamond-shaped hatching on the back and a narrow, dark band from the gill to the caudal fin base.
Size: Usually 3 to 4 inches long.
Habitat: In the upper water column of lotic systems of various sizes; also in estuaries and coastal waters.

COTTIDAE (SCULPINS)

Diversity and distribution: The sculpin family Cottidae includes close to 300 species of both freshwater and marine fishes distributed throughout the world, though mostly in the Northern Hemisphere and within cold waters. Marine sculpin species outnumber those of freshwater. Yet in North America about 28 species occur in lotic and lentic environments, all within the genus *Cottus*. Sculpin are found in cold and cool water throughout the continent, from the northeast to the southwest and north to Alaska.

Sculpin lack swim bladders and reside in the benthic zone all their lives. As such, they are always found on the bottom of aquatic ecosystems. However, this does not much limit their geographic distribution, as sculpin can be found along with trout in the smallest reaches of mountain headwater streams.

Ecology and life history: The feeding strategy that sculpin employ involves lying still while camouflaged in the substrate and ambushing unsuspecting prey. A large mouth allows sculpin to capture many insect species, crayfish, and the occasional fish. Sculpin have sometimes unfairly held a bad reputation as consumers of prized trout and salmon eggs. However, they are rarely if ever capable of reducing fish populations in this way and sculpin are prized prey once trout grow large enough to consume them, so they are more beneficial than harmful.

Sculpin choose nest sites on the undersides of rocks, logs, or bedrock edges where the female deposits eggs while positioned upside down. The male fertilizes the eggs then guards them from predators and fans them with his caudal tail to deliver oxygen until they hatch.

Identifying species: Distinguishing sculpin of *Cottus* from other fishes is very easy. They have large eyes; a very large, upturned mouth that suggests they are frowning; relatively large pectoral fins; brown saddles and mottling; two dorsal fins; and a body compressed top to bottom.

However, identifying freshwater sculpin to species challenges even the most experienced ichthyologist. Traits required to distinguish species include the number of rays in the pelvic and pectoral fins, spacing of pores under the chin, and the presence of a tooth patch, all characteristics difficult to deduce in the field. However, many species possess very limited ranges and one can often identify species by locality. Species outlined below are widespread and common within their ranges.

Genus *Cottus*

All North American freshwater sculpin species are in the *Cottus* genus. Few grow to more than 6 inches (often much smaller), and all exhibit dark brown mottling patterns suitable for camouflage. *Cottus* sculpins feed on any small invertebrate or fish egg that can be captured, with aquatic insect larvae comprising most prey. Larger individuals of some species shift to a diet of small fish.

Cottus asper—Prickly Sculpin

Figure 10.151. A Prickly Sculpin (*Cottus asper*). ROGER TABOR/USFWS

Description: A sculpin with four to five broad, dark saddles and reddish-brown to light brown body. The first dorsal fin often features a large spot and may develop an orange band during the spawning season.
Size: Typically to 4 inches long, rarely to 6 inches.
Habitat: From small, cold rivers to estuaries and the open ocean, but always in waters with limited to no pollution.

Cottus bairdii—Mottled Sculpin

Figure 10.152. A Mottled Sculpin (*Cottus bairdii*), which exhibits A) three broad, dark saddles on the back.
NCFISHES.COM

Description: A common and widespread sculpin with three broad, dark saddles behind the first dorsal fin.
Size: 3 to 4 inches long.
Habitat: Cold, clear waters in primarily headwater streams but also larger lotic systems and lakes.

Cottus cognatus—Slimy Sculpin

Figure 10.153. A Slimy Sculpin (*Cottus cognatus*). ROGER TABOR/USFWS

Description: The Slimy Sculpin has dark and light blotches on the body toward the caudal fin. They typically lack saddles, or if present they are poorly defined.
Size: In lotic systems, usually 2 to 3 inches long, sometimes over 4 inches.
Habitat: Found in cold streams and lakes north to the high Arctic. Individuals may move to depths exceeding 300 feet in the Great Lakes.

Cottus gulosus—Riffle Sculpin

Figure 10.154. A Riffle Sculpin (*Cottus gulosus*). ROGER TABOR/USFWS

Description: A sculpin with mottling but <u>no well-defined saddles</u>.
Size: Rarely above 4 inches long.
Habitat: Headwater streams with cold water and rocky substrate.

Cottus rhotheus—Torrent Sculpin

Figure 10.155. A Torrent Sculpin (*Cottus rhotheus*), identified by A) two forward-slanted dark bars under the second dorsal fin. Roger Tabor/USFWS

Description: The Torrent Sculpin often shows <u>two forward-slanted dark bands under the second dorsal fin</u>. Mottling on the caudal and dorsal fins may form stripes.
Size: Up to 3.5 inches long.
Habitat: Cold, mountainous headwater streams.

SCIAENIDAE (DRUMS)

Diversity and distribution: The drum and croaker family Sciaenidae consists of about 300 species, almost all of which are exclusively marine fishes distributed throughout the world. The only true freshwater North American species in the Sciaenidae is *Aplodinotus grunniens*, the Freshwater Drum, a species that possesses a distribution with an impressive latitudinal range, from the upper Great Lakes drainage in the north as far south as Guatemala.

Ecology and life history: The Freshwater Drum primarily consumes aquatic insects, clams and mussels, and occasionally other fish (especially Clupeidae species). Prey are actively sought after by flushing organisms from the benthic zone using the snout, almost exclusively during the night.

The Freshwater Drum reproduces by broadcast spawning, releasing gametes into the water column that float up near the water surface where they are carried in the current for up to four days until hatching. After another three days, young attain enough strength to swim into deeper water. The high exposure of eggs and larval fish mean that young Freshwater Drum fall prey to many predators in the water column.

Identifying species: The Freshwater Drum is most distinguished by its deep body shape, which appears almost triangular from the side. The head slopes strongly to the first dorsal fin then moderately to the caudal fin.

Genus *Aplodinotus*

The genus *Aplodinotus* is composed of just one species, the Freshwater Drum (*A. grunniens*), which is endemic to the Mississippi and Great Lakes drainages of North America. Drums and croakers get their name from the noise made by compressing their swim bladder when taken out of water. The American Drum primarily consumes aquatic insects; larger individuals also consume fish.

Aplodinotus grunniens—Freshwater Drum

Figure 10.156. A Freshwater Drum (*Aplodinotus grunniens*), identified by A) a tall first and B) long, rounded second dorsal fin. SAM STUKEL/USFWS

Description: A large-scaled, silver- to dull gold-colored fish with a <u>tall first dorsal fin and long, rounded second dorsal fin</u>.
Size: Commonly 12 to 20 inches long, up to 28 inches and over 5 pounds.
Habitat: Medium- to large-sized rivers and occasionally shallow lakes, with turbid water preferred over clear water.

PERCIDAE (PERCHES AND DARTERS)

Diversity and distribution: Percidae is a family of about 200 species entirely of the Northern Hemisphere. Percidae biodiversity is centered in North America, but some species are endemic to Europe and Asia. Large-bodied and widely distributed perches targeted by anglers, including the Yellow Perch, Sauger, and Walleye, are familiar species. However, most Percidae species are small-bodied, often very colorful fishes known commonly as darters.

Perches and darters occupy a very diverse range of aquatic habitats in North America, from small, headwater streams to large rivers and lakes. Most darter species occur in small- to medium-sized lotic systems, and a majority possess extremely restricted native ranges. A sizable number of darters are endemic to single states and/or small watersheds. Although many large-bodied perches and a few darters have been introduced to western North American waters, only one Percidae species (the Mexican Darter, *Etheostoma pottsii*) is native west of the continental divide.

Ecology and life history: Generalizing anything about Percidae fishes is difficult due to the exceptionally high family biodiversity. However, all perches and darters are primarily invertebrate predators, while the largest species consume fishes as adults.

Reproductive strategies vary significantly within the family. Large-bodied Percidae are broadcast spawners that release very large numbers of eggs (in some cases over 500,000) across the benthic zone and offer no further parental care. Most darters bury fertilized eggs in benthic substrate, also offering no further care. A minority of darters excavate moderate nests and defend them from potential predators after depositing fertilized eggs.

A sizable number of darters are considered at risk of extinction, in no small part due to very limited native ranges. The US government lists twenty-seven darter species as threatened or endangered under the Endangered Species Act. Fortunately, full extinctions of darters have so far proven rare: Only one, the Maryland Darter (*Etheostoma sellare*) has gone extinct.

Identifying species: Distinguishing Percidae fishes from other families is relatively easy. Most Percidae fishes have two distinctly separated dorsal fins, a mostly torpedo-shaped body, and fine- to medium-sized scales, and exhibit complex colors and patterns.

Despite the large number of darters, identifying Percidae fishes to genus is straightforward using traits that can be observed in the field. Body size, shape, and color can usually quickly identify a species to genus, especially if the individual is an adult. Within the genus *Etheostoma*, geographic locale helps identify species.

Genus (# of North American species north of Mexico)	Traits, habitats, and/or typical size (*genus not covered further).
Ammocrypta (6)	Slender, elongate, and small darters with a translucent body. Sand-bottomed lotic systems. Up to 2.5 inches.
*Crystallaria** (2)	Medium-sized darters up to 5 inches with similar appearance to Ammocrypta. Now-rare populations of the Crystal Darter *A. asprella* persist in medium-sized rivers with clean, clear water. The Diamond Darter *A. cincotta* is restricted to the Elk River of West Virginia.
Etheostoma (138)	Mostly small-bodied darters, usually with bright colors and/or complex patterns.
Perca (1)	Sole species in the genus is the Yellow Perch. Bright gold to yellow with green vertical bands. Large rivers and lakes. Commonly grows to 7 to 10 inches.
Percina (44)	Small- to medium-sized, elongate darters often with conspicuous, broad, dark vertical bands along the body. Some species resemble those in Etheostoma.
Sander (2)	Medium to large rivers and lakes. Both species grow large, up to 42 inches.

Genus *Ammocrypta*

Darters in the genus *Ammocrypta* are collectively referred to as sand darters. All species are small, slender darters with a translucent body. Sand darters bury their body in benthic-zone sand and ambush invertebrate prey. The two darters in the genus *Crystallaria* are like those of *Ammocrypta* in appearance and behavior. Sand darters primarily consume aquatic fly larvae and aquatic worms, as well as small mayfly nymphs.

Ammocrypta clara—Western Sand Darter

Figure 10.157. A Western Sand Darter (*Ammocrypta clara*), identified by A) faint saddles on the back and B) eight to twelve blotches on the side. KONRAD SCHMIDT

Description: A very slender darter that is nearly transparent except for <u>faint, dark saddles along the back and eight to twelve blotches along the sides</u>.
Size: Usually 1.5 to 2.5 inches long.
Habitat: Large- to medium-sized, clear lotic systems with sandy substrate.
Remarks: The Eastern Sand Darter (*Ammocrypta pellucida*) is almost identical in appearance to the Western Sand Darter except with darker saddles and blotches. The two were previously considered the same species.

Genus *Etheostoma*

With over 130 North American species north of the Mexican border, the genus *Etheostoma* is by far the most biodiverse genus of fishes in the continent. All are small-bodied invertebrate predators that lack swim bladders and primarily inhabit the benthic zone. During the spawning season the males of most species develop very bright colors that rival those of tropical coral reef fishes.

Comprehensively covering *Etheostoma* darters is far beyond the scope of this book. A majority possess very limited native ranges and would not be encountered unless specifically sought. *Etheostoma* diversity is concentrated in the Ozark and especially southern Appalachian Mountains. The 12 species outlined here possess relatively broad native ranges. For a full treatment of all darters, see *The American Darters* by Robert Kuehne and Roger Barbour. Snorkeling is an excellent way to observe darters.

Etheostoma darters consume a diet of small-bodied invertebrates, especially small fly larvae, mayfly nymphs, and amphipods.

Etheostoma blennioides—Greenside Darter

Figure 10.158. A male Greenside Darter (*Etheostoma blennioides*), identified by A) an orange stripe on the first dorsal fin and B) green bars toward the caudal fin. ZACH ALLEY

Description: Spawning males have bright green-colored bars toward the back of their body; face, first dorsal fin, and anal fin are also colored green with an orange stripe on the first dorsal fin. Vertical bands remain present in males outside of spawning season but are less brightly colored. Females are pale brown with U- or W-shaped dark blotches along the body.

Size: Usually to 3 inches long.

Habitat: Lotic systems with swift current, clear water, and gravel to boulder substrate.

Etheostoma caeruleum—Rainbow Darter

Figure 10.159. Male (top) and female (bottom) Rainbow Darters (*Etheostoma caeruleum*). Males have A) orange-red second dorsal and caudal fins with B) blue-green bars on the body toward the caudal fin. Females have C) dark saddles in front of each dorsal fin. ZACH ALLEY

Description: Males have striking colors when spawning, with blue-green stripes along the body, anal and first dorsal fins also colored blue green, and orange to red on the second dorsal fin, caudal fin, and face. These colors fade somewhat outside of spawning. Females are tan with dark mottling throughout the body, often with dark saddles in front of both dorsal fins.
Size: Usually 2 inches long, but up to 3 inches.
Habitat: Small- to medium-sized lotic systems with cool, clear water and sand to rocky substrate.

Etheostoma camurum—Bluebreast Darter

Figure 10.160. A male Bluebreast Darter (*Etheostoma camurum*), identified by A) abundant red spots when spawning. ZACH ALLEY

Description: An olive to dark yellow darter with scattered red spots. Males turn dark blue and develop abundant red spots when spawning.
Size: Up to 3 inches long.
Habitat: Medium- to large-sized lotic systems with fast-flowing water and coarse substrate.

Etheostoma exile—Iowa Darter

Figure 10.161. A male Iowa Darter (*Etheostoma exile*), identified by A) a red and blue first dorsal fin when spawning, B) a dark stripe below the eye, and C) fine spots on the caudal fin. ZACH ALLEY

Description: An olive to brown darter with six to nine dark saddles on the back and a <u>dark stripe below the eye</u>. In males, saddles turn blue green during the spawning season and the <u>first dorsal fin turns bright blue with a red stripe</u>; blue stripes and red squares also appear on the body. Caudal and pectoral fins often show fine spots.

Size: Up to 2.8 inches long.
Habitat: Slow-moving lotic systems, lakes, and ponds with abundant submerged vegetation.

Etheostoma flabellare—Fantail Darter

Figure 10.162. A Fantail Darter (*Etheostoma flabellare*), identified by A) a short snout, B) the second dorsal fin taller than the first, and C) spots or stripes on the caudal fin. ZACH ALLEY

Description: A darter with <u>the first dorsal fin considerably shorter than the second</u> and a <u>short snout</u>. Both sexes are drab olive to brown with dark bars or mottling on the body; the caudal fin is considerably spotted or striped. Males do not develop bright colors when spawning.

Size: 1.5 to 2.5 inches long.
Habitat: Small- to medium-sized lotic systems with cool to warm water and gravel to sand substrate and abundant riffles.

Etheostoma histrio—Harlequin Darter

Figure 10.163. A Harlequin Darter (*Etheostoma histrio*), identified by A) banding through and below the eye, B) orange-yellow spots, and C) dark spots on the caudal, second dorsal, and pectoral fins. BRIAN ZIMMERMAN

Description: The Harlequin Darter is darkly colored with pale yellow-orange spots and banding through and below the eye. Caudal, pectoral, and second dorsal fins have dark spots. Spawning males become colored bright green with a red stripe on the first dorsal fin.
Size: Up to 2.5 inches long.
Habitat: Larger lotic systems with sandy substrate.

Etheostoma microperca—Least Darter

Figure 10.164. A male Least Darter (*Etheostoma microperca*), which develops orange A) on the first dorsal fin and B) the anal and pelvic fins. KONRAD SCHMIDT

Description: The Least Darter is cream colored with an olive-green back and speckles along the body. Spawning males develop an orange band on the first dorsal fin and orange anal and pelvic fins.
Size: One of the smallest darters. Usually to 1.5 inches long.
Habitat: Clear lotic habitat and lakes with abundant submerged vegetation.

Etheostoma nigrum—Johnny Darter

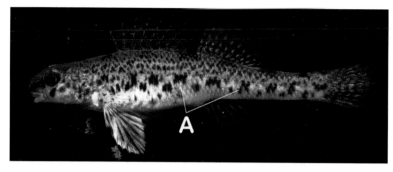

Figure 10.165. A Johnny Darter (*Etheostoma nigrum*), identified by A) M- and W-shaped spots. ZACH ALLEY

Description: The Johnny Darter is pale yellow colored with a row of M- and W-shaped dark brown spots throughout the the body. Males turn dark brown to black during the spawning season.
Size: Commonly 1.5 to 2 inches long.
Habitat: Pools of warm lotic systems.
Remarks: The Tessellated (*Etheostoma olmstedi*) and Johnny Darters were once considered the same species and are very similar in appearance. Genetic studies show that they are distinct and reproductively isolated.

Etheostoma spectabile—Orangethroat Darter

Figure 10.166. A male Orangethroat Darter (*Etheostoma spectabile*), identified by A) striped orange and blue dorsal fins, B) orange bars that becomes less defined toward the head, and C) a blue anal fin. ZACH ALLEY

Description: Both sexes of the Orangethroat Darter are pale yellow with seven to nine poorly defined dark bars on the body and a similar number of back saddles; often the bars transition to spots toward the head. Spawning males develop orange and blue dorsal fins and a bright blue anal fin.
Size: Up to 2.3 inches long.
Habitat: Small- to medium-sized lotic systems with riffles and undercut banks.

Etheostoma tippecanoe—Tippecanoe Darter

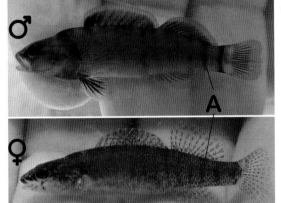

Figure 10.167. Male (above) and female (below) Tippecanoe Darters (*Etheostoma tippecanoe*). The tiny darter has A) bars that fade toward the head in both sexes. ZACH ALLEY

Description: Both sexes of the Tippecanoe Darter are orange with a dark head, a dark band at the base of the caudal fin, and <u>very faint bands that become more developed toward the caudal fin</u>. <u>Male fins become bright orange</u> when spawning.
Size: One of the smallest darters. Usually 1 to 1.5 inches long, rarely to 2 inches.
Habitat: Small- to medium-sized, warm lotic systems with gravel or sandy riffles.

Etheostoma variatum—Variegate Darter

Figure 10.168. A male Variegate Darter (*Etheostoma variatum*), identified by A) a blue and red stripe on the first dorsal fin and B) four to six dark saddles on the back. ZACH ALLEY

Description: Both sexes of the Variegate Darter have <u>four to six dark saddles on the back</u>. Spawning males have a <u>blue and red stripe on the first dorsal fin</u>, orange vertical bands, and red spots on the second dorsal fin.
Size: Up to 4.5 inches long.
Habitat: Riffles with coarse substrate in small- to medium-sized lotic systems.

Etheostoma zonale—Banded Darter

Figure 10.169. A male Banded Darter (*Etheostoma zonale*), identified by A) an orange stripe on the first dorsal fin and B) green bars or Vs on the body. ZACH ALLEY

Description: Both sexes of the Banded Darter are pale yellow with <u>abundant prominent, dark green bands or broad, V-shaped mottling</u>, sometimes with a fainter lateral band. Males develop a turquoise-green chin, anal and pelvic fins, and lower bars when spawning plus a <u>bright red stripe at the base of the first dorsal fin</u>.
Size: Up to 3 inches long.
Habitat: Lotic systems with warm water, rocky substrate, and abundant riffles.

Genus *Perca*

Only one species is included in the genus *Perca*: the Yellow Perch, a widely distributed fish prized by anglers due to its culinary value. The Yellow Perch consumes small invertebrates and zooplankton when young, transitioning to fish in adulthood.

Perca flavescens—Yellow Perch

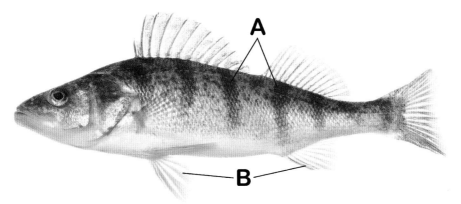

Figure 10.170. A Yellow Perch (*Perca flavescens*), identified by A) five to eight broad, green, vertical bands and B) lower fins tinted red. SAM STUKEL/USFWS

Description: The Yellow Perch is colored yellow with five to eight broad, green, vertical bands from the head to the caudal fin. Lower body fins are tinted red.
Size: Usually 4 to 9 inches long, rarely up to 14 inches.
Habitat: The Yellow Perch is more associated with lakes than lotic habitat, though they also occur in large rivers and pools of smaller lotic systems.
Remarks: Yellow Perch have been introduced far beyond their native range to support recreational fisheries, including in many western rivers and lakes.

Genus *Percina*

The diverse genus *Percina* is composed of mostly medium-sized darters called logperch. Most *Percina* species exhibit broad, dark bands running along the length of the body. The best way to identify a *Percina* species is by a row of enlarged scales running along the bottom of the belly, the number of which varies among species and sexes. However, this anatomical attribute can be difficult to spot on live specimens in the field. Logperch consume invertebrates, including fly larvae, mayfly nymphs, leeches, snails, and amphipods.

Percina caprodes—Common Logperch

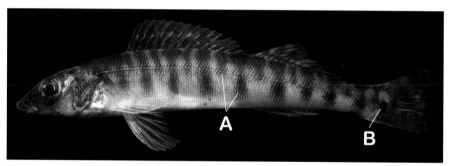

Figure 10.171. A Common Logperch (*Percina caprodes*), which has A) vertical bars with alternating lengths and B) a dark spot on the caudal fin base. ZACH ALLEY

Description: The Common Logperch has a pointed snout, <u>enough vertical bars to give a zebra-like appearance</u>, and a large, conspicuous blotch at the caudal fin base. The <u>bars alternate in length</u>.
Size: Commonly 5 to 7 inches long.
Habitat: Typically riffles of small- to medium-sized, shallow lotic systems with clear water, but also found in lakes and larger rivers.

Percina copelandi—Channel Darter

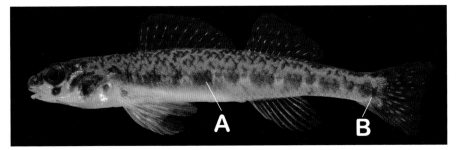

Figure 10.172. The Channel Darter (*Percina copelandi*), identified by A) ten to fourteen dark blotches and B) a dark spot on the caudal fin base. BRIAN ZIMMERMAN

Description: The Channel Darter has a blunt snout, <u>a dark spot on the caudal fin base</u>, and a <u>row of ten to fourteen dark blotches running along the body</u>. Color is pale brown with hints of blue-green iridescence.
Size: Rarely beyond 1.5 to 2 inches long.
Habitat: Medium- to large-sized, warm lotic systems with clear water and sandy substrate.

Percina evides—Gilt Darter

Figure 10.173. A male Gilt Darter (*Percina evides*), identified by A) a bright orange dorsal fin and B) five to eight green-brown, faded blotches. NCFISHES.COM

Description: The Gilt Darter has <u>five to eight large, dark green-brown blotches on the body</u> that merge with saddles on the back. Male spawning colors often include <u>very bright orange on the belly, dorsal fin, and cheek</u>.
Size: About 2 to 3 inches long.
Habitat: Clear-running lotic systems with abundant riffles.

Percina macrolepida—Bigscale Logperch

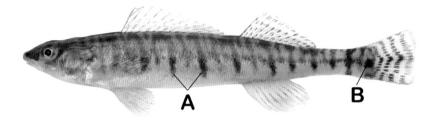

Figure 10.174. A Bigscale Logperch (*Percina macrolepida*), identified by A) fourteen to twenty-two vertical bars and B) a dark spot on the caudal fin base. RENÉ REYES/US DEPARTMENT OF RECLAMATION

Description: The Bigscale Logperch is pale olive colored with <u>fourteen to twenty-two darker vertical bars, all about the same length</u>. The caudal fin base shows a black spot. Similar in appearance to *P. caprodes* but with a blunter snout and vertical bars all the same length.
Size: Up to 3.5 inches long.
Habitat: Small- to medium-sized lotic systems with gravel to sandy substrate.
Remarks: The Bigscale Logperch is one of the few darter species that has been introduced west of the continental divide, where viable populations are found in the Sacramento/San Joaquin drainage of California.

Percina maculata—Blackside Darter

Figure 10.175. The Blackside Darter (*Percina maculata*) has A) a dark bar running through five to eight blotches, B) mottling on the back, C) a stripe below the eye, and D) a cream-colored belly. KONRAD SCHMIDT

Description: The Blackside Darter gets its name from a <u>prominent dark bar running the length of the body contiguous with five to eight large blotches of the same color</u>. Color is <u>cream below</u> the bar and <u>mottled brown above</u>. A <u>narrow vertical stripe is below the eye</u>.
Size: 1.5 to 2.8 inches long.
Habitat: Lotic systems of variable size and temperature but usually in relatively pristine conditions. Primarily inhabits riffles.

Percina peltata—Shield Darter

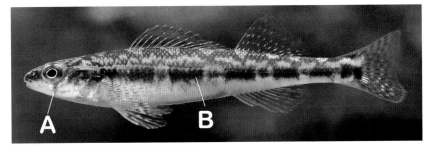

Figure 10.176. The Shield Darter (*Percina peltata*), identified by A) a dark stripe below the eye and B) rectangular brown blotches along the body. CHRIS CRIPPEN

Description: The Shield Darter exhibits <u>rectangular, dark brown blotches along the body</u>, otherwise colored pale olive to gold. Usually with a <u>dark stripe below the eye</u>.

Size: 1.5 to 2.8 inches long.
Habitat: Lowland lotic systems with warm water and sandy to gravel substrate.

Percina phoxocephala—Slenderhead Darter

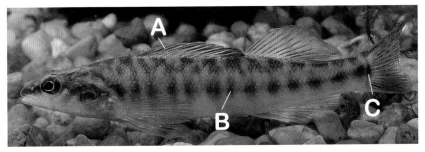

Figure 10.177. A Slenderhead Darter (*Percina phoxocephala*), identified by A) an orange band on the first dorsal fin, B) faded rectangular blotches, and C) a dark spot on the caudal fin base. KONRAD SCHMIDT

Description: A relatively elongate *Percina* species with a moderately pointed snout, <u>faded rectangular blotches along the body</u>, and a <u>dark spot at the caudal fin base</u>. Color is pale yellow with an <u>orange band on the first dorsal fin</u>.

Size: Up to 3.8 inches long.
Habitat: Lotic systems with gravel substrate and free of heavy silt. Sometimes found in high abundance below dams.

Percina sciera—Dusky Darter

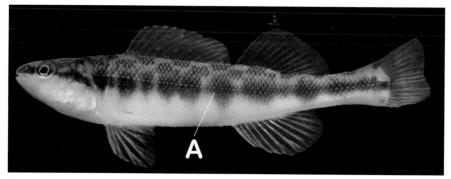

Figure 10.178. A Dusky Darter (*Percina sciera*), identified by lack of a stripe below the eye and A) six to ten dark blotches with a bar running through them. BRIAN ZIMMERMAN

Description: The Dusky Darter has six to ten large, dark blotches running the length of the body, often (but not always) with a dark bar running through them. Similar appearance to *P. peltata* but lacks the stripe below the eye.

Size: 3 to 5 inches long.

Habitat: Medium- to large-sized lotic systems with clear water. Adults are often found in snags of woody debris, juveniles along pool margins.

Percina shumardi—River Darter

Figure 10.179. A River Darter (*Percina shumardi*) has A) a well-developed stripe below the eye and B) four to nine faded vertical blotches. KONRAD SCHMIDT

Description: The River Darter is olive to yellow colored with four to nine very faded vertical blotches along the body and a prominent stripe below the eye.

Size: Usually 1.5 to 2 inches long, but up to nearly 3.5 inches.

Habitat: Fast-moving riffles with boulders in large lotic systems.

Genus *Sander*

The two fishes in the genus *Sander* are by far the largest in the Percidae family. Both typically inhabit larger rivers and lakes and are targeted by anglers. Unlike most other Percidae fishes, both *Sander* species consume fish in adulthood and are active nocturnally. Young *Sander* perch consume zooplankton and insects from the water column.

Sander canadensis—Sauger

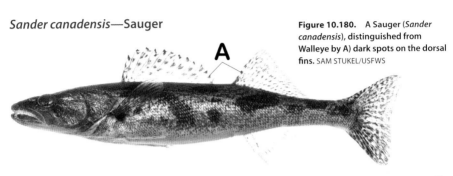

Figure 10.180. A Sauger (*Sander canadensis*), distinguished from Walleye by A) dark spots on the dorsal fins. SAM STUKEL/USFWS

Description: The Sauger is colored dark yellow to olive brown and exhibits dark saddles or mottling with a white belly. Can be distinguished from Walleye by black spots on the dorsal fins and more consistently featuring dark saddles.
Size: Usually 10 to 13 inches long, but up to 30 inches.
Habitat: Large rivers and lakes with turbid water.

Sander vitreus—Walleye

Figure 10.181. A Walleye (*Sander vitreus*). SAM STUKEL/USFWS

Description: A large perch with an olive-green to gold body and dark green to brown saddles or mottling. Walleye eyes appear cloudy white due to crystalline compounds in the retina that improve sight in dark water. Distinguishable from Sauger by a lack of black spots on the dorsal fin.
Size: The largest fish in the Percidae family. Can grow up to 42 inches and weigh over 20 pounds, but more commonly range 24 to 36 inches.
Habitat: Deep waters of large rivers, also lakes.
Remarks: The Walleye has been widely introduced beyond its range to support recreational or commercial fisheries. In the Great Lakes, commercial Walleye fisheries exist in Canadian waters.

MORONIDAE (STRIPED BASSES)

Diversity and distribution: The family Moronidae includes just six species worldwide: two in Europe and North Africa and four in North America. All four North American species are in the genus *Morone* and inhabit freshwater, typically large rivers or lotic systems with connectivity to the coasts or lakes. Each has been widely introduced outside their native ranges.

Ecology and life history: Striped basses form schools to forage in the water columns of large rivers, lakes, or estuaries. All are predators of very diverse prey, usually taken from the water column, from squid and shrimp to many species of fish.

Morone fishes are broadcast spawners that aggregate in large numbers, with some species traveling to river spawning grounds from estuaries. Females release eggs into the water column that can number in the millions released per individual. Fertilized eggs are carried by river currents downstream to rearing habitat, often estuaries or lakes.

All four *Morone* species are targeted by anglers, and the Striped Bass (*M. saxatilis*) is particularly prized for its large size, fight, and culinary value.

Identifying species: Striped basses possess two dorsal fins that are narrowly connected or very slightly separated and color patterns consisting of long, lateral stripes. Both traits separate striped basses from species in the sunfish (Centrarchidae) family. Striped basses hybridize, which can make field identification difficult where more than one species occupy the same water body.

Genus *Morone*

The four North American *Morone* species can be distinguished from one another using the shape of the dorsal fin, striping patterns, body color, and length of the first spine of the dorsal fin using the outline below.

Species	Traits
M. americana	Dorsal fins narrowly connected by ray membrane, deep body, stripes absent. Most likely in lotic systems when spawning.
M. chrysops	Dorsal fins entirely separated, deep body, well-defined stripes near the back
M. mississippiensis	Dorsal fins entirely separated, less streamlined body than M. saxatilis, body colored yellow, well-defined stripes with more than one reaching the caudal fin
M. saxatilis	Dorsal fins entirely separated, streamlined body, very well defined stripes with more than one reaching the caudal fin

Morone fishes rear on zooplankton caught in the water column then transition to a diet of primarily fish as adults. Common prey species include darters, minnows, smelts, anchovy, silversides, and herrings.

Morone americana—White Perch

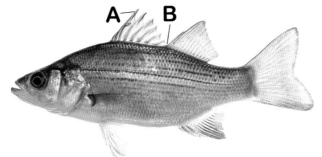

Figure 10.182. A White Perch (*Morone americana*), identified by A) first dorsal fin rays that are longer than those on the second dorsal fin and B) narrowly separated dorsal fins. NCFISHES.COM

Description: The first dorsal fin rays in White Perch are relatively longer than those on the second dorsal fin and the two are narrowly separated. Stripes are absent and the body is deep.
Size: The smallest *Morone* species. Typically 5 to 9 inches long, but can exceed 12 inches.
Habitat: Most often associated with estuaries and river mouths; moves into lotic systems to spawn. Widely introduced to reservoirs.

Morone chrysops—White Bass

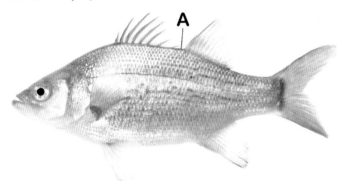

Figure 10.183. A White Bass (*Morone chrysops*), identified by A) separated dorsal fins. SAM STUKEL/ USFWS

Description: The White Bass has a deep body and stripes toward the back. The two dorsal fins are separated.
Size: Usually 8 to 12 inches long, rarely to 18 inches.
Habitat: Open, clear water in lotic systems, lakes, or reservoirs.

Morone mississippiensis—Yellow Bass

Figure 10.184. A Yellow Bass (*Morone mississippiensis*), identified by A) well-defined stripes and B) a yellow hue. ZACH ALLEY

Description: The Yellow Bass is distinguishable from other *Morone* species by its yellow body color and well-defined brown or black stripes.

Size: Up to 18 inches long, but usually smaller.

Habitat: Slow-moving, clear water with little vegetation. Often in pools of large lotic systems; also lakes and reservoirs.

Morone saxatilis—Striped Bass

Figure 10.185. A Striped Bass (*Morone saxatilis*), the largest Morone species with A) well-defined stripes that reach the caudal fin. NCFISHES.COM

Description: This largest and most streamlined *Morone* species has very well defined stripes, many of which continue into the caudal fin.

Size: Adults 18 to 36 inches long are common, but can be up to 55 inches and over 50 pounds.

Habitat: Cool to warm lotic systems with deep, clear water.

Remarks: Anglers go to great lengths to target striped bass, including hiring charter boats. Popular destinations include the Chesapeake and San Francisco Bays. In the latter, Striped Bass are nonnative and voraciously consume young salmon as they migrate to the ocean. Commercial fisheries also exist for Striped Bass.

CENTRARCHIDAE (SUNFISHES)

Diversity and distribution: The family Centrarchidae includes about thirty-eight species, all native only to North America. The center of sunfish biodiversity is the southeastern United States, and all species except one, the Sacramento Perch (*Archoplites interruptus*), possess native ranges east of the continental divide. The most recognizable species are those targeted by anglers, such as the Largemouth and Smallmouth Basses, which have been widely introduced around the world and can cause ecological damage where they are not native. Yet most sunfish are lesser-known, smaller-bodied species that often have bright, iridescent colors and beautiful patterns.

Sunfishes exclusively inhabit freshwater. Ideal habitat for most sunfish consists of warmwater lotic systems with abundant pool habitat, though many thrive in lakes, ponds, wetlands, and reservoirs.

Ecology and life history: All sunfishes are predators specializing on aquatic invertebrates such as insects, small-bodied crustaceans, zooplankton, and terrestrial insects. Larger species like bass feed on fish and frogs.

Male sunfishes excavate nests in the benthic zone by forming a circular cavity. Such nests are often found in aggregate, although only one male is associated with each nest. Sunfishes are sexually dimorphic, with males developing very bright colors during the spawning season. However, some males adapt an alternative breeding strategy and display a female-like appearance that gives them access to nests and allows them to fertilize females alongside the unsuspecting males that built the nest. Males continue to guard the nest after eggs are fertilized. Some defend young from predators after they hatch.

Identifying species: Most Centrarchidae species are round- to oval-shaped and flattened side to side, with large, sharp rays on the first of two dorsal fins and the anal fin. The two dorsal fins are broadly connected, in some cases appearing as one contiguous fin.

The sunfish family consists of seven genera with considerably varying body shapes, typical colors and patterns, and characteristic habitat. Genera can be distinguished by body shape and size, number of anal fin spines, and caudal fin shape.

Genus (# of North American species)	Body shape and size	Anal fin spines	Other distinguishing traits
Acantharchus (1)	Small-bodied and elongate to oval, compressed side to side.	5 to 7	Exhibits green to brown mottling that usually forms a lateral stripe pattern on body.
Ambloplites (4)	Oval to elongate, only moderately compressed side to side.	5 to 7	Colored drab shades of green but three species with bright red eyes.
Archoplites* (1)	Oval to elongate, compressed side to side with slightly concave head.	5 to 7	Native only to California and endangered. Light silver body with dark, irregular blotches.
Centrarchus (1)	Compressed side to side, with oval profile and slightly concave head.	5 to 7	Always with stripe below eye and young with dark spot on base of second dorsal fin. Colored silver green.
Enneacanthus (4)	Oval to round and very compressed side to side. Very small sunfishes.	2 to 3	Often exhibits bright, iridescent blue spots throughout body and fins.
Lepomis (12)	Highly compressed side to side, with oval to round profile. Medium to large species.	2 to 3	Often with bright colors and complex patterns.
Mictropterus (13)	Elongate and less compressed side to side. The largest fishes in family.	2 to 3	Usually colored shades of drab, dark green. Very large mouth.
Pomoxis (2)	Oval to elongate and compressed side to side, often with concave head.	5 to 7	Mottled shades of gray throughout body.

*not covered in detail further.

Genus *Acantharchus*

The sole member of the *Acantharchus* genus is *A. pomotis*, the Mud Sunfish. True to its namesake, the Mud Sunfish occupies swampy, blackwater habitat and feeds on crayfish, amphipods, and aquatic insects. Larger adults consume fish.

Acantharchus pomotis—Mud Sunfish

Figure 10.186. The Mud Sunfish (*Acantharchus pomotis*), identified by A) loosely defined, yellow lateral stripes.
NCFISHES.COM

Description: The Mud Sunfish is colored shades of dark yellow to olive brown that form loose, lateral stripes. The compressed body is oval shaped in lateral profile.
Size: Up to 8 inches long, but rarely above 6 inches.
Habitat: Swamps, wetlands, and associated lotic systems. Strongly favors acidic blackwater aquatic habitat.

Genus *Ambloplites*

The four species in the genus *Ambloplites* are collectively referred to as rock basses. Three species, *A. ariommus* (Shadow Bass), *A. cavifrons* (Roanoke Bass), and *A. constellatus* (Ozark Bass) possess very narrow native ranges in two to four states. In contrast, the Rock Bass (*A. rupestris*) is widespread and abundant. Like many other sunfishes, rock basses consume aquatic insects, crayfish, and small fish.

Ambloplites rupestris—Rock Bass

Figure 10.187.   A Rock Bass (*Ambloplites rupestris*), in a genus identified by A) bright red eyes. SAM STUKEL/USFWS

Description: The Rock Bass is brassy to green colored with spots on the body scales forming loose rows along the back. Like other *Ambloplites* species, the <u>eyes are often bright red</u>.
Size: Commonly 7 to 10 inches long.
Habitat: Medium-sized lotic systems with clear water and abundant cover for hiding, especially rocks or submerged vegetation.

Genus *Centarchus*

The genus *Centarchus* includes just one species, the Flier (*C. macropterus*). The Flier feeds on any aquatic invertebrate that can be captured, including snails, worms, and leeches.

Centarchus macropterus—Flier

Figure 10.188. A Flier (*Centarchus macropterus*), identified by A) a dark band running through the eye and B) a dark spot on the second dorsal fin. RYAN DOUGLAS

Description: The Flier is a dark yellow- to olive-colored sunfish with irregular small spots forming horizontal rows on the body. A broad, dark stripe runs through and below the eye. Young Flier show a large, dark spot on the second dorsal fin.
Size: Usually 8 to 10 inches long.
Habitat: Very slowly moving and acidic water, either in lakes or lotic systems. Prefers habitat with abundant submerged vegetation.

Genus *Enneacanthus*

Fishes in the genus *Enneacanthus* are small and often strikingly beautiful sunfishes, as they typically exhibit abundant small, iridescent blue spots. All three species are commonly kept in home aquariums. *Enneacanthus* sunfishes feed on very small invertebrates, especially fly larvae.

Enneacanthus gloriosus—Bluespotted Sunfish

Figure 10.189. A Bluespotted Sunfish (*Enneacanthus gloriosus*), distinguished from others in the genus by A) blue spots under the eye rather than a stripe. NCFISHES.COM

Description: The Bluespotted Sunfish has <u>iridescent spots under the eye rather than a stripe</u>, lacks well-defined bars on the body, and sometimes has a red or orange anal fin.
Size: Typically to 4, rarely to 6 inches long.
Habitat: Slow-moving lotic systems with muddy or sandy substrate and abundant submerged vegetation.

Enneacanthus obesus—Banded Sunfish

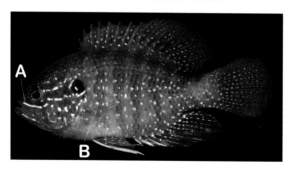

Figure 10.190. A Banded Sunfish (*Enneacanthus obesus*), identified by A) an iridescent stripe under the eye and B) vertical bands. ROBERT AGUILAR/SMITHSONIAN ENVIRONMENTAL RESEARCH CENTER

Description: The Banded Sunfish has <u>dark vertical bands</u> throughout the body and <u>a thin, iridescent stripe (the same hue as spots) under the eye</u>.
Size: Never more than 4 inches long.
Habitat: Very slow-moving lotic systems, especially blackwater habitat.

Genus *Lepomis*

Sunfish in the genus *Lepomis* are well known as colorful gamefish. They are among the most widely distributed sunfishes, and many species have been introduced to waters far beyond their native ranges. The dark-colored flap of tissue covering the gill can be used to identify *Lepomis* species.

Lepomis sunfishes are mostly predatory generalists of all invertebrates and are capable of consuming large quantities of mosquito larvae. Most tend to feed in the water column. The Redear Sunfish (*L. microlophus*) specializes on snails in adulthood.

Lepomis auritus—Redbreast Sunfish

Figure 10.191. A Redbreast Sunfish (*Lepomis auritus*), distinguished by A) a long, dark gill flap and B) orange-red belly. NCFISHES.COM

Description: The Redbreast Sunfish has a <u>bright orange to red belly</u> and a very <u>dark and long gill flap</u>.
Size: 3.5 to 7.5 inches long.
Habitat: A wide range of lotic system sizes and environmental conditions.

Lepomis cyanellus—Green Sunfish

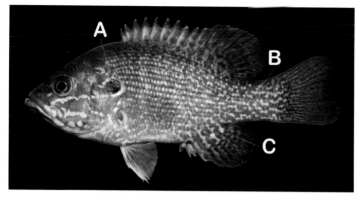

Figure 10.192. The Green Sunfish (*Lepomis cyanellus*) exhibits A) bright blue to green-blue iridescent stripes and spots, B) a short gill flap, and C) dorsal and anal fin spots. ZACH ALLEY

Description: A sunfish with brilliant iridescent green stripes and spots, a short gill flap, and spots on the second dorsal and (usually) anal fins. Spawning males show orange in their fins.
Size: 4.5 to 6 inches long.
Habitat: Tolerates a very wide range of conditions in lotic and lake habitats, including urban waters.

Lepomis gibbosus—Pumpkinseed

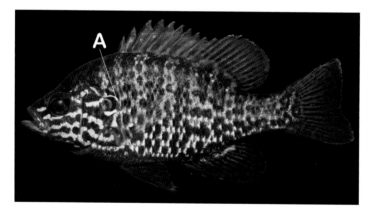

Figure 10.193. A Pumpkinseed (*Lepomis gibbosus*), identified by bright blue mottling and A) a red edge on the gill flap. ZACH ALLEY

Description: The Pumpkinseed can be identified by bright red on the gill flap edge and abundant iridescent blue mottling throughout the body.
Size: Usually 6 to 8 inches long, but up to 10 inches.
Habitat: Lotic systems with deep pools and abundant submerged vegetation.

Lepomis gulosus—Warmouth

Figure 10.194. A Warmouth (*Lepomis gulosus*), which has A) a larger mouth than other Lepomis species. RENÉ REYES/ US DEPARTMENT OF RECLAMATION

Description: The Warmouth has abundant leopard-like mottling and a relatively large mouth (compared to other *Lepomis*). Males show a bright red spot at the base of the second dorsal fin, and their eyes turn red when spawning.

Size: Usually 4 to 10 inches long, but can exceed 12 inches.
Habitat: Chiefly lakes and ponds, but also lotic systems with slow water and lots of vegetative cover.
Remarks: Warmouth hybridize with both Bluegill and Green Sunfish.

Lepomis humilis—Orangespotted Sunfish

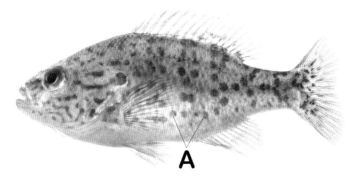

Figure 10.195. An Orangespotted Sunfish (*Lepomis humilis*), easily identified by A) large, orange spots. SAM STUKEL/USFWS

Description: The Orangespotted Sunfish shows large orange spots throughout the body. The head is often somewhat concave.

Size: Up to 7 inches long.
Habitat: In lotic systems, usually slow-moving and turbid waters; also lakes and reservoirs.

Lepomis macrochirus—Bluegill

A

B

Figure 10.196. Bluegill (*Lepomis macrochirus*) have A) a very small mouth and B) an orange-yellow belly. SAM STUKEL/USFWS

Description: A sunfish with a <u>round body</u>, <u>small mouth</u>, and <u>orange to yellow belly</u>.
Size: Up to 16 inches long.
Habitat: Lakes and very slow-moving lotic systems; capable of surviving in a range of environmental conditions.
Remarks: Bluegill are among the most abundant freshwater fishes in North America thanks to their ability to thrive in reservoirs, lakes, and farm ponds.

Lepomis megalotis—Longear Sunfish

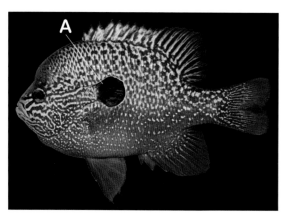

A

Figure 10.197. The Longear Sunfish (*Lepomis megalotis*) is easily identified by A) a long, teardrop-shaped gill flap with a white edge. ZACH ALLEY

Description: The Longear Sunfish possesses a <u>long and teardrop-shaped gill flap</u> with a <u>white edge</u>. Color is orange on the belly with a gray-blue back and bright iridescent blue spots.
Size: Usually no more than 9 inches long.
Habitat: Shallow, warmwater lotic systems with clear water and abundant aquatic vegetation.

Lepomis microlophus—Redear Sunfish

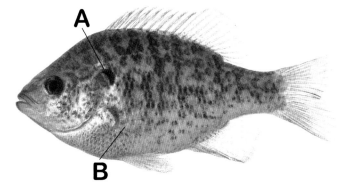

Figure 10.198. A Redear Sunfish (*Lepomis microlophus*), identified by A) a bright red gill flap edge and B) large pectoral fins. SAM STUKEL/ USFWS

Description: The Redear Sunfish has a conspicuously red gill flap edge and very large pectoral fins, and lacks the iridescent blue markings of similar *Lepomis* species.
Size: Up to 14 inches long.
Habitat: Warm, slow waters in large rivers, lakes, reservoirs, and ponds.

Genus *Micropterus*

The genus *Micropterus*, commonly known as black bass, includes thirteen species prized by anglers, including perhaps the most sought after North American sportfish, the Largemouth Bass (*M. salmoides*). *Micropterus* sportfish have been introduced far beyond native ranges, where they often outcompete or prey on native species. The Alabama Bass (*M. henshalli*) is also a rapidly expanding invasive species in eastern North America that locally hybridizes with and outcompetes native *Micropterus* species. All are elongate and less compressed side to side compared to other sunfishes.

Micropterus basses are voracious predators of any invertebrate, amphibian, or fish prey that can be captured.

Micropterus dolomieu—Smallmouth Bass

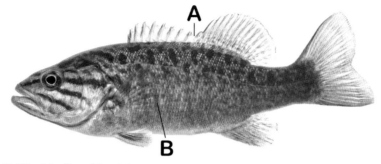

Figure 10.199. A Smallmouth Bass (*Micropterus dolomieu*), which has A) weakly separated dorsal fins and B) sometimes faintly visible vertical bars. SAM STUKEL/USFWS

Description: The Smallmouth Bass is olive to dark green on the back and yellow on the belly with eight to fifteen broad, vertical bars. The dorsal fins are weakly separated.
Size: Usually 12 to 20 inches long, but up to 28 inches.
Habitat: Resides in cooler, swifter lotic waters compared to other *Micropterus* species.
Remarks: The Smallmouth Bass is a highly prized sportfish due to its legendary fight.

Micropterus henshalli—Alabama Bass

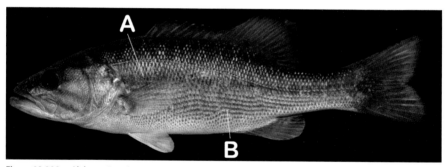

Figure 10.200. Alabama Bass (*Micropterus henshalli*) look like Largemouth Bass but have A) a less well defined lateral band and B) rows of spots below the band. ZACH ALLEY

Description: Looks very similar to (and hybridizes with) Largemouth Bass but with less well defined lateral bands and rows of spots below the lateral band.
Size: Up to 38 inches long, but usually 12 to 24 inches.
Habitat: Warmwater and slow-moving lotic systems.
Remarks: The Alabama Bass is more aggressive than others in the genus and has displaced native basses in its introduced range, which is rapidly expanding.

Micropterus punctulatus—Spotted Bass

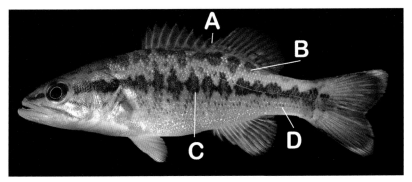

Figure 10.201. A Spotted Bass (*Micropterus punctulatus*), with A) connected dorsal fins, B) mottling above a C) broad band, and D) rows of fine spots below the band. BRIAN ZIMMERMAN

Description: The Spotted Bass has a <u>thick band running from the gill to the caudal fin with lateral rows of fine spots below and mottled dark spots above</u>. The <u>two dorsal fins are also broadly connected</u>.
Size: Up to 24 inches long.
Habitat: Cool, clear lotic systems with gravel to rocky substrate.

Micropterus salmoides—Largemouth Bass

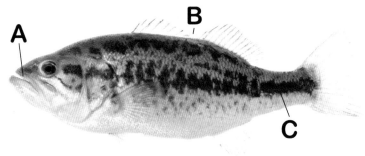

Figure 10.202. A Largemouth Bass (*Micropterus salmoides*), identified by A) a large mouth, B) separated dorsal fins, and C) a broad, dark band. SAM STUKEL/USFWS

Description: An olive-green, elongate sunfish with <u>separated dorsal fins</u> and a <u>very large mouth</u>. Sometimes a broad, dark band runs from the gill to the caudal fin.
Size: Up to 38 inches long, but usually 12 to 24 inches.
Habitat: Warmwater lakes, ponds, slow-moving lotic systems, and reservoirs.
Remarks: The Largemouth Bass is highly sought after by anglers and even inspires fish competitions with large monetary prizes.

Genus *Pomoxis*

The two *Pomoxis* species are known as crappie or calico bass. Both are nocturnal predators of fish as adults. Both species have an <u>obviously concave head</u>, are colored shades of gray to white, and have <u>dorsal fins broadly connected by a membrane</u>. Crappies prey on aquatic insects and fish, especially herrings.

Pomoxis annularis—White Crappie

Figure 10.203. A White Crappie (*Pomoxis annularis*), distinguished by A) five to six dorsal spines and B) faint vertical bars. RENÉ REYES/US DEPARTMENT OF RECLAMATION

Description: The White Crappie is primarily white with <u>faint vertical bars</u> and <u>five to six dorsal spines</u>. More elongate than Black Crappie.
Size: 7 to 20 inches long.
Habitat: Prefers lakes and ponds but also occurs in slow-moving lotic systems with sandy or muddy substrate, clear water, and abundant cover.

Pomoxis nigromaculatus—Black Crappie

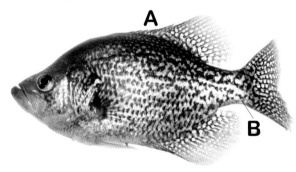

Figure 10.204. A Black Crappie (*Pomoxis nigromaculatus*), identified by A) seven to eight dorsal spines and B) abundant black spots. SAM STUKEL/USFWS

Description: The Black Crappie shows abundant black spots throughout the body and has <u>seven to eight dorsal fin spines</u>.
Size: 5 to 12 inches long.
Habitat: Lotic systems with cool, clear water and deep current.

REFERENCES

INTRODUCTION

Crandall, Keith A., and Jennifer E. Buhay. 2008. "Global Diversity of Crayfish (Astacidae, Cambaridae, and Parastacidae—Decapoda) in Freshwater." In *Freshwater Animal Diversity Assessment*, edited by E. V. Balian, C. Lévêque, H. Segers, and K. Martens, 295–301. Developments in Hydrobiology. Dordrecht: Springer Netherlands.

Lévêque, C., T. Oberdorff, D. Paugy, M. L. J. Stiassny, and P. A. Tedesco. 2008. "Global Diversity of Fish (Pisces) in Freshwater." In *Freshwater Animal Diversity Assessment*, edited by E. V. Balian, C. Lévêque, H. Segers, and K. Martens, 545–67. Developments in Hydrobiology. Dordrecht: Springer Netherlands.

CHAPTER 1

Schlesinger, William H., and Scott Jasechko. 2014. "Transpiration in the global water cycle." *Agricultural and Forest Meteorology* 189–190 (June): 115–17.

CHAPTER 2

Clow, David W. 2010. "Changes in the timing of snowmelt and streamflow in Colorado: a response to recent warming." *Journal of Climate* 23 (9): 2293–2306.

Eltahir, Elfatih A. B., and Rafael L. Bras. 1996. "Precipitation recycling." *Reviews of Geophysics* 34 (3): 367–78.

Hendriks, Martin R. 2010. *Introduction to Physical Hydrology*. Oxford; New York: Oxford University Press.

Holland, G., B. Sherwood Lollar, L. Li, G. Lacrampe-Couloume, G. F. Slater, and C. J. Ballentine. 2013. "Deep fracture fluids isolated in the crust since the Precambrian era." *Nature* 497 (7449): 357–60.

Naman, Sean M., Jordan S. Rosenfeld, and John S. Richardson. 2016. "Causes and consequences of invertebrate drift in running waters: from individuals to populations and trophic fluxes." *Canadian Journal of Fisheries and Aquatic Sciences* 73 (8): 1292–1305.

CHAPTER 3

Joshi, Sanjeev, and Y. Jun Xu. 2017. "Bedload and suspended load transport in the 140-km reach downstream of the Mississippi River avulsion to the Atchafalaya River." *Water* 9 (9): 716.

McKergow, Lucy A., David M. Weaver, Ian P. Prosser, Rodger B. Grayson, and Adrian E. G. Reed. 2003. "Before and after riparian management: sediment and nutrient exports from a small agricultural catchment, Western Australia." *Journal of Hydrology* 270 (3): 253–72.

Mossa, Joann. 1996. "Sediment dynamics in the lowermost Mississippi River." *Engineering Geology* 45 (1): 457–79.

CHAPTER 4

Baxter, Colden V., Kurt D. Fausch, Masashi Murakami, and Phillip L. Chapman. 2004. "Fish invasion restructures stream and forest food webs by interrupting reciprocal prey subsidies." *Ecology* 85 (10): 2656–63.

Beacham, Terry D., Clyde B. Murray, and Ruth E. Withler. 1989. "Age, morphology, and biochemical genetic variation of Yukon River Chinook Salmon." *Transactions of the American Fisheries Society* 118 (1): 46–63.

Bevis, Michael, Douglas Alsdorf, Eric Kendrick, Luiz Paulo Fortes, Bruce Forsberg, Robert Smalley, and Janet Becker. 2005. "Seasonal fluctuations in the mass of the Amazon River system and Earth's elastic response." *Geophysical Research Letters* 32 (16).

Dias de Paiva, Rodrigo Cauduro, Diogo Costa Buarque, Walter Collischonn, Marie-Paule Bonnet, Frédéric Frappart, Stephane Calmant, and Carlos André Bulhões Mendes. 2013. "Large-scale hydrologic and hydrodynamic modeling of the Amazon River basin." *Water Resources Research* 49 (3): 1226–43.

Fukui, Dai, Masashi Murakami, Shigeru Nakano, and Toshiki Aoi. 2006. "Effect of emergent aquatic insects on bat foraging in a riparian forest." *Journal of Animal Ecology* 75 (6): 1252–58.

Helfield, James M., and Robert J. Naiman. 2001. "Effects of salmon-derived nitrogen on riparian forest growth and implications for stream productivity." *Ecology* 82 (9): 2403–9.

Jenkins, Robert E., and Noel M. Burkhead. 1993. *Freshwater Fishes of Virginia*. American Fisheries Society.

Kubitzki, Klaus, and Albrecht Ziburski. 1994. "Seed dispersal in flood plain forests of Amazonia." *Biotropica* 26 (1): 30–43.

Minshall, G. Wayne, Robert C. Petersen, and Curtis F. Nimz. 1985. "Species richness in streams of different size from the same drainage basin." *The American Naturalist* 125 (1): 16–38.

Mulholland, Patrick J., Robert O. Hall, Daniel J. Sobota, Walter K. Dodds, Stuart E. G. Findlay, Nancy B. Grimm, Stephen K. Hamilton, et al. 2009. "Nitrate removal in stream ecosystems measured by 15N addition experiments: denitrification." *Limnology and Oceanography* 54 (3): 666–80.

Murakami, Masashi, and Shigeru Nakano. 2002. "Indirect effect of aquatic insect emergence on a terrestrial insect population through by birds predation." *Ecology Letters* 5 (3): 333–37.

Oberdorff, Thierry, Eric Guilbert, and Jean-Claude Lucchetta. 1993. "Patterns of fish species richness in the Seine River basin, France." *Hydrobiologia* 259 (3): 157–67.

Vannote, Robin L., G. Wayne Minshall, Kenneth W. Cummins, James R. Sedell, and Colbert E. Cushing. 1980. "The river continuum concept." *Canadian Journal of Fisheries and Aquatic Sciences* 37 (1): 130–37.

Wollheim, W. M., C. J. Vörösmarty, B. J. Peterson, S. P. Seitzinger, and C. S. Hopkinson. 2006. "Relationship between river size and nutrient removal." *Geophysical Research Letters* 33 (6).

CHAPTER 6

Clausnitzer, Viola, Vincent J. Kalkman, Mala Ram, Ben Collen, Jonathan E. M. Baillie, Matjaž Bedjanič, William R. T. Darwall, et al. 2009. "Odonata enter the biodiversity crisis debate: the first global assessment of an insect group." *Biological Conservation* 142 (8): 1864–69.

Twardochleb, Laura, Ethan Hiltner, Matthew Pyne, and Phoebe Zarnetske. 2021. "Freshwater insects CONUS: a database of freshwater insect occurrences and traits for the contiguous United States." *Global Ecology and Biogeography* 30 (4): 826–41.

CHAPTER 9

Etnier, David, and Wayne Starnes. 1993. *The Fishes of Tennessee*. Newfound Press, 1993.

NatureServe. 2010. "Digital distribution maps of the freshwater fishes in the conterminous United States." Version 3.0. Arlington, VA.

Schramm, Harold L., Jay T. Hatch, Robert A. Hrabik, and William T. Slack. 2016. "Fishes of the Mississippi River." *American Fisheries Society Symposium* 84: 53–77.

Tedesco, Pablo A., Olivier Beauchard, Rémy Bigorne, Simon Blanchet, Laëtitia Buisson, Lorenza Conti, Jean-François Cornu, et al. 2017. "A global database on freshwater fish species occurrence in drainage basins." *Scientific Data* 4 (1): 170141.

ABOUT THE AUTHOR

Ryan Utz is an assistant professor of water resources at Chatham University in Pittsburgh, Pennsylvania, and an outdoor enthusiast with an obsession for backcountry camping. He has published more than forty scientific articles on subjects ranging from Chinook Salmon restoration in California to long-term rising river salinity levels throughout North America. Less academic but more fun, a few of his outdoor forays into the wilderness have appeared in *Backpacker* magazine. Ryan earned an MS in wildlife and fisheries management from West Virginia University and a PhD in environmental science from the University of Maryland. He lives in Pittsburgh, Pennsylvania, but spends the night in a tent every chance he can get.